WILL APPALACHIA – FINALLY – OVERCOME POVERTY ?

by

Anthony J. Salatino

ISBN 0-913383-37-6
Library of Congress 95-79614

Cover design and book layout by James Asher Graphics.
Cover illustration by James Asher from a photograph courtesy
of Alice Lloyd Library Archives
Photographs used in the book courtesy of
Alice Lloyd Library Archives,
The Christian Appalachian Project, Evelyn Bernitt / Hazard Community College
and The City of Hazard, Kentucky
Back cover photograph by Village Photographers, Tampa, Florida.

Manufactured in the United States of America.

McClanahan Publishing House
Kuttawa, Kentucky 42055

All book order correspondence should be addressed to:
Dr. Anthony J. Salatino
Suite 264
3837 Northdale Blvd.
Tampa, FL 33624
813-273-1739

CONTENTS

Dedication

To the people I love

Foreword

When I, a confirmed Vermonter, hear "Appalachia," I think of a faraway place in America, a rural land of "hillbillies" and poverty.

I vaguely remember many plans and promises to change things there, such as the War on Poverty! Surely we must have won the "war" by now? If we haven't, why not?

This book, a history and commentary about the area, is written by a compassionate, thoughtful human being, a wise educator, who has lived and worked in Appalachia. He tells the story of this troubled land as seen through the prism of an educator who had served at Alice Lloyd College in the heart of Appalachia. He has strong feelings for this place. He cares. It's a tale rich in anecdotes and wisdom. It has heroes, heroines, and villains. Certain bad guys through the years have stifled progress. That needn't continue. The people are changing, education is working. There's hope and with "champions" brought to the forefront in this book, maybe they will make it. A. J. Salatino proposes plans, based on grass roots experience. I hope the politicians will listen.

Jerold F. Lucey, M.D.
Professor of Pediatrics
University of Vermont
Editor in Chief, _Pediatrics_

Introduction

My first exposure to poverty in Appalachia occurred during the Great Depression, when I was just a child. Father had received news of his longtime friend's fatal illness — the dreaded black lung disease. He was a coal miner in Appalachia and they had been "army buddies" during World War I. My family was residing in upstate New York at that time, and immediately upon hearing the news, dad drove with us to eastern Kentucky. Compounding the sorrow and heartache of an impending pneumoconiosis death, my father's friend and his family were destitute, brought on by every conceivable economic and social ill. I remember that we did not have much to spare, but dad gave everything he could, and I will never forget his compassion and concern. For many years thereafter, he told me that one had to live among the needy, in order to realize how cruel and demeaning it is to be dealt a hand of despair and deprivation, yet how good and giving these people are. Later on in life, I visited Kentucky many times, but it was not until the early 1960's that my work placed me in the heart of Appalachia. Only then did I fully understand the ravages that destitution leaves on the poor and their surroundings.

In my position as Academic Dean of Alice Lloyd College at Pippa Passes, I found that the people, including my colleagues, fellow workers, neighbors, friends and students, were the warmest, kindest, and most honest human beings I ever came in contact with. The intrinsic goodness of these individuals is unmatched because of their common cause. They have contributed their part to make eastern Kentucky a better place to live, and help the less fortunate achieve success in a poverty-stricken environment. This region was one of the poorest and lowest income areas of our nation in the early 1960's, and still is the most deprived to this day. In fact, poverty has been identified in Appalachia as an ongoing problem since the time of its settlers.

Through the years many undertakings have been made to overcome impoverishment in eastern Kentucky. Even the most extensive and comprehensive action by our government in the 1960's attempted to eradicate conditions of the poor with little success. Yet, the results have left us with researched information to understand the problem of poverty and how to fight it. Some experts are of the opinion that there is no clear cut or agreed-upon solution. However, certain humanitarian efforts have left an imprint for betterment of the downtrodden and underprivileged in Appalachia. No matter how "modestly successful" that change, the importance is that it came about, and mainly through action beyond the call of duty. Knowing why people are poor does not cure the ills, but doing something about it certainly makes a big difference for those in need. Concerned citizens have shown that any form of success in helping the less fortunate is of significance, for it may provide some answers to the overall problem of poverty. This in turn could lead to positive change for the future of Appalachia. Perhaps the most important lesson one can gain from this book is that there are answers to overcoming destitution.

My central purpose is to present a biographical sketch about eastern Kentucky's long standing problem of poverty since settlers came to this region. Needs of the poor are so voluminous and persistent that a study of conditions and circumstances from past to present is necessary, in order to understand why they exist and have become more complex. It is evident that individuals and groups are an integral part of solutions for change. The momentous foundation that the grass-roots movement has spawned constitutes a necessary facet of Appalachia's direction in overcoming poverty and should be viewed in this perspective. Those I have written about are part of the overall picture of many people who are playing a leadership role in helping the needy. Therefore, it is important to understand the significance of their actions, and could be used as a model to guide others in bringing an end to impoverishment.

Included in this book is a brief description of economic, social, political, physical, and cultural conditions, which were evident from the late 1700's up to the present. Poverty's presence stands out as the focus of each period in eastern Kentucky's history. Emphasis is given to the changing over from agriculture to an industrial structured economy and its consequences. Inherent throughout the book are issues related to education, health and health care, living and environmental conditions. The never ending problem of poverty is being challenged and recommendations for solutions are outlined.

EASTERN KENTUCKY AND SURROUNDING AREAS

Area Enlarged Above

Atlantic Ocean

Chapter I

1750 — 1899

Poverty From the Beginning

T he history of Appalachia has been told many times due to a unique folk culture, which was built on strong individualism and self-reliance, brought about by living in isolation. However, this image is shattered by the fact that constant poverty has extended into all aspects of people's lives since arrival of the settlers. Eastern Kentucky during the late 1700's and early 1800's was no different than the rest of America, when poor people came from other countries, seeking a new and happier way of life. Many immigrants arrived in "the new world" to achieve success and prosperity, yet, stories of this region's settlers have a different tale to tell.

The mountainous terrain, which these individuals chose as their home, was looked upon as protection from persecution by outside forces. An example of grandeur, the Cumberland Appalachian range, with its rugged forested mountains and many winding streams, was first explored by Dr. Thomas Walker in 1750. This land was beautiful in its entirety, bountiful with natural resources, and abundant in "food" and wild animals. Other adventurers, like Daniel Boone, followed immediately thereafter and traveled the region through the same mountain pass as Dr. Walker. This is now part of Cumberland Gap National Historic Park, located in the far southeastern tip of Kentucky, bordering Virginia and Tennessee. Unfortunately, these majestic mountains would also create a barrier against growth of the region for many generations.

Right from the start, Appalachia's settlers brought with them an unwarranted label of their past. When the westward-moving English, Scottish and Irish settlers staked their claims in eastern Kentucky, they were described as "people of poverty." Suffering from personal and religious oppression led them to this region in search of freedom, however, they faced an unknown and unpredictable future. This was also the beginning of a culture that had to endure social, economic and political obstacles, which would play havoc with their lives.

Historically, poverty in Appalachia is traced back to English indentured servants, who were held in bondage and brought over to this country by wealthy landowners. Many of these servants originally landed on the eastern seaboard of North America, mainly in Virginia, North Carolina, and Maryland, subservient to their "task masters." Hoping to escape persecution from England, they came across similar abuses in the colonies. A variety of stories handed down through generations told about many experiences of servitude and hardship that the poor had to endure in colonial America. One elderly gentleman in the 1960's described how his great-great-great grandfather was forcibly brought over as an indentured servant. An orphan, and penniless at age 14 in one of the seacoast towns of England, he was kidnapped and transported illegally to America. During that period and until after the Revolutionary War, the English laws were not fair to those who lived in poverty. "Ridding the burdens" of society meant sentencing a poor man to indentured service in the colonies. The canon of judicial ethics prohibited poor individuals from defending themselves against their accusers, even if it was a minor incident like taking food for their hungry family. It was also obvious that certain courts were favoring the rich at the expense of indigent people.

Passage of the poor to colonial America was provided by their employer, namely a "plantation" owner, and servants were required to pay them back by toiling the soil. A signed contract generally defined that indentured persons meet their debt in seven years. Historians cite that in the 1700's there were only "two classes of whites" in the colonies: wealthy planters and poor people. Harsh and unfair treatment by landowners had been unbearable and life on the plantation was full of abuse, leading in certain cases to maiming of servants, or death. The poor indentured people could not accept this kind of injustice, and whenever possible tried running away to nearby communities, hoping to melt into the population. However, when captured, iron collars were placed around their necks to signify bondage and distinguish them from the free colonists. Those fortunate enough to escape, either sailed on pirate ships, or traveled far away to avoid not only persecution from landowners, but also the "Church of England," located in eastern seaboard colonies. Escapees who forged inland to Appalachia's Cumberland region became the first "Kentucky mountaineers," and were later joined by more "poor whites," when their bondage expired.

There were other English, Scottish, and Irish settlers who migrated from the colonies to Appalachia, assuming that this region was part of the last frontier. Some of these folks were the offspring and followers of Daniel Boone or other explorers, scouts and surveyors, who claimed the land. They were rugged, individualistic in their nature, desiring to build a life of personal and religious freedom and succeed in the unknown wilderness. Included in this group were people with a natural gift of making farming implements, hunting and household utensils, by using basic hand tools.

As a result of living in the wilderness, settlers encountered a new kind of freedom, but experienced greater dependency on their family. This meant that a person could make his own choices and live in an environment where standards of control by others were non-existent. However, people now had to find their own direction and bear total responsibility for survival. They were also able to bind themselves to their own ethical and religious standards that would provide guidance throughout life. Free thinking and self-responsibility, as taught by family and church, became their foundation and gave them strength. At the time Appalachian society was developing this type of individualism, it also struggled with numerous obstacles. The mountaineers were penniless and disadvantaged in many ways, encountering a new life. To survive, they had to skirmish native Indians, who inhabited the region long before white settlers arrived. This land was revered by Indians not only for its beauty, but also because of abundant wild animal life that made it their "hunting ground."

One of the first problems that confronted early settlers, after finding a piece of land they wanted to farm, was temporary shelter. Stories were told how the first settlers occupied hollowed tunnels of giant sycamore trees as temporary homes, while building their log cabins. Others stayed temporarily under cliffs, or were ingenious by digging a hole into the side of a hill, and covering exposed areas with bark from trees. This dugout proved to be effective against mixed elements of nature and the uncertainties of human and animal presence. People lived a hard life, fought Indian wars, cleared land for farming and built log cabins. The family's world evolved within the confines of their cabin's small single room, which served as gathering place for children to grow up in, pray together, and socialize as a close-knit unit. At night a cabin ensured safety against unknown variables of the primeval forest.

Decades of relative isolation and lack of economic growth demanded self-determination. These settlers had to persevere, be self-sufficient and imaginative. In comparison to other parts of the colonies, this

land did not offer very good conditions for farming. However, the mountaineers' practical attitude prevailed, by eking out a meager living on small
tracts of land, which provided just enough sustenance for day-to-day living. Their interest was not in seeking wealth like the detested plantation
system, instead they treasured liberty and family, which made them more
determined to overcome many difficult situations.

The people of these remote areas began to build a culture that
solely existed to meet their basic needs. They were without a class system,
as religious and personal independence remained strongly intact. Freedom
to the mountaineers transcended all boundaries of life. They were private
people, who wanted to be left alone, and in turn did not impose on others or their beliefs. Unlike groups of colonists on the eastern seaboard,
they were not educated or prosperous. Even though Puritans and other
colonists left England in search of religious freedom, their beliefs were
deeply rooted in bigotry. If someone did not have the same kind of religious conviction, they became intolerant. Punishments, such as having
people hounded out of communities, as well as whippings or fines, were
normal types of action by Puritans. The Appalachian settlers did not
approve of this religious fervor and behavior, which is an admirable and
distinguishing characteristic that personifies the hillfolk in their advocacy
for human liberty. Freedom of speech and belief was and is nowhere else
more democratically entwined than within the culture of eastern
Kentuckians.

Family tradition did not lose ground like in other parts of the
country, where cultural pluralism developed as small urban communities
were built. The culture of mountain families was based on simple wants
and needs, and a moral structure that embodied its closeness. As the people of urban areas in our nation began to surrender their traditions to
exposure of life's changes relating to economic, political, and social patterns, Appalachian culture remained singular in direction. Mountaineers
maintained their ways, as the rest of the country experimented with adapting to new life styles. Traditions of the hillfolk were preserved, and important values continued to serve as their strength for generations.

To live in eastern Kentucky during the late 1700's meant that
education in a formal sense was non-existent. Most adults were illiterate,
and children did not have schools to attend or teachers to train them.
Offspring had to assist their parents at an early age either by helping on
the small farm, doing household chores or caring for their younger siblings. As children grew older, they were given greater responsibilities.
Boys would go hunting and trapping with their fathers, and girls helped
with housework, such as cooking, caring for the family and domestic animals. Knowledge of new and diverse ways of mankind was secondary to
putting food on the table, since agriculture was the basis for their exis-

tence. Children learned in the traditional informal way by watching their parents, whether it was working the land, doing household tasks or other daily activities. Observing and imitating by practicing the skills of every-day life over and over, was their way of learning. However, this practical hands-on experience did not eliminate the need for formal education. Unfortunately, the lack of it presented an obstacle for child development. It is a paradox that each culture of our society stands as a monument to man's achievement, but it can also deter human potential. Due to lack of education, people of this region would experience a long tradition of illiteracy.

As the population grew, a homogeneity of purpose in daily life continued. The mountaineers kept their habits, customs and speech, which goes back to the time of Queen Elizabeth I and Shakespeare. Even today, a person brought up in a diverging society would be amazed by the archaic use of language. In spite of many hardships, these people were self-sustaining by living in harmony with their environment. They were poor, yet they built, repaired or mended in their own unique way. Isolation from the outside world made them dependent on each other, and as areas within the region of eastern Kentucky developed, little hamlets and villages began to spring up. Local artisans with special gifts were providing farm and household implements. Other community members contributed their services as basket makers, spinners and weavers, blacksmiths or craft makers.

As a practical matter of survival, family life demanded constant toil of the land, with time off on Sunday, observing the Christian Sabbath. Religion and attachment to land and surroundings were underlying factors in the settlers' everyday activities. Their most important institutions were family, church and community, upon which personal and social relationships evolved. Whatever few opportunities children had for learning were brought about by the closeness of church members. They worshiped in Primitive and Free Thinking Baptist churches, attended the same camp meetings, recited tall tales, and shared humor that brought out the honesty and simplicity of hillfolk. Stories were plenty, ranging from hunting and farming to family. Mountaineers built their own musical instruments, such as the dulcimer, "cornstalk fiddles," and gourd banjos. They sang about the Shakespeare era, told about their roots and experiences of life. Courting-and answer-back ballads, work and topical songs were also popular. The Appalachian dulcimer, a folk instrument made by craftsmen, served as the basis to accompany oral traditional mountain music.

Even though they were considered "people of poverty," showing strength in their character and culture presented a unique quality, which carried forth through generations. They were aware of the significant struggles in life, and had the ability to proudly maintain and cherish their

13

heritage, along with oral traditions in communicating history. The arts and crafts they produced were ingrained in an ongoing aesthetically pleasing way of life. Continuing this style of existence through the years can be attributed to the fact that hillfolk adults had instilled in their children enlightenment of cultural beliefs. In turn, assimilation into Appalachian life was done with ease and dignity, as each succeeding generation committed itself to preserve their heritage.

Unwanted Outside Forces

Since the time of settlement, mountaineers and their families had to strenuously fight for independence by staving off outside forces. No group was more tenacious than the land companies, in trying to claim huge portions of Appalachia's vast frontier. Their motives were very questionable and involved leading figures of the Revolutionary War era as investors. In 1774, the Transylvania Land Company made plans to claim huge areas of eastern Kentucky and signed a treaty with the Cherokee Indians to gain land. Chief Dragging Canoe, one of the signers of this agreement in 1775, stated that the Company was getting "dark and bloody ground." It probably was no darker and bloodier than when the Indian people fought settlers over hunting rights. The Land Company, with its eastern seaboard financial influences, attempted to establish the State of Transylvania that consisted of Appalachian land between Kentucky and Tennessee. This action led to government intervention and extensive work to nullify the treaty, which was declared illegal in 1776. Thus, the proud mountaineers survived the first onslaught of many outside forces that in coming years would have a positive or negative effect on their future. However, intrusions were a major cause of great problems for these hillfolk through generations.

From the American Revolution to the Civil War, during which the mountaineers tried to maintain independence, armed conflict impinged on them and forced their involvement. The intention to be left alone was first and foremost their concern, however when war occurred, the history of being held in bondage made Appalachians strongly advocate the "Freedom of Man." In 1860, Kentucky-born Abraham Lincoln, who was against slavery, became President of the United States. It was a time in the history of our country that probably produced the bloodiest and most violent conflict of American society. During the Civil War, farmers of Appalachia were still poor, eking out a living from their land. They did not enjoy prosperity like wealthy landowners who inhabited more fertile, flatter lands of the central and western regions. Politically, outspoken factions from this part of Kentucky were pro-slavery. Mountaineers favored fighting against it, insisting on the right for each individual to be free, and believing that no man should own another person. Native Kentuckians had a strong sense of pride, therefore great bitterness existed on both sides. Being a border state, it experienced the burden of trying to remain neutral. Eventually having to choose sides, most of the state supported the Union with 90,000 soldiers, of which 24,000 were blacks. The Confederacy had 45,000 Kentuckians fighting on their side.

Strong division of feelings about the Civil War was nowhere else as extensively experienced as in Kentucky. This led to greater tragedy among its people than in any other state. Father was fighting against son, brother against brother, cousin against cousin, neighbor against neighbor, which confused outsiders as to the mixed loyalties of these people. President Abraham Lincoln's strongest backer, Robert J. Breckinridge, had two sons who fought for the South. Mary Todd Lincoln, the President's wife and a native Kentuckian, had a divided group of relatives fighting for both sides. The heart rending experiences of senior United States Senator John J. Crittenden, found him with one son a general in the Union Army, and the other a Confederate general. Even though there were people who sided with the South, State government throughout this War was steadfast behind the Union. Most eastern Kentuckians had a feeling of pride and wanted the states unified as one nation.

The Civil War left scars upon many hillfolk, which continued to create ill feelings with friends and neighbors. In certain instances, strong sense of pride, culture and lifestyle made it difficult for mountaineers to forgive one another for their differing loyalties during the conflict. Some differences were simmering before the war and increased, if one family or individual sided with the Union, the other faction supported the Confederacy. During this period, one such disagreement led to the most infamous feud in American history. For more than a quarter century after this War had ended, the Hatfield family, living in Mingo county on West Virginia's side of the border, and the McCoy family of Pike County, from eastern Kentucky, were still battling over disagreements. In 1863, the first McCoy family member, a Union soldier, was killed by a Hatfield clan member, and constant revenge continued through the years. Approximately one hundred McCoys and Hatfields died before their bad feelings subsided. This conflict is one of the most legendary tales of Appalachians and their personal struggles with each other. Clannish feuds of mountain folk go back to the time of their forefathers, and yet these people have always been noted for their hospitality. Stories are told that they welcomed strangers into their homes with open arms, the same way they greeted their relatives or neighbors. Before the Civil War, this type of hospitality exemplified the spirit of Appalachian families, in spite of violence that took place.

After the Civil War, reconstruction problems and suffering prevailed in Kentucky, as well as other border and southern states. Financial conditions of the poor hillfolk did not improve, however, certain factors brought slow change to the economic system. Small rural villages were beginning to spring up and serve as centers for newly formed county governments. The village became a meeting place for people to gather and tell stories and tales about feuds of the War, disgraceful acts of soldiers and Quantrill's guerrillas, who destroyed mountain country and plundered property of defenseless hillfolk. Bands of guerrillas torched corn fields and killed or stole animals. There were other situations, where women and children starved in their cabins because they were unable to grow food due to destruction of their land, while their husbands and fathers went to war. Some men never returned, and their families carried on the best they could, even though poverty and its many ills created a greater burden.

Local Government

When Kentucky became a state in 1792, there were nine counties spread throughout the total central, western and eastern regions. As the Civil War began, they increased to 110 counties, and a major reason for this expansion was the distance and rugged terrain that Appalachians had to travel, in order to participate in government matters. This made it possible for county seats to be reached within a day's journey for all constituents living within a given area. After the War, local governments of Appalachia were still too inconvenient to reach and warranted further divisions by the State Legislature to total 120 seats.

With the formation of county governments in the 1800's, local political power gained opportunities to control economic and social structures of the community. In some counties, politicians were often more inclined toward self-serving interests, rather than representing the people fairly. Folks even suggested that "real" political power was at the county rather than state level, when certain officials ignored America's principle of separating the three branches of government. The county court's power was all encompassing, which included authority to regulate certain business, supervise collection of taxes, and sit in judgment of all cases brought forward by the community. They were a small but powerful "elite" group, and their domain was both judge and jury of the people. This type of control also gave justices of the peace power to appoint officials, such as sheriffs, constables, surveyors, coroners, inspectors, county clerks, and other officials and workers.

It is ironic that the Constitution of the United States lists duties of federal and state governments and their limitations of power. Yet, there were no guidelines relating to local governments, such as the county. Even though the state constitution determines how many and what kinds of local governments are to be established, flexibility without checks and balances allowed county officials in those early days to control, make and carry out the laws. This concerned the fair-minded people, and their fear of authoritarian control was well-founded. Some county justices of the peace "played out their role to the hilt." County courts consisted of non-elected justices, who were appointed by the governor of Kentucky. Upon retirement, justices filled their own vacancies by recommending two candidates. The governor would invariably choose one of them, thus assuring continued control of power by a "selected few."

During the 1800's, county seats were gathering places for mountain men and their families. However, living in the backwoods and having no roads, people had to walk over mountains, through winding creeks, deep gullies and steep ridges, which made it difficult getting to the county seat. As a result, court sessions were limited to once a month. People had to deal with the county in one way or another by recording deeds, processing wills, and bringing various petitions before them. Many legal papers revealed an "X", marking the place of signatures, which indicated a high illiteracy rate of the populace. Abuses of power and undemocratic practices by courts were the rule. Hillfolk growing up with unfairness, came to the county seats objecting to this type of government. Their distrust increased and plans at the state level were developed to overcome unjust conditions. The State of Kentucky eliminated these undemocratic practices by rewriting their constitution in 1850. Even if it was disputable whether county government was good or bad, it appeared evident, as one views the history of action by state officials to reform the structure, that people were at the mercy of a few individuals with Machiavellian intentions.

As county government developed, a major concern that had to be dealt with was its inefficiency and quite possibly corruptness. The term "domination by a few elite" during this period is used to summarize conditions and experiences of power. Counties were not democratically organized, and it was obviously true that not all had exercised their power wisely. Another concern of county government during that time was the "saga of financial inability." As expected, small population communities of the region had limited income resources to sustain adequate services. The immense disparity in financial resources between growing urban Louisville and Lexington and small rural villages, exemplified from the beginning how revenue-raising for larger communities was much easier. Essentially those cities grew, since wealth created jobs as well as opportunities and the standard of living increased, which in turn provided for more available and better services. From the start, eastern Kentucky communities were without any solid form of income, yet had greater needs that could not be met. Lack of tax revenue and process of assessment gave rise to suspicions regarding capabilities of rural communities toward progress. Financially, many of Appalachia's counties were not able to respond. Consequently, this failure to generally improve functions of service to communities within their domain would weaken the effectiveness of county government.

Health and Health Care

To understand the significance that lack of good health had on Appalachians in early years, one has to visualize that people were living under very undesirable and disadvantaged circumstances. Their poor health status was further perpetuated by non-existing basic professional health care services. Since the time of the settlers and continuing for over a century, health care was largely an individual situation between the sick and their families. Often, there was no doctor for hundreds of miles, or near enough to call upon for aid, when sickness occurred. People were born, lived and died without ever seeing a physician, or let alone know what a hospital was all about. Mothers were considered "the medical practitioner" for the family and responded the best they could to every need of these perilous times. Even though many premature deaths occurred, lives were saved by intuitive knowledge and self-developed skills.

Poor health conditions and the lack of medical care were major reasons why these people had large families, for they knew that some of their children would die at a young age. By frequent pregnancies and childbirth, the mother became physically weak and more susceptible to illness and disease. This unfortunate circumstance placed her in an untenable and vulnerable position of early death. A sad commentary regarding this situation is to look at recordings of early settlers in eastern Kentucky or visit graveyards, and one would be amazed at the number of mothers and children that died prematurely. Unfortunately, the high rate of infant-parent mortality continued mercilessly throughout the 19th century.

Since doctors or medicine were not available for decades to mountaineers living in remote areas, home remedies became instinctively the procedure for care. Though people did not understand how or why they worked, these remedies were used for many generations, and some still have a purpose today. Handed down from English, Irish, and Scottish ancestors, they included prescriptions based on plant derivatives, such as bloodroot, which was used for skin rash, irritation, and snake bites. Dock, a genus of the buckwheat family with long tap roots, was also used in Appalachian folk medicine. Even though home remedies did not stave off any epidemic that spread throughout the region in early years, they were still used in one form or another. People easily fell prey to disease, however it was accepted as a normal process of life.

During the Civil War and until the late 1800's, general family physicians had been the only medical persons providing care and surgery related to all medical ills. These doctors were not prepared to be surgeons and lacked special training. Their skill with a scalpel was largely self-taught. In Kentucky, practitioners generally settled in the Louisville/Lexington areas, near hospitals that were built to meet the needs of urban growth. Any doctor working in Appalachia was considered a humanitarian. The medical man in those days traveled by horse, which took him to places that were difficult to reach, yet many people in remote areas never saw a doctor in their lifetime. Operating on patients and traveling to widely separated places in one day compounded the many problems these doctors had to face, and sleeping overnight at a patient's cabin was common. Physicians had no medical assistant, unless visiting county seats and a self-taught nurse was available. In general, a doctor would need assistance from a family member or friend. Any minor or major surgery was performed in the home, and the medical man would boil surgical instruments in a wash basin on a kitchen stove, often using a table as a makeshift "operating table."

During the late 1800's, increase for medical help was warranted by certain uncontrollable circumstances. Many counties and pockets of the region were without medical assistance, and growth in population continued adding to problems that faced the small group of Appalachian practitioners. Handicaps that doctors and people endured during this period became unbearable. Epidemics such as typhoid fever, smallpox and other diseases, like the dreaded bubonic plague and cholera, were difficult to overcome, and premature death was a common occurrence in every family.

Education

From early times through the late 1800's, there was no formal education for the hillfolk and their offspring. Most adults were illiterate and children did not go to school. For decades, education was a self taught luxury that had its limitations. Like their fathers and mothers, children helped on the farm, breaking and digging rocks from the land. Long hours of work and strength were required, with little or no time for education. In certain county seats or villages, where parents could afford an education for their children, a one room log cabin was built, and either a parent or teacher would provide educational lessons. As a result, only the privileged few learned to read and write. However, as years progressed through the middle and later 1800's, church schools along with individual community schools and academies formally opened. Church schools used reading and writing to pass religious knowledge of the Bible from generation to generation, which had an effect on values and morals that contributed to the development of good character. It brought a sense of belonging to the family, in which goodness and understanding were inherent by believing that each human is equal. Thus, education gained from the Bible helped them in their daily living and learning experiences.

During the late 19th century, a class system was beginning to surface in Appalachia, where villages appeared to be organized. Certain parents had the wisdom to understand the importance of education for the future of their children. However, the underprivileged, who lived in backwoods hollows, were unable to walk the many miles to a one room cabin in the local village for formal learning experiences. Even though the first statewide public school system operated in Kentucky by 1847, education overall was not important to Appalachian mountain folk. Life in the back country area, where most farmers lived and worked, remained self-sustaining. Unfortunately, lack of access to education combined with illiteracy throughout the mountain population became a nagging problem for generations.

Coal Mining

It was not until the late 1890's that the mountains would open doors for opportunity, which occurred with the discovery of coal. Since the arrival of settlers, agriculture was the sole economic base for this region. Eastern Kentuckians did not envision that the mineral-rich land, which had been their home for years, would fulfill unforeseen expectations of wealth for outsiders. The mountains provided natural beauty and were a reason for pride in maintaining an independent life. However, during latter years of the nineteenth century, hillfolk saw for the first time a disruption of that physical beauty. To wealthy outsiders, called the coal barons, these mountains were not only valuable by themselves, but also for what they contained: "Black Gold." Moving from agriculture to coal mining opened up jobs, and many mountaineers had to decide whether it was worth going into coal mining or keep on farming.

Along with discovery of coal, English steel interests found that the mountains also contained low-grade iron ore, specifically in Bell County. The building of an iron and coal empire in the late 1890's brought steelmaking to Middlesboro, which led to an increase in Bell County's population. Migration into coal mining and steel-making areas transplanted many workers from the highlands. Mountaineers left the farms for mining jobs, and their families worked the land. Middlesboro was born overnight and built alongside the new tracks of the Louisville and Nashville Railroad, where blast furnaces and coke ovens were placed. Thousands of workers, including people from other parts of the country and Europe, poured into Bell County to work in steel manufacturing. In spite of all the steel factories and mines, English steel processing bottomed out "with a bust" at the end of the 19th century. New communities that had sprung up in a short time became ghost towns. Appalachian miners went back to family and farming, while men that came from Europe and others left for different parts of the country to work in factories, where the Bessemer process of steel-making was being used.

Lumber

Toward the turn of the century articles appeared in "Harpers" and "Geological Survey" magazines, containing stories not only about vast amounts of coal and iron ore, but also citing that the highlands of Kentucky had the greatest concentration of forest land. Nearly 75 percent of the land was virgin forest, which included giant trees such as oak, poplar, hickory, beech, maple, and sycamore. Lumber companies and speculators surveyed the region's land and legally claimed thousands of acres. They purchased trees from illiterate mountaineers "dirt cheap" as well as through county or state government. Whenever possible, land was bought by lumber companies from those counties that needed income to run their government. The start of the timber industry in this region also brought employment opportunities, even though it was not as great an impact as the "coal boom." Some eastern Kentuckians went to work in logging camps, leaving the tilling of bottomlands to their women and children. The mountaineers' work situation was slowly changing, even though their lifestyle remained the same. They also did not realize the implications of yielding their rights to owning the trees, and it is sad, but ultimate results of actions for immediate financial gain, which amounted to a few pennies, would lead to a future of anguish. Their children and generations of offspring had to suffer the consequences of subsequent mineral rights battles.

Summation

From the beginning, Appalachia was moving to a different beat of the drum than other parts of our nation. Differences were running deep as conditions and circumstances for eastern Kentucky took a course that would profoundly affect its future. While America began to grow economically and socially, Appalachia's situation remained almost unchanged. During this period, mountaineers adhered firmly and faithfully to their culture, yet the rest of our country expanded in different directions. The nation was changing, as other people migrated from their rural areas to burgeoning urban cities, assimilating into mixed-structured societies. However, hillfolk were living in a region that made them bond together by the nature of physical surroundings as well as economic and social conditions. The fact remained that directions taken during this time, would have long lasting consequences for these people.

As one looks at the path eastern Kentuckians took, it appears obvious that the aim was toward a sustainable society, which tried to satisfy needs the best way it could, even though human and material resources were very limited. These people endured life by patterns of their own design, but as years progressed, it became evident that eastern Kentucky was caught in a cycle of deteriorating circumstances, affecting every fibre of existence. Despite wanting to be left alone due to past victimization, they were unable to help themselves, thus their problems began to accumulate. With each generation, new economic, social and political crisis would perpetuate the scene of Appalachian life. People were in need and encountered barriers such as lack of education, poor health status, minimal health care, and an inadequate economic structure that jeopardized the prospects of future generations.

These poor and illiterate people had no access to education, which could have guided many to escape impoverishment. Necessities of these mountaineers were never met and made them more vulnerable to situations of exploitation. Had Appalachians been educated and more knowledgeable of their mineral-rich surroundings, they might have been able to effectively change the outcome that benefited only a few elite. Honesty, loyalty and trust were part of eastern Kentuckians cultural strength, yet, this became a weakness that would carry them into the next century, being even more exploited. Unable to read, they were misled into signing away the mineral rights of their land, and greedy actions by certain outsiders would be the bane of mountaineers' lives through the 20th century.

These people were not seeking personal wealth as other societies of our country, because their ideology cherished human values over materialism. It is difficult to argue about their common cause that included democratic principles, freedom, respect for human rights, and acceptance of life's burdens. Love of family and friends was their gratification of personal wealth. Appalachians were strong and independent, because they knew how to live in harmony with their surroundings. As the population grew from within, this region's families maintained their role as stable units that not many Americans have been able to preserve. Mountaineers had built a solid foundation within their confines, by embracing the strength of immediate family and extended clan. This tradition still stands today as a monument to the Appalachian family. Clan gatherings or festivals can bring together up to 3,000 people from the same family that go back to the earliest roots of settlers. Even though eastern Kentuckians experienced more adverse conditions than the rest of our nation, closeness of family, religion, singular class structure and sense of community held them together.

Finally, as one looks at Appalachia during this period of history, a pattern of poverty had been established that was more than economically based. Lack of social and political movement also produced ills that became the foundation for a "tradition" of indigence, which would carry on through the 20th century. Appalachians had very few initiatives for growth, and in order to build a thriving, sustainable society, meant that they had to develop new choices. Otherwise, disparities and inequities that were evident during this time would lead to uncontrolled conditions. Poverty in eastern Kentucky has existed since the formation of its society, and as the 19th century came to a close, it was inevitable that many obstacles had to be overcome.

Chapter II

1900 — 1929

Emergence of an Industrial Giant

During the 20th century's early years, a most obvious consequence for change in Appalachia was the declining dependency on agriculture by its people as their main source of income. Opening eastern Kentucky to mineral rights speculators went beyond the knowledge and understanding that its rural population had of this land, as the purpose for buying mineral rights was external and unfathomable to them. At the same time they were coerced into believing that a new industry would bring prosperity and a better way of life. What was central to this projected future and distinguished it from past living conditions, is that the hillfolk saw possibilities of improving their situation, which meant an escape from being poor. Knowing that they were dealing with easy going illiterate people, speculators and coal companies did not have a difficult task buying up mineral rights to most Appalachian land.

Coal Mining

Employing lawyers, politicians and officials of county seats as their emissaries of "good will," coal corporations began exploiting the Appalachian people. These corporations moved with such "sleight of hand slickness" that eastern Kentuckians did not realize they were giving away certain mineral rights, which proved to be a devastating decision. The "richness" of these mountains was obvious to speculators and coal companies, yet common people could not foresee the financial values. To the illiterate hillfolk, getting twenty-five cents per acre for mineral rights was a lot of money, which meant that those who had 200 acres of land received fifty dollars in full settlement of all claims. They were ecstatic having this much money, which helped sustain their immediate existence, however, it was a short-lived experience that left people bewildered and questioning implications of their hasty decision. A typical cartoon in newspapers, exemplifying the coal owner's gains and downfall of the hill-folk, showed a baron as a huge pompous man with a cigar in his mouth, money bulging out of pockets, and a deceitful smile. With one hand he gave a few coins to a poor mountaineer, while shaking the other hand of this thoroughly confused man. Thus, with mineral rights virtually given away to outsiders, development of a new industry would change the economic picture of this region for many decades. Though it is important to emphasize that the coal boom opened doors for Appalachia's population growth, equally notable is that this industry also became responsible for the addition of a myriad of problems to already existing ills.

With the discovery of coal, Appalachia would play an important role in America's economic history. In the early 20th century, eastern Kentucky became an important base for the coal industry and supplied not only the United States, but went beyond its borders. The railroads extended new lines to places such as Hazard, Benham, Wheelright, and McRoberts, which added to existing tracks that were built during the coal boom of the late 1800's. It became evident that with construction of rail lines and buying huge land areas for coal mining, the region was no longer closed to outsiders. The railroad system had expanded to encompass back country areas, so that coal resources of eastern Kentucky would be transported throughout the nation. Laborers built tracks, including tunnels through mountains for railroad companies like the Chesapeake and Ohio, and men were hired to clear the "land and its wilds," so that coal camps and towns could be built.

Although man-made paths existed in many mountain areas, they were not passable by vehicles, and around 1910 a movement to build dirt roads began. Generally, road construction was under the jurisdiction of counties. However, since governments in Appalachia lacked revenue, they were limited to finance projects, but utilized the "free workins" approach to construction of roads. The phrase "working your tax off" was an expression used in those days, for many men were in debt. Local law required these men to work on the roads in a team, using basic tools, such as a hand-operated scraper. Even though it was backbreaking, tiring, slow and demanded long hours, mountaineers developed a sense of satisfaction in doing something for the benefit of fellow Appalachians. Due to limitations of available money, communities that benefited from building those few roads were county seats, instead of back country villages and towns. The coming of change and population growth, which included an additional 300 coal towns and camps, made matters worse for the region. Added to this, areas and communities were still being reached by foot or on horseback. As was expected, Appalachia's county governments could not sustain an adequate range of services and also lacked financial resources, which for many years would be a constant deterrent for community growth.

Coal mining towns and camps were born overnight, as corporations made plans to mine the rich mountains that contained "Black Gold." Mountaineers, and outsiders brought in by coal companies, worked side by side to build shanties that were put together in hurried fashion with "much to be desired materials." These structures stood on cinder blocks or poles, two to three feet off the ground, with unpainted boards nailed directly to the frames of shanties. The roofs of these poorly built dwellings were made of thin composition, which after a few hard winter seasons would deteriorate and fall apart. These "simple homes" had the same indoor and outdoor plan throughout the community complex. In fact, as one viewed coal towns and camps, a homogeneous architectural style prevailed all over this region. Living quarters were built in close proximity to the mining area, because each community had to be designed so that everything would evolve around the workplace.

It was not easy to plan around the base of mountains, because there were complications in combining a coal camp and operations buildings, along with equipment, to support miners who worked underground. Engineers with local help and workers from other states built the total complex and organized necessary equipment that was required for the operation. A formidable task of planning services for a coal mine is the development of an effective transportation system, and railroads were the only major source in this region for carrying coal to other places. Building trunk lines for railroads to haul coal out of the area presented numerous problems to coal company planners, since mountains in their natural design could not be moved, and in certain cases where there was not enough flat bottom land, camps were built further away from the mining center. Unique construction for trunk lines going into rich veins of the mine area was a necessity for easy accessibility of transporting coal onto railroad cars. Engineering ingenuity created opportunities for railroads to bring out the product. In spite of hairpin curves and twisting passes, one of the most expansive networks of rail lines was established, leading to and from Appalachia.

Coal camps and towns were generally located in isolated backwoods country, where transportation by road in and out of the areas or to local mountain villages was difficult. Workers did not have automobiles and had to depend fully on the company-owned store (commissary) in their town, which contained goods, ranging from food, drugs, clothing, hardware to furniture. These stores were so diverse that they even sold coffins for the dearly departed. Political structure and management of coal communities was important to the role commissaries played, making them the only choice for miners and their families to shop. Even though the stores were stocked with a variety of merchandise, everything was over-priced. These businesses were run to benefit coal companies, as miners were mainly paid in scrip, which could only be used in the commissary. The power that coal corporations had over workers was all encompassing, relating to the miners' work and their overall daily living conditions.

Since companies required that workers live in coal communities, men from tiny hamlets and hollows of Appalachia moved from the hills, leaving their farms in the hands of wives or relatives to maintain them. Various estimates reported that between 25 and 35 percent of the moun-taineer working population toiled in underground mining. In a short period of time, inexperienced hillfolk were joined by coal company recruited newcomers from all parts of the United States. Added to these two groups in mining towns and camps were immigrants from Europe with Italian, Polish and other origins. The "John Henrys," who had been building railroad lines in Appalachia, and impressed coal company owners with their hard work ethic, were also employed to work the mines. These strong black men were eventually joined by others who came from Alabama. In 1910 the population of eastern Kentucky had increased at a greater percentage than the State as a whole, and the upsurge of people was a picture of constant migration, both into and within the region. The mining boom brought a great bustle of activity not only to coal towns and camps, but overflowed into other communities that served as business cen-ters for rural residents.

Local Communities

Overabundance of workers and a housing shortage in coal towns at the peak of mining between 1912 and 1926, brought many people into county seats and local villages. Boarding houses, room rentals, and quick rising shanties on hillsides and hamlets added financial gain for some local people. Differing cultural backgrounds began to melt within the com-munities and were changing them with all the nuance that growth brings. Population increase boggled the minds of local folks. For example, Perry County grew from approximately 11,000 people in 1910 to over 26,000 by 1920, and the population of Harlan County mushroomed from about 10,000 to over 31,000. Lynch, the biggest coal town in the region, doubled its population to 10,000 by the early 1920's.

Growth in the Appalachian region also attracted Jewish and Syrian merchants from cosmopolitan areas, who were creative and ambitious, enhancing the communities. A combination of the new and existing stores in county seats and villages presented competition problems to coal company commissaries. Prices in coal camp and town commissaries were higher, and miners who shopped at lower priced stores in other villages were penalized, or let go from their jobs. This feudal system of control would present problems to workers and families for many years to come.

Although there were mountaineers who did not join the mining labor force, a fair percentage was able to benefit from local growth of the coal industry. Farmers in particular, limited in selling their crops, hogs, poultry and eggs at a market, had ready-made customers in miners. If a town was near a mine, various merchants and farmers were able to gain from the added revenue. Housing was at a premium, and miners working for smaller companies often did not have to live in a coal camp. The local folk would rent rooms or space to these miners. With slices of the population benefiting from the coal boom, even the lumber industry profited, as local companies were in need of providing wood that was necessary for mining purposes.

Moonshine Profiteers

An interesting enterprise during this period was the development of moonshine stills, which were located in back country rough terrain and impossible for strangers to find. With the region's population growing, opportunity for some hillfolk to economically benefit, brought to light the making of corn whiskey. This practice was not new, for it can be traced back to the settlers of Appalachia. Since not all hillfolk had been able to gain employment in the coal industry, some resorted to making corn whiskey for economic reasons. Making and selling moonshine produced a good income for those mountaineers who committed themselves to this illegal operation. The rationale as to why these people got involved in this unlawful occupation was explained to me in later years. One of my college students stated that his granddaddy and uncle "had been making moonshine, in order to keep their families going." He clarified that farming of the land had taken a downturn and was no longer feasible, and they did not want to live under conditions that were best described as indigent. In these isolated backwoods areas, the hillfolk did not have opportunities for growth, and they became trapped by a combination of physical, economic, social and cultural factors, which helped intensify poor living situations.

The reason for being involved in this illegal activity was generally contrary to the belief held by many Appalachians. In fact, there have been very few mountaineers who illegally made moonshine, yet this negative image had plagued citizens of the region for decades. The perception Americans had about such activity was developed through the media, which categorized all Appalachians as participating in this way of life. People did not try to understand causes and circumstances of the conditions that led to breaking the law. Very few participated in illegally making a living and if they did, it was out of necessity.

Local (County) Government

The term "corporate dominated power structure" is used to summarize conditions and experiences that were new and different from what the people had been exposed to in the past. The "big coal giant" had conquered Appalachian society in one fell swoop for self-serving purposes, to never release its reigns. Even though local community government was lacking in many ways before arrival of coal mining, their inadequacies were further compounded by new conditions that this industry created, which affected nearly every person in the region.

Difficulties that existed in county seats and villages in the past became greater because of growth, which in turn required local government to develop or expand services more than before. However, money to provide for these services was not available. Tax revenue, based on property value, was weakly structured, and the process of assessment gave rise to suspicions of favoritism, which added to the fact that counties were incapable in responding financially to community demands. They desperately needed police, public works, education, health care and other services. As all these necessities mounted, many communities were too small and not able to provide a full range of municipal services, consequently responsibilities fell on the county government. However, the new set of conditions differed from past experiences, and county government inadequacies became very evident. What exposed their weakness even more was the inability to function, as counties were unable to adequately make change or incapable of handling complex problems. Nevertheless, it is important to emphasize that the influence of coal corporations became a strait jacket to not only "controlled politicians", but even honest community leaders, who were limited by the ways in which they could act effectively.

Coal towns and camps were totally under the control of corporations. The hand-appointed governing administration generally consisted of company officials or managers. Coal barons extended their power into county seats through various ways and means, as complete domination by a corporation was not an exception and led to corruption and plain dishonesty. The corporations built a power structure through the backing of politicians, who would respond to their desire of control. These governing few elite, geographically concentrated in county seats, were eager to compromise with coal companies in order to climb the ladder of financial benefits, and did so without consideration for their fellow Appalachians. Very little was done by politicians and county government to improve daily problems in communities that fueled conditions of poverty, leading to insecurity in people.

It was evident that county government did not progress, as building of necessary roads, facilities, and community services was ignored. As a result, backwardness of the region haunted people for many years. Most roads were mere trails and game tracks that mountaineers developed for free "road workins." County seats lacked government buildings as well as other facilities, and dismal school situations prevailed. The quick change from an independent agricultural environment to an industrial base, along with the mixing of already existing towns and county seats, caused poor health and other social conditions to increase unceremoniously.

Ineffective county officials and government were not the only problem that communities had to contend with. They also had to deal with coal corporations' lack of commitment to the region. Many were operating tax free or without regulation, and their desire to keep it that way was unquestionable. In turn, they were depriving communities of government services, direly needed to keep the region from sliding backward. Unjust inaction brought disdain by concerned citizens toward the power structure. The social consciousness of these people created endeavors of trying to change the political direction during this period. However, lacking a power base and material advantages of the coal corporation-backed politicians, the common man met with organizational problems and inconsistent direction in most communities. Deterrents were so expansive that it was difficult for mountaineers to develop an ideology for finding the right ways to improve life in Appalachia. They were poorly educated, and the reliability of leadership was open for scrutiny. People were hurt too many times and did not even trust their own kind, and unity was a lacking ingredient. Wherever common folk leadership potential looked evident, the county power structure was able to control the situation, by employing methods that used fellow Appalachians to stifle social and economic reform efforts. The political power structure had created a controlled community, completely under the domain of a few elite.

Transportation

As the United States progressed through the 1920's, there appeared to be an increase in prosperity. Thus, the "roaring twenties" came about, with most Americans living in the fast lane, even though they were not spending money beyond their means. During this time, the automobile opened up travel in our country. By 1929, approximately three million new cars were purchased each year, and a total of 26 million traveled over roads in the United States. People throughout the country started using their vehicles for recreational purposes, therefore longer and more extensive vacations were becoming a part of the American way of life. Appalachia on the other hand, did not benefit financially like other parts of the nation. The control that coal companies had over community and workers was further evident, for even car dealerships were owned by company stores. The buyers of automobiles consisted mainly of coal executives, professional people, businessmen, and others, whose "take-home pay" made it possible to buy a vehicle. For the common man, miner or farmer, a car was unaffordable, because this purchase would have meant the largest single financial transaction they had ever made. It was a luxury that poor people could look at, but not enjoy.

Continuing into the end of 1929, Appalachia's roads did not improve, as two lane travel was an exception to the rule. In back country areas, one-lane dirt roads followed the established foot paths over and around mountains. They were narrow, winding, with numerous dangerous curves and other obstacles that created frustrating experiences for the traveler. Many roads, built alongside creeks or rivers, became treacherous during winter or rainy weather. Washouts were the norm after thawing of snow or during a rainfall, with parts of the road sliding into a creek or river.

Health and Health Care

As one views the health status of Appalachia during the early 20th century, poverty had extended to all facets of a persons life. Susceptibility to disease and illness, lack of health care services, unhealthy living situations, and hazards of working in the most dangerous occupation caused mental conditions that took a toll on the human spirit and self-respect. Unfortunately, the region was not ready to deal with the onslaught of poor health conditions that evolved through growth of population and its resultant problems. Trying to meet these head on by an understaffed health care system proved to be a demanding challenge, and the most needy communities that warranted services were newly developed coal towns and camps.

Journalists who traveled into the hill country, came back to big cities of the Northeast with stories condemning coal barons, who lacked concern for their employees and families. Articles from the *New York Times* cited Appalachia as being reminiscent of Dark Ages, rather than the 20th century. Water, which required purification processes by health departments, presented a constant concern to many coal camps, because it was drawn from open springs and polluted wells, creating disease and illness. Coal company health services became a necessity for the miners and their families, and corporations had to "contract" outside physicians to work in the camps and towns, because there were no rural doctors available. Hospitals also were needed, but existing dwellings had to be used, ranging from a one room structure with a few beds to nursing home style facilities that originally served as residences.

A company doctor was difficult to find in certain camps, making families and neighbors more dependent on home remedies. In the beginning medical people were scarce, because the coal companies had not been able to entice enough physicians and other professional personnel from different parts of the country. However, intensive recruiting efforts showed an increase in health services, though not sufficient. Overall, most hospitals lacked adequate facilities, qualified doctors, nurses and other health personnel, and consequently functioned below normal standards. Nevertheless, a few hospitals were organized and ran efficiently, for communities such as Lynch, Benham, and Jenkins had been fortunate enough to have coal companies that were concerned about the health conditions of their workers and families. Care was important to assure not only effective worker response, but also family satisfaction. During the early 1900's, approximately 300 mining camps and towns existed in eastern Kentucky, and not all communities had a "so called" hospital. In certain situations, two camps built a centrally located medical facility, which was shared by both. Along with a few beds, these "hospitals" had basic emergency medical equipment and supplies for minor operations.

During this period, hospital development in Appalachia had proceeded with feverish haste, and many were not planned in respect to people's convenience and necessity or sound financing. As a result, most of the so called "medical facilities" had a difficult time making ends meet. The people themselves did not have the understanding and knowledge as to intangible values that make a "good hospital," like quality and capabilities of professional staff, customs and practices in vogue, and innumerable variables, which affect functions of such a facility. The result was that good health standards were unheard of, and the only concern people had was to get medicine that would free them from pain and illness.

As the 20th century progressed, medicine in the United States eliminated plagues, such as yellow fever, cholera, and typhus. Today, we take for granted the control of diphtheria, malaria, smallpox, chickenpox, tuberculosis, and typhoid fever, all of which were real menaces to a great number of people during that time. Plagues, illnesses, and diseases led to many premature deaths during the early part of this century, and Appalachia was no exception, for it became one of the hardest hit regions in the nation. Problems arising from inadequate living conditions of communities were inevitably linked to the people's poor health status, which resulted in part from lack of sanitation and water purification services, as well as overall inefficiencies. Many people living in poorly kept coal towns and camps were caught in deteriorating situations, affecting their physical, social and mental well-being.

The health status of children during this period was of great concern, as they became most susceptible to diseases and illness. Even poor school conditions affected their health and made it difficult for proper learning experiences. In talking with a group of senior citizens recently, who had grown up in these communities during the 1920's, they verified that poor school facilities hindered learning. One elderly gentleman told of how schools in those days were cold in the winter time and "overcoats" and "stocking caps" had to be worn in class. Children took breaks from studying at half-hour intervals and stood around a pot-bellied stove to keep their hands and bodies warm. He further explained how the wind would whistle through cracks of non-insulated walls, which was a daily annoyance, affecting learning experiences. As an anecdote to this story, the gentleman told how howling of the wind brought on an irascible situation, when a student tried to whistle as loud as he could in harmony during class. As he paused and looked around in embarrassment, his classmates joined in chorus. The elderly man further stated that the conditions continued to prevail, yet nothing was done to help alleviate these types of obstacles that children had to endure everyday.

Local Youth in Medicine

Even though health conditions did improve slightly, eastern Kentucky's medical services still lagged far behind the rest of the nation. However, changes taking place during the coal boom had a vast impact on mountain communities that bore little resemblance to their counterparts of earlier years. The coal industry brought many problems to these transformed rural areas, and the already inadequate medical profession was confronted with obstacles, trying to accommodate the burgeoning of existing and new communities. As the population grew, certain young men were interested in becoming doctors, and families would fund a medical education for them by selling their mountain land. In other situations, parents let their sons leave home not only for college studies, but also to attend secondary school in metropolitan areas of the state. The University of Louisville became a favorite medical school for Appalachian youth, and upon completion of their respective internships, they returned to open practices in native counties. It was between 1912 and 1922, with the infusion of "home grown" accredited doctors and an increase of coal company imported physicians from other parts of the nation that medical services gradually improved.

Mary Breckinridge

In the 1920's, Appalachia struggled with its many health problems, yet there was a woman who cared about what happened to less fortunate people and tried to make things better for them. That person was Mary Breckinridge, who would set standards for success in nursing service work, which became a model for health care not only in eastern Kentucky, but throughout the world. Born in 1881 at Memphis, Tennessee, Mary came from a well-to-do family. She was one of Clifton and Katherine Breckinridge's four children. Mary's father had been a former U.S. Representative from Arkansas and Ambassador to Russia in the 1890's. Her schooling included a registered nurse's diploma at St. Luke's Hospital in New York City, along with a public health nursing graduate degree from Columbia University's School of Nursing.

During the course of Mary's early married life, she encountered two tragedies that would profoundly affect her goals in the nursing field. Mary had lost her two children: a daughter shortly after birth, and a son just four years old. As an outlet for her sorrow over the deaths of her children, she made a commitment to raise the health status of mothers and their offspring. Mrs. Breckinridge had explored the Hyden area and decided that this was the place where she wanted to help. During the 20's, Appalachia was one of the poorest and most isolated regions in America and Mary felt that its greatest needs for health care were not being met. One area of concern was the high maternal/child mortality rate, and the State's inability to do something about it, gave Mary a purpose to initiate a new innovative approach in combating this tragic situation. In the fall of 1923 Mary Breckinridge departed for London, England, engaging in post-graduate work pertaining to midwife nursing. She also traveled throughout Scotland, observing the effectiveness of medical care in the Scottish Highlands.

When Mary Breckinridge returned from England, she settled at

Hyden, Leslie County, where the mortality rate of mothers and young infants was the highest in Kentucky, and this area lacked social as well as medical agencies. In 1924, this county like many others of the region, had no licensed physician or registered nurse, and the only so called medical personnel consisted of elderly, untrained midwives. The challenges of working with these people, who were deprived of good health and care, encouraged Mary Breckinridge to initiate a nursing service. She traveled to the State capital at Frankfort and met with the health commissioner and governor. They became her strongest backers, and Mary's proof for maternal and infant health care was so convincing that in 1925 with support of the State, she started the Frontier Nursing Service (F.N.S.). For the first three years, Mary Breckinridge underwrote the entire operation of this organization with money she inherited from her mother. One of her first objectives was to enlist support from prominent citizens all over the state, in establishing the Kentucky Committee for Mothers and Babies, which eventually became part of the F.N.S. Effectiveness of nurse-midwifery as a solution to Appalachia's as well as America's alarmingly high maternal and infant death rates gained acceptance throughout the country. From the beginning, Mary's work was medically sound and meticulous, therefore results of keeping complete statistics through the years were valuable in researching maternal and infant mortality rates.

Since there were very few roads in Leslie County, F.N.S. set up outpost nursing centers approximately ten miles apart from each other. Nurse-midwives traveled on horseback no more than a few miles from any outpost. Realizing that the 300 square mile area required people to help with certain health needs in rural hamlets and hollows, Mary Breckinridge developed one of the first community involved health programs. She also initiated the regional health care concept, with Hyden Hospital serving as medical center for nursing outposts.

This operation was viewed by medical personnel as Hyden hospital being the palm of a hand, with services extending to outposts like fingers pointing in different directions. With one physician on staff, who was the medical director, F.N.S. provided preventive medicine as well as crisis nursing. Within five years, F.N.S. had served thousands of families in the area. Dr. Wallace Campbell, at present Academic Dean and Vice-President at Alice Lloyd College, attests to the fact, if Mary Breckinridge had not helped to bring him and his siblings into this world, their chances of survival would have been questionable. This petite woman, dearly admired and revered by thousands of Kentucky hillfolk, left a standard of excellence in health care that was recognized and praised not only in the United States, but also internationally. The success of F.N.S. methods to deliver quality healthcare services and lowering the rate of death in childbirth, was Mary's gift to Appalachia. She also proved that cost-containment of nurse-midwifery was effective. Breckinridge had been an astute administrator and always conscious about the importance of research, in justifying her approach to nursing and health care practice.

In 1939, F.N.S. and Hyden Hospital initiated the Frontier Graduate School of Midwifery. Mary Breckinridge, who had used her maiden name, was a very effective communicator. During the early 60's, I remember the opportunity of meeting with her as well as Peggy Elmore, Mary's longtime assistant and faithful confidante, for that day will always stay in my memory. Mrs. Breckinridge stated that as a seeker to help others, she found what she was looking for not far from where her search began — in Appalachia, and her dream to "improve the status of mothers and their children" was realized. Mary Breckinridge died May 17, 1965, at the age of 84. As I look back and remember what this good-hearted woman's contributions meant to the poor, I found that she was one of the most significant health care contributors for Appalachia's people.

Right after Mary's death, her nephew John Breckinridge came to visit Ralph Lewis, Alice Lloyd College Publicity Director, and me. John was former Attorney General of the State of Kentucky and later served as U.S. Representative to Congress. He told how his aunt was a woman of drive and insurmountable energy. We compared the similarities of Mary Breckinridge and Alice Lloyd, two great humanitarians who both "came from elsewhere to help the people of eastern Kentucky." Like Alice Lloyd, Mrs. Mary Breckinridge was constantly raising funds to keep F.N.S. going. John mentioned how she traveled throughout the country, spreading goodwill about people of Appalachia. She was a very plain looking woman, who dressed like the hillfolk and cut her own hair. This of course, did not meet the style of fashion among the wealthy of America, who were her contributors. However, they still supported Mary Breckinridge's cause, for the good she was doing far outweighed this insignificant matter. The most dramatic example of this giver is that she understood the intensity of suffering that the poor had to endure, and she persevered to do something about it.

Education

As in previous years, intended beneficiaries of education, the children of eastern Kentucky, were continually overlooked. They suffered from a range of problems, with lack of formal education being a major hindrance to improve their situation. Life had been hard for children from small farms in the mountains, as well as those living in towns and villages. The late 1800's and early 1900's saw changes in education for the rest of the state, as an abundance of "schooling" opportunities blessed the central and western regions, but bypassed children of isolated Appalachian highlands. To a certain extent, education in eastern Kentucky was available, but those children that benefited belonged to a select group of people who lived in villages and towns. Mountain families from backwoods hollows and farms were mostly illiterate and their children learned in the traditional hillfolk way, by observing and imitating their elders. They were not encouraged nor eager to attend school in the village, and travel distance was still a deterrent for many. There were other factors that played a role when children did not benefit from formal education. Families, through illness or some other misfortune, were forced to depend on older children in many ways.

Closeness and commitment to the family were inherent characteristics that children of Appalachia enjoyed, and if money was needed, which most often occurred, the oldest boy worked rather than attend school. Daughters stayed home to watch younger siblings while mothers helped their husbands with farming. These self-sustaining mountain families in this isolated region preserved their customs and even speech, while persons from other parts of Kentucky had the chance to improve their lives through education. Appalachians were content with quiet pride of their independence, and needs were simple and basic. The things that children were able to do, they learned from their parents. They knew that milk did not come from a bottle, flour from a sack, or eggs from the store. To study the sky and predict weather for the next day was their way of gaining an educational experience. The many things they "got to know" were best-described by one senior gentleman back in the early 1960's, who said to me: "We learned things that can't be taught in the classroom, but they were valuable."

Formal Learning Experiences

With the arrival of coal mining, outsiders played an important part in changing the educational environment. Combined desires of coal company executives and their wives, along with coal miners that migrated from other parts of the country, brought one-room schools into coal mining communities. They realized that a boy or girl who went into the "world" uneducated, would encounter economic and social problems. Teachers, recruited from other parts of the country, provided a more effective learning environment, which eventually "rubbed off" onto local county seats and surrounding mountain towns and villages.

Qualifications for educators during the early 1900's were extremely lower than today's requirements. Most teachers were women, and a teenager after graduating from the eighth grade was qualified to instruct in a one-room school. Today, an appropriate bachelor's plus a master's degree certifies a person to teach. Memories of the school years during the early 20th century were pleasant, even though one-room learning had quite a few inadequacies, which included large numbers of unqualified teachers. Another problem was that more than one grade level of children had to be taught in the same classroom. Each child needing his or her own course of study led to a very heavy and tedious schedule for the teacher.

In the last quarter of the 19th century the "McGuffey Reader" was published. Known as the "bible of education" and written by Kentuckian William Holmes McGuffey, the Reader was used not only in this state but also extensively throughout the nation. I have had the opportunity through the years to talk with highly respected educators, sharing their feelings of this well-known Reader, and the consensus was very favorable. As one individual who grew up with the McGuffey Reader so aptly stated, "You knew that children were well-educated by the time they left school." Of course, this may appear primitive compared to today's standards, however one has to understand the limitations placed on teaching at that time. For better or worse, the McGuffey Reader was a tool of ambitious proportions, largely successful in its day and by no means a total curriculum, as some people unfortunately espoused. Yet, it did create a loyal and dedicated group of followers, because some schools were still using this educational "material" up to the end of World War II. It was not until the latter part of the 1800's that Kentucky organized a formal structure of education. Nevertheless, Appalachia was slow in responding, for life in the mountains where people lived on farms, needed a minimal amount of formal upbringing. Back-breaking work required man's brawn, and the children learned from their parents by being exposed to every day living experiences.

While education was available in one-room schools at coal towns, certain miners' families reacted unfavorably toward learning, as did some of their counterpart mountaineers. Parents who lacked education often did not understand why their children had to go to school. Coal workers' sons sometimes helped in the mines, and were eager to work beside their fathers. This was a kind of apprenticeship through which people learned skills in the early days. However, working in the mines was abusive, as young boys were overworked, underpaid, and their life span shortened through injuries or hazards. The eastern Kentucky region did not lead the crusade against child labor abuses, yet as a result of the unspeakable conditions throughout the country, laws were passed to restrict child labor.

Leadership For Change

The greatest impact of educational reform during this period occurred through individuals and schools, which established an unprecedented tradition for change and leadership in order to meet the needs of young people in eastern Kentucky. Settlement schools, such as Pine Mountain, founded in 1913, and Henderson School near Middlesboro, recognized depressed problems of their areas and provided educational opportunities for the youth. In certain instances, mountaineers themselves realized the importance of education and enlisted the aid of "outsiders" to provide learning experiences for their children.

Uncle Sol Beveridge

Hindman Settlement School, the first of its kind in Kentucky, started through efforts of "Uncle Sol" Beveridge. His story, how at age 82 he trekked a long, hard twenty miles through rough and rocky stretches of mountain land to interest two women in becoming schoolteachers in his area, is still a legend today. The determination as an individualist made him decide that his grandchildren and great-grandchildren should get an education that he never received.

Katherine Pettit

In August 1902, Katherine Pettit of Lexington and May Stone from Louisville founded the Hindman Settlement School. After going through some very difficult early years, the school was able to survive and flourish. Its reputation of success was reaching other parts of the region, and in 1911 enrollment increased to 200 students, supported by a resident staff of thirteen. A natural leader, Katherine Pettit cultivated the good will of these people to combine their survival skills with academic learning. She explained to them that crafts and manual skills, such as sewing, cooking, woodworking, and other handicrafts should be a part of their total learning experiences.

During this time, Katherine Pettit and May Stone embarked on providing other services to people of the area. Trachoma, a contagious eye disease that can lead to blindness and is common in the mountains, had spread out of control, and realizing the consequences, Miss Pettit decided to take immediate action by contacting her Lexington friends, Linda Neville and Dr. J.C. Stucky, who had devoted their lives to combat this disease. At Katherine's request, they treated many trachoma patients, however, it was spreading and something more had to be done to overcome this situation. Through her efforts, the United States Public Health Service was able to develop a plan to fight this disease, and the good deeds of Katherine Pettit were heard throughout the mountains and never forgotten by many Appalachians.

In 1913 she accepted an invitation to open a similar school in Harlan County. Accompanying her was Ethel de Long, who had been a teacher at Hindman. Miss Pettit and Miss de Long met with William Creech, a mountaineer of vision, who contributed 250 acres of land for the development of Pine Mountain Settlement School. Working as a team, Katherine Pettit, Ethel de Long, and Mr. Creech created the same type of learning experiences that had been successful at Hindman. Local needs of the area called for setting up extension programs in isolated one-room schools, along with founding health centers in remote areas of Big Laurel and Line Fork.

After seventeen years at Pine Mountain Settlement School, Miss Pettit left to help farmers in this area. Through her experience of growing up on a large plantation in Lexington, she encouraged Appalachian farmers to improve methods and techniques of working the soil. She also went among the people to help them sell their handicrafts in gift shops of Lexington and Louisville. In honor of her contributions to people of Appalachia, the University of Kentucky awarded Katherine Pettit the Algernon Sidney Sullivan Medal. In 1936, at age sixty-eight, Katherine Pettit died of cancer in Lexington. However, her gift of helping others lives on in those people she touched.

Abisha Johnson

There were other mountaineers of the same spirit as Solomon Beveridge, and through strong determination they wanted to generate a better environment for their families, which included education as the foundation for change. Each knew that their offspring had a better opportunity to be viable members of the community to elevate themselves in society, if they were educated. One such person was Abisha Johnson, a Caney Creek resident and hard working well-respected farmer. For Mr. Johnson and his family to be educated was realized in his chance meeting with Alice Geddes Lloyd, which also proved to be an unexpected benefit for the people of Appalachia. "Bysh" Johnson's meeting with Mrs. Lloyd started an important development of long range strategies, in assisting many Appalachians to become literate in order to break the chains of poverty. Above all, people were motivated to be educated and become effective citizens.

Jim Bergman, of Alice Lloyd College writes of Abisha Johnson's meeting with this "stranger:"

> "....One day in the fall of 1916, Caney Creek citizen Abisha Johnson walked up to the porch of "Hope Cottage," and rapped on a porch post to draw the attention of the residents inside. Presbyterian missionaries had made this house on Troublesome Creek at Ivis, Kentucky, available to Boston native Alice Geddes Lloyd and her mother a year earlier. Mrs. Lloyd, who was married at that time to Arthur Lloyd, had been advised by doctors to seek a warmer climate, because of ill health.
>
> When Mrs. Lloyd came to the door, "Bysh" was quick to inquire if she was the foreign woman. "I was born in the Cradle of Liberty; you may consider me foreign in these parts," she replied.
>
> This unlike visitor had come with a special request. Would Alice come across the mountain to Caney Creek to teach his family? If she would consent to come, he would offer a "strip of land" (about fifty acres), and build her a home.
>
> Sometime before the end of the year, Alice and her mother made the journey to Caney Creek. It marked the beginning of what is now one of the most unique educational communities in America."

Mr. Johnson, a common man, could not foresee that this "outside woman" would do extraordinary things to help improve the lives of others. For years after that eventful meeting, "Bysh" Johnson was seen walking around the Alice Lloyd College campus, proud of this "great humanitarian's" achievements. Thus, Alice Lloyd's personal war against illiteracy and poverty had begun.

Alice Geddes Lloyd

One of the most imaginative and influential leaders of eastern Kentucky was Alice Geddes Lloyd, a little frail woman who persevered against all odds, battling physical disability and partial paralysis. She lived a dynamic life of leadership by providing an educational impact, and became a social force for many people of Appalachia. Alice, born and reared in Massachusetts, attained her college education at Radcliffe, and was later employed as a reporter for the Boston Globe. Afterwards she edited the Cambridge Women's Chronicle and became publisher of Cambridge Press. When Alice Lloyd moved to Caney Creek in 1917, she chose to settle in an area that had only one college graduate. Few of its citizens could read or write, and there was no public high school that encompassed Knott and three surrounding counties. The average annual income in these counties was under 25 dollars. Coal, which ultimately revolutionized the economy of this area, was the only way to make money. Mrs. Lloyd had recognized the needs of these people and immediately provided basic social services and education for the community.

Alice Lloyd wrote fund raising letters to her northern friends, collecting enough money for the construction of a six-room schoolhouse and purchased the rest of Mr. Johnson's farm to be used as Caney Creek Community Center. Over the next 46 years until her death, Alice Lloyd laboriously typed hundreds of letters on her battered Oliver #9 typewriter, soliciting funds to support her educational endeavors. Right from the start, her mission was to train mountain youth to be leaders in their communities. The first years in Appalachia, Alice worked in cooperation with surrounding counties to develop and improve over 100 grammar schools and established community organizations. In 1919 Mrs. Lloyd was joined by June Buchanan, a graduate of Wellesley College, who became her confidante and assistant.

Alice Lloyd and Miss Buchanan opened the first high school in this area with a total of two pupils. They immediately set out encouraging the youth to enroll in secondary education. Enrollment increased immensely and accreditation, which was unknown to people, became a challenge for Mrs. Lloyd. Knott County High School at "Pippa Passes" became accredited in 1924. Alice Lloyd suggested this name for the growing community on Caney Creek and selected it from a poem by Robert Browning about a young girl in Italy, who had touched the lives of many people in a small rural village. Approximately five years after Alice Lloyd's arrival in Pippa Passes, she opened seven other high schools in the surrounding areas of eastern Kentucky. With no federal aid available, each of these schools started with gifts of money solicited from friends and people all over the nation. The schools recruited teachers from the northeast with Alice Lloyd's letter in hand. College graduates who came from other states to Appalachia often volunteered their time and effort, and in many instances paid their own expenses.

In 1922, Alice Lloyd was not satisfied with high school education and felt that the area needed local college graduates who would come back to communities and lead the fight to improve life for less fortunate hill-folk. She had the vision of upgrading education by including the college level. With the belief that higher education was a necessary instrument for greater effective change, Mrs. Lloyd gave the youth of this region a sense of purpose for their future, thus, Caney Junior College was founded in 1923. It became her central concern, even though Caney Creek Community Center continued to provide basic social services to the area with June Buchanan serving as Director. Mrs. Lloyd ran almost single-handedly the College for over forty years, relying entirely on contributions from individuals and groups throughout America, with no state or federal aid during her lifetime. In fact, I remember traveling to Washington, D.C. in 1964 to request a National Science Foundation Grant for an experimental project that Professor Roy Reynolds had initiated. It was a small grant, but the College began proudly to receive further aid not only from private individuals or organizations, but also from government agencies. Still, no tuition was charged and total scholarships were given to all students. Alice Lloyd was able to attract trained professional faculty members, who were impressed by the college's purpose and dedication to students.

As I look back, Alice Lloyd College was the most gratifying experience for me while working in education. Many traditions established by Alice Lloyd in early days of the college persisted through her lifetime, and for years thereafter. Even though Mrs. Lloyd had been an "outsider," she was welcomed right away by mountaineers. The hillfolk usually do not accept strangers that readily, because they had been taken advantage of. Yet, being a free thinker, Alice Lloyd earned the immediate respect and support of mountain people by pledging never to interfere with their politics, religion, or "moonshining." She was a "task master," demanding strictness of conduct. There was neither tobacco, whiskey or playing cards allowed on campus. Even though firearms had been very common in the mountains, none were allowed on college grounds. The mixing of young men and women in a classroom was also prohibited. However, in the early 1960's Alice Lloyd allowed them to attend the same classes.

Mrs. Lloyd believed that the spartan way of life would thrive best in an isolated environment, and opposed building a road to the college. Nevertheless, this changed after a few years and in 1960 Alice acknowledged that a paved road was needed. She was convinced that students who came to her with lack of training should be challenged with a rigorous traditional curriculum, which included Latin, Greek, Literature, Mathematics, Philosophy, and the sciences, with emphasis on liberal arts. During its early years, the college did not participate in intercollegiate sports. Students were involved in activities that helped people of eastern Kentucky communities in different ways. They called themselves

"Crusaders," who toured the United States to arouse interest in their college and make people aware of the deprivation in Appalachia. The message sent forward emphasized that these students were not supported by government, but through private contributions. During Alice Lloyd's lifetime, many graduates went on to successful careers, serving as physicians, dentists, lawyers, congressmen, engineers, psychologists, educators, ministers, businessmen, and healthcare professionals.

Those students entering college for the first time knew that this education was "their gift of life" and would have never happened, if they had stayed at home or in their local community. Very concerned that these young people came from families where poverty existed for many years, Alice Lloyd's desire to motivate them to succeed was one of her major objectives. Even though Mrs. Lloyd focused on an academic program that improved their learning skills, she felt that values and ethics needed to be taught right from the beginning, not superficially but in depth, reinforcing the students' higher education experience.

Alice Lloyd's personal life was completely entwined in her work, and throughout these years her mother had been a devoted supporter, until she passed away in 1945. Although Mrs. Lloyd was devastated by her mother's death, she carried on with the help of dedicated friend and associate June Buchanan, as they continued to expand services of both the College and Community Center. Alice Lloyd was not a well woman, her right arm had been helpless, and she walked with constant pain after a leg fracture in the 1940's. Yet, crippled and even as she stooped, Alice carried herself with the strength of a mountain. Mrs. Lloyd avoided publicity and refused remuneration for her work. Her one-room apartment was located next to Caney Creek Community Center, on the grounds of the College campus. On December 7, 1951, Alice Lloyd was persuaded to visit California by the prospect of raising funds, and found herself the subject of Ralph Edwards' television program "This is Your Life." Asked by Mr. Edwards how she felt about all the attention given to her, Alice responded that it was embarrassing to receive such acclaim and further commented, "Caney is what matters the most, not me." Edwards appealed for funds and over one hundred thousand dollars were given to the College. Alice Lloyd never left Pippa Passes, and over half of her eighty-six years were devoted to serving the isolated mountain people of eastern Kentucky.

When Alice Lloyd died on September 4, 1962, Appalachia lost one of its greatest humanitarians. She is buried on a hillside, overlooking the College campus. Immediately after her death, Caney Creek Junior College was renamed Alice Lloyd College. Her goal of providing leaders to serve the people in Appalachia continued to dominate the institution's outlook. Today, this College is a unique and outstanding four year institution in higher education. The challenge that Mrs. Lloyd faced in educating Appalachian youth was difficult, but she persevered by giving them an opportunity to succeed. Students who came to the college from impoverished family backgrounds struggled and overcame many burdens. Alice Lloyd had faith and hope for their future, and in those graduates that stayed on in the hills of eastern Kentucky to carry out leadership roles, Alice Lloyd's legacy lives on.

Education Impact On Families

When education was introduced to eastern Kentucky it brought about an astonishing response by individuals and families. Their attitude toward education led to a chain of events, carrying on Alice Lloyd's humanitarian efforts. Her concept of education for these small rural communities brought to light the importance of effective schools that developed an atmosphere of close relations among teachers, children and families. In turn this became paramount to creating a strong base for learning. The distinct uniqueness of motivated children, who had never been reached before, gaining academic success brought fulfillment. Family environment and values made it possible for youth to find themselves and determine their identity. The impact that opportunities provided for those with humble beginnings, is an example of what people can achieve when given a chance. Results of living in poverty and its consequences have been overcome when individuals experienced education, which changed their attitude and brought on the yearning to succeed.

Children Of Isaac And Leanor Slone

An example of one family, whose drive and desire to achieve success through education, were the offspring of Isaac and Leanor Slone in Knott County. Mr. and Mrs. Slone had nine children, and one can marvel at the zeal and dedication with which these children pursued the complicated task of overcoming many obstacles that were placed in front of them, as they undertook individual opportunities with determination.

Isaac and Leanor Slone demonstrated love, energy and firmness, which was necessary to raise their children to become achievers, in spite of poor economic and social conditions. With the premature death of patriarch Isaac Slone, family leadership and father role fell on the shoulders of seventeen year old J. Commodore Slone. When losing a parent at an early age, a family can either fall apart or pull together and move on in life. As oldest male in the family, Commodore understood his role that bound him to responsibility not only for himself, but also for his siblings, so that

45

unnecessary suffering of this loss would be minimized. Born at the turn of the century, he overcame adult obstacles at a young age, and his life was full of action and activities. Strong values, high standards, religious belief, and love, made him demand perfection from his younger siblings. Years later, his brothers and sisters told Commodore's daughter, Charlotte Madden, that he was like a pussy cat to his own children compared to the way he had treated them. However, they understood that by being strict he only wanted the best for them.

At a young age Commodore Slone went through various challenges and learning experiences that were considered awe-inspiring. He served in World War I, was one of Alice Lloyd's first students, went on to college in Ohio, and came back to Appalachia with his "papers" of achievement in engineering and architecture. Joining the college staff to build Alice Lloyd's campus, he continued on as a faculty member. I met J. Commodore Slone in the early 1960's, and he epitomized to me the type of person that my dad had been: someone that I admired and respected. As Commodore and I would meet many times between classes or walk along the campus, he reminisced about World War I experiences, and the time when he was getting his education and "it was a privilege to go to school."

Commodore Slone's younger sister, Rilda Watson, who for years was Alice Lloyd's and June Buchanan's secretary, had a very pleasant personality and made people feel welcome. Rilda was a pillar of strength to Alice and June, and always had a smile for everybody, whether in the administrative offices or on campus. Rilda Watson exuded kindness, cared for others, and was the type of person who had a positive attitude, regardless of the situation. Commodore's other siblings included Jim Slone, a math teacher in Hazard, Kentucky; Robert Worley Slone, who built a fine reputation in vocational education at the Kentucky State Department; Mrs. Bertha Whitacker, teacher for many years at Lotts Creek Community School; Mrs. Frankie Jane Reynolds, mother of former Alice Lloyd College faculty member, Roy Reynolds; and Mrs. Luhetta Owens, whose son, Devert Owens, is a well-known eastern Kentucky educator.

Besides working with J. Commodore and Rilda Watson, the other family member that I met in the 1960's was Alice Slone. At that time Miss Slone had established a reputation of her good deeds for the people in Lotts Creek, reminding me of Alice Lloyd's accomplishments. The economic and social conditions, along with strong influence from Alice Lloyd led this disciple to Lotts Creek, where she started a community center in the early 1930's. She joined her sister, Mrs. Bertha Whitaker, who taught at the private, non-profit community school. Alice Slone had dedicated herself to work with children of the Lotts Creek area, who needed to be educated as well as clothed and fed, because they had so little in life. One of Alice Slone's students, whose success can be attributed to the encouragement and leadership of this giving woman, is Dr. Wallace Campbell. Wallace came from a poor background, but Miss Slone saw in him a child with a brilliant young mind, bound for high educational attainment. Supporting Wallace Campbell and others through high school and college was a trademark of her work. Each year the students of Lotts Creek Community School were accepted with open arms by colleges and universities, for it was known that the solid and strong tradition of education offered by Alice Slone and her faculty was outstanding.

Alice became one of the most loved and recognized educators in eastern Kentucky. Her contribution to the many children of Lotts Creek Community School who benefited from this gifted woman, will always be in their grateful memories. She never lost her love to help people, especially the children of Appalachia. Alice Slone passed away in March of 1994. Fortunately, her tradition is capably carried forth by her niece, Alice Whitaker, who also believes that opportunities have to be given to the poor, so that they can help themselves succeed in life. Miss Slone came to a small community and achieved state recognition for a school that was not large. The importance is not size, but the strength of an educational program. Graduates of Lotts Creek Community School can attest that the high standards, caring, concern and understanding they received, is an unmatched legacy. As a result, Alice Slone's impact on the students and community will never be forgotten.

Summation

During the first part of the 20th century, Appalachia was greatly affected by a profound change from traditional farming to coal mining. The population increased dramatically, and Appalachia's countryside was altered to accommodate the boom of coal towns and camps. Presence of rich mineral resources was brought to the attention of Americans and Europeans, who invested in the new found economic and strategically important "black gold." The discovery of coal not only opened opportunities for people outside Appalachia and immigrants, but mountain farmers as well.

De-emphasizing farming was part of the most striking alteration that the region had seen since their forefathers came to Appalachia. Farming that once seemed so stable to mountain people for over a century, weakened with the discovery of coal and was unable to withstand the rising tide of this new industrial giant. However, the decline of farming would prove to be lengthy and continuously painful for future generations, often marked by poverty and despair, which ultimately ended up in disbandment. The beginning of coal industry's "big boom" led from one form of existence to another. Old ways of being free and independent changed to dependency, controlled by the corporation community life. Mixing the traditional life style with new choices and experiences presented conflicts to mountaineers, and eventually old ethical and religious standards, as well as the family structure would change.

Corporate communities, which controlled the miner's life, were so powerful and impersonal that individuals came to believe there was very little they could do to change or improve their situation. Many had been illiterate and ended up being forced into a pattern of existence, which made them feel that this was all they were worth. At first, miners assumed that economic advantages and higher wages would be provided for their hard work. However, power wielded by large coal owners threatened the workers with a mode of operation that exposed them to harsh labor and living conditions, creating bottom levels of human despair. Miners were angry about dangerous working conditions and upset with low pay. Many men died or were maimed, because safety measures were virtually nonexistent. Any open flame or spark resulted in disastrous explosions, and inhaling of coal dust led to miners contracting black lung disease.

Living under such societal conditions resulted in the need for greater understanding of the eastern Kentucky communities' health status. It was unimaginable to see the breadth and scope of health problems that confronted these people. Disparity between the population outside Appalachia and the region's citizenry was even more evident in health and health care. The health status of most American citizens was showing some form of improvement, whereas eastern Kentucky headed in the opposite direction. Appalachia's situation had deteriorated and access to care was in dire need. Probably the greatest single factor for lack of health care was the insufficient number of physicians and other medical personnel. Whatever health care improvements occurred in eastern Kentucky were not shared by all people. Poverty seemed insurmountable, as poor health and nutrition, illness, prevalence of infectious and chronic diseases brought about higher infant and adult mortality rates than in the rest of America. More effective commitment from government and the private sector was needed to improve the health status of Appalachians.

One fundamental concern during this period was the condition of the educational structure. As isolation proved to be a deterrent to people in many ways, educational opportunity was also inadequate for intellectual growth of its people. New ideas and theories presented in classrooms throughout the country were delayed in getting to Appalachian schools. In 1916, John Dewey introduced a new theory, essentially stating that each child is unique and learns in different ways. What appears to be important for one child may not necessarily be applicable for another. Modern concepts of education had not yet arrived in most of eastern Kentucky. However, a select group of humanitarians were setting standards for success, which was built on a philosophy of "making education personal to each child." Creating these kinds of schools in eastern Kentucky required the patience of people, who were totally committed to educating the underprivileged. Possibly the philosophy and techniques of pragmatism, functionalism as well as innovations by John Dewey may not have reached all of Appalachia at this time, but there was evidence that it occurred in certain areas. Educators such as Alice Lloyd and Katherine Pettit, through perseverance and ingenuity, foresaw their schools democratically run with a close relationship of teachers and students, supported by parents and community. The results have shown that through this kind of conceptual thinking these mentors knew what their community needed and attended to the individuality of each student.

Other essential services for the people were transportation and communication not only out of Appalachia, but also within the region. Communication between communities did not exist at all. Furthermore, towns and villages were self-contained, and everything evolved within each community. One part of the region was unknowing of other areas. In trying to develop a transportation system, many obstacles had to be overcome. Roadways were lacking within eastern Kentucky. Still, the greatest priority were railroads because coal was hauled out of the region. At first, railroads were not providing passenger service between inhabited places. However, this changed during the twenties when railroads not only transported coal but also people, as passenger cars were added. Improved transportation and communication was important for Appalachia to achieve a measure of unity and growth, economically, socially and politically. Unlike other regions of Kentucky, where roads and communication were able to bring people together, Appalachia still lingered behind, as continued "backwardness" was largely due to its isolation.

Chapter III

1930 — 1939

The Great Depression

In 1930, American society experienced its greatest economic down-turn, and Appalachia was no exception. The Great Depression's first sign was the Stock Market Crash of 1929, and dark clouds ascended over every phase of our economic structure. In spite of the Administration's assurance that this "temporary situation" would be cured, banks failed, corporations closed their doors and small companies went out of business. The tactical retreat by our government's later statements that this would be a long haul, did not provide a solution to those millions of Americans who were without jobs. Industry in eastern Kentucky suffered similar conditions and the number of jobless multiplied unceremoniously. Unemployment in America before the Wall Street crash was about 3.2 percent of the labor force, but in early 1932 jumped to 25 percent. However, the average rate for Appalachia was between 45 to 50 percent and reached a higher percentage in certain pockets of backwoods areas. Unfortunately, the Administration at that time was not meeting its obligations to establish policies which would invigorate the nation with economic transformation. In 1932, during this unprecedented crisis, the Democratic Party Convention in Chicago came forth with an extraordinary and popular man as candidate for President, Franklin Delano Roosevelt. He promised a "new deal," by taking this country from the brink of disaster and turning it in a direction of prosperity.

By the end of 1932, unemployment was climbing further and increased to 33 percent nationally, while Appalachia had gone beyond 50 percent. The situation was so devastating in the highlands that some coal communities were forced to close. In other towns and villages, small businesses failed, including banks that had very little capital to function during these hard times. Poverty reached its highest level, as federal government progress in public aid was slow to come by, and local, county and state governments were not able to contribute much in helping the needy. Lack of aggressive action by Herbert Hoover's administration, which had appropriated insufficient expenditures for welfare, would lead to the Republican Party's defeat in the national election. In 1932, between federal, state, and local governments, approximately 200 million dollars for relief and welfare were allocated. Ironically, private charities, individuals, and religious groups contributed more than the government. However, to sustain never ending daily needs of the people, resources were drained from these groups of good samaritans and humanitarians. Soup kitchens became bare and the lines of homeless were endless, as some private charities, engulfed with financial demands and great burden, had to shut down their operations.

FDR — The New Deal

Since the early settlers, people of eastern Kentucky had very few opportunities to benefit from federal action. Prior to Franklin Delano Roosevelt and the New Deal, government's attitude toward Appalachia was one of unconcern for its many economic and social ills, which left people frustrated and angry. In turn, the government was viewed with askance and hesitancy, and rightfully so. However, F.D.R. affected these people so profoundly that his picture was part of the "family gallery" in mountain shacks for many years. I remember an occasion back in the 1960's when visiting a former Alice Lloyd College student's family that one picture caught my eye: it was a discolored old photo of Roosevelt. The reverence that people had for this leader lasted through all those years. Even today, Appalachians who had lived through the Great Depression still compare the greatness of Roosevelt to subsequent presidents. They believed there would never be another influential and humanitarian leader like F.D.R., and one best not disagree, especially in Appalachia.

In 1933, when Franklin Delano Roosevelt took office, the New Deal was put together to overcome crumbling American economic and social conditions. He immediately responded to relieve this distress, and with the help of Congress appropriated 500 million dollars for direct relief. The Federal Economic Recovery Agency (FERA) was organized under Harry Hopkins' direction to prevent further suffering and help maintain a standard of living. This program which was purposely designed for a short period, had federal, state, and local financial implications attached to it. However, Hopkins' influence through astute administrative leadership played an important part for its success. Such accelerated action had never been experienced before, as money and goods were rushed to poor and needy throughout the country. Work relief was part of the program and at the center of significant economic changes, and even though some Appalachians benefited, a major portion of backwoods folk were not reached. The Civil Works Administration (CWA) provided immediate necessities for a potentially disastrous winter in 1933-34. James T. Patterson's book "America's Struggle Against Poverty 1900-1980" describes the impact of this brief action program and concluded that without its implementation the country would have faced widespread hunger. However, as the Depression continued, the dream to liberate America from poverty was by no means achieved. Government funding, whether it called for federal, state or local level contributions encountered insufficient funds to lift the numerous burdens of hunger and sorrow.

Yet, from 1933 until World War II, more progress was made in public welfare and relief than at any time in the history of our country. At the beginning, our nation's poverty conditions were too great and the frustration of federal government to offer assistance for all people continued to plague whatever effectiveness each program brought forth in fighting poverty. Certain programs still stand as a monument to Roosevelt and the most brilliant minds of that era, which included the Civilian Conservation Corps (CCC), National Youth Administration (NYA), and Works Progress Administration (WPA). However, some critics were concerned that public assistance was heading in a direction which would lead our country toward a welfare state, while others felt that not enough had been done to meet the needs of all Americans.

The New Deal programs were not intended for long term relief or welfare, because F.D.R. felt the government needed to prudently provide assistance to poor people, so that they could make it on their own as soon as possible. His actions were aimed toward families, to avoid getting them entwined in a "cycle of poverty." One program of the Roosevelt administration that still exists is Social Security. On August 14, 1935, F.D.R. signed the Social Security Act, which became the most massive welfare program in our country's history that included income maintenance on a planned basis of social insurance. The different aspects of this program began with the federal government providing grants to states for developing old age assistance, aid to dependent children and the blind, along with other designated categories.

The Works Project Administration (WPA) was the basic social and economic program of President Roosevelt's New Deal. Like other programs, it was directed at establishing employment for the "down and out." During the years that WPA functioned, some eastern Kentuckians joined the more than eight million unemployed men and women across America to build schools, hospitals, libraries, gymnasiums, and even government buildings. Some courthouses and city halls, constructed throughout the country by WPA, are still standing today. Projects also included building water and sewer lines, and mile after mile of rural roads where none existed before.

Despite success of certain New Deal programs there were pitfalls that exposed vulnerability, which occur with the magnitude of such undertakings. The aggressiveness of county and state leaders and the know-how of certain persons in charge of programs were responsible for their success or failure. In some situations, the relief setup in counties was controlled by small political groups with self-interests. Other people in politically appointed positions at local levels frustrated federal government through bureaucratic ineptness of administering the various programs. The incompetence of local government employees in not carrying out their duties created an outrage by the people, as poorly structured criteria and procedures for justifying a family in need created irascible situations that brought humiliation. For example, to dispense aid under the FERA assistance program, recipients had to appear at the relief office and pass a battery of tests to justify receiving assistance. They had to go through certain procedures, such as declaring their need, and passing the "means test" to establish that they were poor. In other unnecessary bureaucratic shortcomings of administering the federal programs at local levels, red tape became a deterrent in applying the budget system. Also, the processing of applications took an expansive amount of time, based upon non-sequitur actions.

In the end, there were many families that continued to suffer and did not receive aid. The reasons were based on people's inability to comprehend the welfare and relief programs, or because government lacked in informing needy persons that assistance was available. Critics during this period felt that the amount and description of various New Deal programs may have been too complex for the illiterate poor to understand, for it had been in many respects a difficult and awkward bureaucratic maze. However, learned historians today consider that it was the most extraordinary work of human dedication in giving to the less fortunate. One noteworthy result during this period was the revelation of an increasingly wide range in human need, and social workers had to expand their professional skills. This became evident in many ways as their work dealt not only with individual need, but also in the application of skills relating to social needs of groups and communities. Thus, the profession of social work emerged with great knowledge, which would serve as the basis for its modern graduate courses of study.

Looking back, it is hard to find an area of American life not touched by the Roosevelt administration's worthwhile programs. Most notable is that we had a president whose belief and strong will to "do good" for people surely outweighed the negativism that was expressed about this great man. If you were to travel the roads of time and meet individuals who experienced this period when Roosevelt was president, it would be obvious that he was one of the most admired leaders of our country.

Coal Mining

As the Great Depression continued spiraling out of control during 1932, coal mining had to increase production in order to show the same amount of income as in 1929. Unsurprisingly, this proved financially beneficial to corporations, for with high unemployment they were able to demand more from fewer workers, who had to put in longer hours for less pay. It was evident from the onset of mining in the early 1900's that these coal industry power forces were not concerned with working and living conditions of miners, thus this situation appeared not to get better. Safety in the mines was a nonentity, which made workers aware that this was a most hazardous and unrewarding occupation. Overwork and lack of oxygen in unventilated mine shafts began to deteriorate man's mind and body. By pushing miners to the limit, fatigue became a major reason why injuries and deaths increased. One cannot imagine the despair and hardship that coal mining brought upon the workers. Studies in later years of retired miners showed that physical and mental results of working the mines were beyond comprehension. Yet, the power structure in its position of control did nothing about the extreme inhumane working conditions.

Coal Barons

Many miners were concerned about deteriorating underground conditions, and their constructive criticism to coal companies for change proved to be futile. They often talked to "deaf ears", because unconcerned corporation owners who were interested in making more profit, did not want to listen. However, if coal miners continued to complain or tried to strike, some companies resorted to physical abuse, often having them beaten up by hired "goons," guards, local police or constables. Along with callous and degrading treatment, many unfair practices and actions by coal barons were the order of the day. Civil rights abuse and violation of the code of ethics had been common, which intimidated certain people who were supposed to be leaders of the community. Politicians, either "owned" or favorable to coal bosses, "extolled" the virtues of these "paternalistic godfathers" rather than criticize.

The wide sphere of the coal barons power and hidden actions inevitably overtook the people, as corporations continued their control of coal towns, camps and some local independent communities. They exercised domination and self-perpetuating control of politicians, including certain unscrupulous lawyers who had represented them in land title suits. These men, through illegal methods, were elected to prominent political office, including the United States House of Representatives. One such notable case pertained to the *Butler versus Roberson* suit, alleging violation of Kentucky's Corrupt Practices Act. It was discovered that in certain districts of Pike and Letcher counties individuals received money for their votes. Appalachians had been known for their disdain of those who were corrupt, however, when living in a society where people are hungry and poor, some will cross the line of legality to make a few "bucks" in order to survive. Indeed, one of the strongest contradictions was the vast amount of energy used in corrupting hundreds of hillfolk to vote for a certain candidate. The brazenness of this situation expanded to one specific precinct, where people openly auctioned their votes to the highest bidder. Deceitful individuals devoted boundless energy to entrap the poor into believing that their vote meant a great deal, by compensating them with a few dollars.

It was obviously true that corporations were well organized to protect their interests through buying votes and exercising power over the poor of eastern Kentucky. Nevertheless, certain circumstances must be explained to better understand why these conditions existed: this was a region where society was highly illiterate and unskilled, but hardworking in their endeavor to provide for themselves and their loved ones. Experiencing very little freedom but many constraints, control from corporations led to inevitable subjugation of people's participation in the community. The industry was so powerful, their "bosses" were free to perform in an inflexible, impersonal manner, and people believed there was no hope to overcome such domineering control. This of course, led to the resolve that they might as well live with the situation, and many reconciled to exist in an atmosphere of submission.

The poor had very few chances to experience opportunities for growth economically, socially, politically or culturally, forcing a breakdown of the human spirit. People became magnetized to the point where they were coerced into believing certain promises, which in reality only benefited purposes of the power structure. It was not difficult for the coal industry to maximize corporate profits, rather than improving situations of workers and the communities. People's fear to oppose this totalitarian power led to the industry's control of minimal social change. Coal company despots projected themselves as benevolent givers in providing services like health care, which was ironically paid for by the employees. It was a society in which people lived under the physical and human jurisdiction of coal companies, whose purposes and direction became more unfathomable to miners as time moved on.

With company-controlled towns came company-owned "dwellings," and each employee had to pay higher rent than people in other villages or hamlets. These facilities were poorly constructed and deteriorated at such an accelerating pace that it reminded one of a third world poverty atmosphere. In many places there was no indoor plumbing, inadequate heating and electricity, and overall poor living conditions existed. By holding back financial assistance for the general maintenance and upkeep of housing and necessary services, corporate leaders appeased their stockholders. The result was that miners and their families experienced many housing inequalities with each passing year, but had no other choice than to live in these shacks, or risk losing their job and be homeless.

Besides ensuring their own wealth and power, those who belonged to the corporate elite had a pernicious effect on the total outcome of a miner's life and his family. They were the supreme determining influence in deciding what people could or could not do in their living situation. This was done by determining where a miner and his family had to spend their income, because paychecks were still in scrip and only good for use in the purposely overpriced company store. Miners became frustrated that independent stores in surrounding villages charged much less than commissaries, yet company policy called for workers and families to shop in the coal town, which "bound" them even more. Many families lived on day to day "credit," and since they did not have the cash to pay for food or other goods, it led to increase in commissary prices that gouged the livelihood of these people.

Years later, Kentuckian songwriter Merle Travis, wrote about some of the hardships that miners and their families endured. Merle's father worked in the mines, slaving long hours each day, digging "16 Tons of Coal." Still, the meager paychecks miners received went back to the corporation's coffers. As Travis wrote, "the miners had owed their soul to the company store," which is a sad and true picture of those times. Since death in the mines and communities was on the increase, selling coffins became a flourishing business for commissaries. To coin a familiar phrase, coal miners and their families felt that the coal company owned them from "cradle to grave."

Overbearing domination by the power structure meant brutalization of man's dignity, and the ability to handle one's own life was completely ignored. Instead, the important element of any creative behavior was subdued to a passive form of existence. No wonder socially derived disorders were on the increase, such as alcoholism, mental illness, and suicide, which suggested that life in coal communities was not producing much semblance of human happiness. Outside critics expressed great concern about the control that corporations had over coal towns and camps, but were not aware of how widespread and persistent this power really was. Anyone who viewed the conditions placed on this region would have quickly realized that the people had not been living in a democratic society, but were dominated by a few self-serving individuals. Thus, hardships that miners and their families experienced gave rise for the need of organizing to fight back. Newspapers throughout America continued their "assault" on coal corporations, commenting that the contrast between "millionaire owners" and "poor miners" was reminiscent of "robber barons" during the Dark Ages when serfs populated their industrial kingdoms. Consequently, union activity came into existence because of stubborn resistance by coal corporations toward the miners' call for better working and living conditions.

Mine Workers Union Activity

Unionism in Appalachia had undergone enormous changes in size and power during the Depression years. From relatively small splintered groups in the early period of this movement, 6,000 miners out of a possible 10,000 men came from Harlan County to join the United Mine Workers Union of America in 1931. Harlan had been the center of organizing during that time, and with a majority of miners representing this county in the Union, their leadership voice became evident. Other counties did not have the union strength as Harlan, which was called "the capital" of eastern Kentucky's coal empire. However, with the Great Depression being a hindrance for miners to organize, this presented an opportunity for coal operators to use repressive measures against their workers. Coal miners from the mountains and "outsiders" labored in harmony for years, but when the Depression set in, workers were let go regardless of where they came from. In turn, those still working were more concerned with preserving their jobs and income than in union participation.

In the early thirties, federal government wallowed in a period of indecision with its lack of experience on how to handle rural unemployment, and workers were left stranded while unions had not yet been in a strong position to bargain for better conditions. Miners and their families encountered many problems depriving them of spirit and virtue. The splinter union groups could not function, losing members they had gained. Not being able to provide jobs for the workers, they became unimportant to the jobless. In certain communities where coal companies closed, the town or camp would cease to exist, and it was difficult for unemployed miners to find work elsewhere in Appalachia. Wherever possible, people did not stick with the hand that was dealt and tried to do something about their dilemma. Those who were able to go back to their homestead to farm, did so. When a coal miner was lucky enough to have an automobile, he piled his family in and headed for other parts of the country. Common scenes on the narrow winding roads of eastern Kentucky during that period showed coal miners carrying gear on their backs, hitchhiking out of the mountains. If a miner had saved some money, he and his family took a train to seek work elsewhere.

However, most of the unemployed could not move away. In 1932, the majority of miners were unskilled laborers, and approximately 78 percent had a limited educational background, having attended only elementary school. Lack of job opportunities in Appalachia made it impossible for miners to find or do other types of work, and county welfare or relief programs were not available for the unemployed. The tax base in eastern Kentucky counties was practically non-existing since whatever funds they had were meager, and in some instances local government became financially strapped, leading to bankruptcy.

Harlan County

Harlan County's splintered union groups arrived at a consensus that one large organization would have greater strength in dealing with the many degenerating conditions. Three years after the Great Depression began, coal production in Harlan County halved. Wages of some workers were reduced more than fifty percent and other miners placed on a part-time basis, while over three thousand men lost their jobs. There was acknowledgment that this Depression had fueled the harm that coal corporations had inflicted on workers. Thus, Harlan County miners organized under auspices of the United Mine Workers Union.

This Union was a temporary solution and miners did not anticipate that corporations would profoundly increase anti-worker activity. In some respects, the United Mine Workers Union's inability to take proper action became a symbol of deeper problems that led to moral and social breakdown. The U.M.W.U. had been fully aware of these troubles, but was unable to fight effectively for the miners because laws were not established to protect the role of unions. Constraints placed on unemployed and working miners brought on frustration, which created dispute and confrontation with the coal companies. Consequently, violent incidents occurred, leaving Harlan County with the reputation of being remembered as "Bloody Harlan."

From the beginning of miners' vocal objections to coal companies "unionists" started to go downhill, and corporations circumvented ways to overcome their discontent. Several hundred union miners found themselves on the hit list and were fired from their jobs, however they retaliated with disgust and anger by damaging and looting company property. In turn, a surge of abusive force by coal company henchmen led to an incident, which resulted in the killing of four mine guards and one union member. The "coal bosses'" determination to oppress workers had existed prior to this violence, which became more evident as they summoned state government intervention and Kentucky's National Guard was called in to put down any future rebellious action. This angered miners further, and thousands walked off their jobs. They were looking for leadership from the United Mine Workers Union, instead it withdrew support and left the county in haste, and as a result another organization, the National Mine Workers Union, represented the Harlan county coal workers. Years later, a retired miner told me that this transformation did not usher a "savior" for the workers, but created a strange relationship. The background of this organization had communistic tendencies, however, when men are down and out, have families that are hungry and live in poverty, they will do almost anything to salvage their desperate situation.

J. Wayne Flynt, the author of "Dixie's Forgotten People," offers insight into six years of terror and oppression that Harlan County miners endured. Flynt states that their constitutional rights were violated, and local government agencies had been under the control of coal barons. Two sheriffs that served the county from 1930 to 1938 were pawns of the coal companies, and one of them accumulated in three years an unbelievable ninety-two thousand dollars on an annual salary of five-thousand. Even certain Harlan County judges usually turned their heads away from illegal doings. The appointment of 169 deputy sheriffs, of which 64 were indicted and 37 convicted of felonies, 8 for manslaughter, and 3 for murder, was an example of the disregard for law and order. It was not unusual for a union member's home to be dynamited or workers being ambushed. Anti-union tactics extended beyond members, and even led to the killing of a union representative's teenage son. The "thug-like mafia tactics" included bombings, beatings and murders, leading to outright public disgust of these actions.

At first, the miners plight and necessity to fight the "bosses" was viewed by the populace with ambivalence. State government did not extend itself to overcome the inequities that were occurring, or tried to end corruption in Harlan County. Anti-union feelings ran high, not only in the State, but also with some eastern Kentuckians, who unfortunately did not take a stand for their fellow downtrodden people. On the other hand, there were those who viewed coal miners as selfless, dedicated men, struggling against the entrenched exploitive power of coal magnates. Moral drive and idealism of miners fitted in with those highlanders who also experienced poverty and identified with them. Coal barons were condemned by newspapers, and people outside Appalachia became aware of the miners' desperate situation and deprivation, causing outrage and indignation by the majority of Americans.

As our nation slid deeper into the Great Depression by 1933, Franklin Delano Roosevelt became president. He immediately encouraged the National Recovery Administration to develop guidelines for the coal industry. As a result, the Bituminous Coal Labor Board was appointed to administer and oversee the Fair Standards Act, and hear complaints of violations by coal corporations. The Board received many charges of constant unlawful actions, and Harlan companies were among the top violators, for out of 708 nationwide complaints over 90 were from this county. Yet, the arrogant attitude of coal bosses was evident through their refusal to abide by the Fair Standards Act.

Violations regarding constitutional rights of Harlan miners gained such national recognition that the La Follette Civil Liberties Committee investigated the county in 1937. The result was devastating, and Harlan County as well as the coal companies were exposed for their corruptness and control, which had subjugated miners for so long to a serf-like existence. The La Follette Congressional Committee denounced the use of private sheriffs, who had been illegally superimposed as lawmen by the mines and county government. All were participants in Harlan county's violations of miners' civil liberties, and deputies' positions were eliminated. As an outcome of this government action the United Mine Workers Union came back into the picture, started to organize under federal protection, and grew from 1,200 members in 1935 to over 9,000 by 1937, as Harlan County's Local assumed a more influential role at the end of the Depression.

Newspaper articles portrayed the miner as a "gallant knight" battling the "tyrant coal baron" on behalf of "oppressed workers." Under the U.M.W.U., miners believed that wages, benefits, working and social conditions would improve. They hoped there would be unified strength in eastern Kentucky locals, and being able to meet the opposition on equal terms became a driving force of the union movement. Harlan was no different from other counties in Appalachia, for they all had their share of bloodshed, death and tears. However, due to long years of fighting injustice, Harlan County coal miners became the symbol of resistance and union resolution.

Miners realized, in spite of their victory, belonging to the National Mine Workers Union would create problems. There were many reasons, but some underlying factors appeared in the open. For example, the United Mine Workers Union, under leadership of John L. Lewis, had gained strength throughout our nation, and received acknowledgment from the federal government, as being "the voice of miners" from Pennsylvania to western states. Also, there were too many philosophical differences between the National Mine Workers Union and Harlan County miners, and it became difficult for the N.M.W.U. to state clearly and realistically to workers how a communistic ideology could serve them. When people's beliefs are to the contrary, it is very evident that the goals of communism cannot function. Only out of dire need did Appalachians grab onto anyone for help, but could not devote themselves to this ideology. Their cultural environment and individualism made it impossible for the National Mine Workers Union to continue functioning in eastern Kentucky.

Farming

During the Depression, farmers came across the same economic uncertainty that engulfed coal towns, camps, county seats and villages throughout Appalachia. Mountain farms had played an important part in the region's existence, going back to the time of settlers, however, they were experiencing a crisis that gradually led to their extinction. Agriculture's decline in the 20's and 30's occurred when products did not sell and local farmers had sustained great losses, because during the Depression people ate little and bought less food. By 1932, an Appalachian farmer's net income was only 30 percent of what he made in 1929, and in order to survive, producing more was a necessity. Unfortunately, mountain farms were not conducive to providing a greater amount of crops. Limited land space and lack of modern machinery were two major obstacles that very few farmers were able to overcome. Many could not expand their land ownership because of physical barriers. Furthermore, new machinery was not a commodity that farmers could financially afford; after all, they were still using the old oxen or horse-drawn farming techniques.

Eastern Kentucky farmers became victims not only of the hard times and limited growing opportunities, but also in regard to the New Deal agricultural policies that called for controlled production of major crops. Consequence of this action was not advantageous for family farms. The New Deal had not intended to force small farmers out of business and work, however its policies turned out to benefit the few large producers. Federal bonus payments and higher farm prices automatically guaranteed an income of generous proportion for them. Yet, the New Deal developed a double standard that left the small farmer feeling neglected and frustrated. The lack of administrative "know how" in the agriculture department and the Administration's miscalculation for appropriation of funds deterred correcting this mistake. Thus, many of Appalachia's small farmers were forced to give up toiling the soil.

There were those who tried to improve their low income status during early years of the Depression by increasing output and getting rid of surplus food through lower prices, yet they were not able to benefit financially. Many Appalachian farmers became delinquent in paying taxes and debts, thus some had to sell their property. County officials in certain areas were tolerant because of the economic conditions, and extended time for farmers to meet their financial obligations. However, this prolonged the agony and frustration of not being able to pay taxes and other bills. Trying to sell land also proved to be difficult. At this time, farmers were not alone in facing a debt quandary, as financial problems were transcending all boundaries of the region's communities, and land speculators, coal company representatives, or a bank benefited from the debt-ridden farmers' demise.

In the past, farming was the most important occupation for mountain people to survive. They grew livestock and crops to support themselves and surrounding communities. Farming was once the only way of life for the region's people, and nearly everyone lived off a piece of land. During this period, it was clear that the position of agriculture in the economy would continue as one of chronic depression and uncertainty. After the Great Depression, despite America's upward progression in the level of living, the position of farming in Appalachia would fail to improve materialistically.

Health and Health Care

Americans who lived in urban areas were accustomed to health care changes which improved their quality of life, however, the precariousness of Appalachian's lack of access to basic medicine was difficult to conceive. Even during the Depression years, urban settings had greater advantages for people to stay healthier, and benefits of medical care far outpaced those of rural Appalachia. Statistically there was no way to compare health care services of urban versus the rural population, but an astounding fact was that many eastern Kentucky areas were without doctors and other health professionals. In comparison, a person living in the city generally had access to a physician, and in many cases house calls were made. With deteriorating conditions created by the Depression, people of the mountain region had greater need for medical care. Access to health care for rural eastern Kentuckians had been a critical issue for years, but the combination of circumstances and factors brought on a more complex health crisis.

As coal industry's big boom era ended, and the Depression was beginning to set in, health conditions in coal camps and towns took a turn for the worse. Companies went bankrupt and many of their "imported" doctors, nurses, and technicians moved away to other parts of the country. This left greater depths of poverty and inadequate medical and health service for those folks who could not afford to leave. Hospitals closed, and if a doctor, along with other professional staff decided to remain, they opened "clinics" to handle the workload. These facilities varied in size, were vastly inferior to hospitals, and could not afford laboratories or services. Many people struggling for day-to-day survival had very little money to pay for a doctor's visit, and as an alternative, they resorted to home remedies for curing their ills and diseases. Poor nutrition, low housing standards, polluted water and sanitation problems created ideal situations for the spread of diseases throughout the region.

A gentleman employed at Alice Lloyd College for quite a few years as a carpenter told me the following story of maintaining sanitary conditions in a coal camp during the early 20's and 30's. His friend was a "honey dipper" at one of the coal camps. "Honey dippers" were hired to clean outhouses, generally located a good distance behind shanties, and service was required to avoid unsanitary conditions. With a lamp on their coal miners' hat, they quietly emptied the privies periodically late at night in order not to be noticed. This was the kind of job nobody would be proud of. However, it was necessary to maintain this service in all areas. The severity of health conditions in communities that lacked this service led to epidemic proportions of disease and illness.

As the Depression deepened in the thirties, greater hardship was pushed on an unemployed populace, which shattered many family situations, and created an atmosphere of abandoned dejection. For the poor in coal camps and towns, health and care became a greater concern. Miners were in constant fear of pneumoconiosis (black lung disease), a disorder resulting from exposure to respirable dust, generated from the mines. Prevalence of pneumoconiosis and its progressiveness became a major worry for Appalachian miners, as prolonged retention of dust in lungs created chronic conditions. This debilitating ailment set off a new social and personal crisis that tended to perpetuate the problem. Medical men were concerned, observing the miners' downward spiral of physical and mental well-being, but were not able to help in many cases due to the complexity of pneumoconiosis. Physicians felt that gaining more knowledge was necessary, since most knew little about this illness, and recommendations were inadequate. Overall, physicians in Appalachia during this period did not have the medical expertise to justify their diagnosis of Black Lung disease. During the early 20th century, doctors overall received exceedingly less education than today's general practitioners, for over 75 percent of medical schools during that period required a high school diploma or its equivalent, and medical study was four years of higher education. This of course, is much less than today's requirements for becoming a physician.

As the years progressed into the Depression, mining injuries grew at a critical rate. Some hospitals and clinics that remained in business through the 30's, treated as many fatal and non-fatal coal miner injuries as other illnesses that needed medical care. Non-fatal work injuries were frequent and the highest in the country, because of neglectful action to maintain safety standards in the mines. Inability of doctors to diagnose the many daily injuries properly, along with inadequate surgical practices and procedures, created situations that led to unwarranted maiming of patients, long range injury implications, or deaths. Some doctors who called themselves surgeons, lacked this specialty in their training and professional background. Handicaps relating to deficient surgical practices and procedures became intolerable for not only the miner, but also his family. Diagnostic errors, viewed over a long period, became more frequent, and deaths of infants and young children were common. A baby dying of whooping cough, pneumonia or diarrhea was inexcusable. Parents were not knowledgeable of how to use food more effectively, or prevent and cure conditions like rickets, scurvy, and pellagra, which were prevalent in coal camps.

During the 1930's diabetes-related illnesses had been consistently high, and poor sanitation created infectious diseases that led to an increase in deaths of young and old. Because of limited statistics at that time, unnecessary suffering or lifelong handicaps had not been recorded, as treatable conditions like asthma and epilepsy went unrecognized or were neglected. Children had been unable to go to school because of seizures, or could not function due to lack of medication. In those days people with untreatable conditions were hidden away, and tuberculosis was one such illness in which this backward practice prevailed. The State of Kentucky had very little control over medical practices in the highlands, and no "agency for setting standards of operating a hospital" existed. It was like exploring a new frontier, as coal camps and towns faced poorly organized hospitals. Coal company practices for recruiting outside doctors had not been different than procedures of employing miners and other personnel. As long as persons were willing to work employment was assured. Generally, in all fairness to doctors, company efforts of enticing top medical professionals proved fruitless.

Stories abounded about doctors during the Depression, and after hearing one such story more than once, the embellishments make it more exciting: A man was hired as a company-contracted doctor, whom some folk used to call a "Dapper Dan." Generally, he would dress in riding boots and jodhpurs, and underneath his jacket was an ascot on a white silk shirt. Functioning like a doctor, people did not know if his medical background was authentic. He had the charisma to fool, dispensed medicines to those who needed it, until someone in town finally found out that he was not a medical man. However, before anything could be done about this fraud, he had disappeared.

Even though quality of medicine in Appalachia lagged behind the rest of our country, there were some physicians truly committed to helping eastern Kentuckians. However, many coal towns and camps lacked either a doctor or clinic services, deterring halfway decent health care. Some folks did not know how to care for themselves or do something about their ills, until pain or discomfort forced them to seek medical treatment. Small communities were also at a disadvantage, because they had been without any form of medical help. For example, people living in Pippa Passes had to travel many miles over winding mountain roads and hairpin curves to a drugstore in Hindman for "life saving pills and other medicinal needs." To some folks, the druggist played an alternative role by giving advice for simple ills.

During the Depression, county, public health and F.N.S. nurses were the unsung heroines to many children and adults in Appalachia. However, work was demanding, their schedule very hectic, and the shortage of nurses combined with overpowering health needs made it difficult to accommodate the many poor people. Prenatal health care was nonexisting in many areas, and babies were dying before their first birthday at twice the national rate. When visiting some graveyards in eastern Kentucky today and reading the tombstones, one will find sad and shocking testimony of circumstances that led to many premature deaths. Nurses saw deteriorating health conditions in the context in which they occurred: unemployment and hopelessness, inadequate housing and sanitation, abysmal education situations, and poor health habits. The high incident of communicable disease through flooding warranted F.N.S., public health, and county nurses to visit schools and homes, administering shots to reduce diseases, such as typhoid.

Back in the sixties, I had some lengthy conversations with a local public health nurse. She served in eastern Kentucky coal towns during the Depression, and stated that very little research had been done by the government on illness and disease. As a public health nurse, she was concerned that children and adults were dying prematurely from simple diarrhea and more complex diseases, reminding her of scenes straight out of underdeveloped countries, when doctors experimented for the first time with conditions not found in medical books. Fortunately, medical and health personnel occasionally received public health newsletters on illnesses that were "springing up," along with information on any new life-saving treatments.

Where coal companies established hospitals to provide care for their workers and families, these medical facilities, along with contracted doctors were prepaid by deducting a fee from miners' paychecks, thus many critics saw this as the forerunner of socialized medicine. The basic health care plan guaranteed income for the hospital and physician, as it offered miners and their families a so-called "wide range" of services. People were now able to see a doctor who made house calls, visit his office and receive hospital care. If a major sickness or operation required a better equipped hospital and medical specialists, people were sent to cities such as Lexington, Louisville, or Ashland by train, which was the most efficient and quickest way of transportation at that time.

For centuries home remedies were the basic foundation for a family's care. During the Depression, mountain folk used medications such as mineral oil, Epson salts, castor oil, clover leaf salve, and rubbing compound, along with age old remedies. Preventive medicine was given little attention by the people at that time, however if a family had the opportunity to have a nurse visit their home, a mother was better prepared to handle various crises that she would experience in the daily care of her loved ones.

Education

With the opening of new educational horizons the reticence that mountain folk had toward education in the past began to reflect a change of attitude in this region. The Depression brought an awareness to people about the importance of education for their children. Leading dynamic educators, such as Alice Lloyd, June Buchanan, Alice Slone, Katherine Pettit, and others, opened doors for educational opportunities. There were many other dedicated teachers who taught in towns and villages, and those that labored in backcountry one-room school houses. These individuals may not have had educational tools like today's professionals, however, in limited ways they proved to be very successful. Early childhood education, as we know it today, was virtually non-existent in the Depression years. Teachers were not trained extensively, or fully aware that children needed certain cognitive, social-emotional, perceptual and physical motor skills for effective learning experiences. The sophistication of education, such as "understanding the child," had not been introduced to all teachers.

However, in fairness to educators of that time, they were pioneers in their profession, whereas today's teachers experience different, complex, and more sophisticated challenges than in the past. It is difficult to compare them adequately or fathom accurately what teachers in those days were capable of, other than the fact that they spread good will throughout their community. Actually, their aim was to teach and work out the everyday issues of school and community within the limits of their educational and professional background. Many individuals during this period attended college for two years and received a teaching certificate, which allowed them to function as educators. There was a mixture of teachers from outside Appalachia as well as mountaineers, who came back from schooling at Morehead, Eastern Kentucky, the University of Kentucky, Western Kentucky, Murray and other state colleges. Alice Lloyd College also served a major role as a provider of educators.

With the discovery of "black gold" in the early twentieth century, migration of coal company executives and managers, businessmen and other professionals, reinforced communities with their positive attitude toward education for children. These people also were responsible for expanding the societal structure into two classes. They had enormous potential for improving education in eastern Kentucky, and the hillfolk that lived in villages and towns benefited by having recognized the importance of education for their children. However, the expanding class structure did not have a unifying impact, instead it produced the "have and have nots" in regard to formal learning experiences. Thus the inevitable happened: children in towns and villages were provided with learning opportunities, whereas those who lived in backwoods country did not have equal access to schooling.

The social milieu created by the region's geography had also determined to some extent the educational direction that school districts took. Those children living in towns and villages had better chances to succeed educationally. These communities had schools with grade level teachers, and in certain instances, where parental involvement occurred, showed signs of encouragement. On the other hand, in desolate backwoods areas, a "one-room schoolhouse teacher" had to work with more than half a dozen grade levels, all in one day. For those children living in the rural backcountry, long daily treks to and from school required great determination. Old-timers have told how they would walk "a good ten miles to school," which was not uncommon. Rural families were penalized in many ways when it came to their offspring's education. Most children came from poverty-stricken families, and being born into these circumstances, chances were almost automatically reduced regarding any educational opportunity. It is understandable that in a situation such as this and an environment of limited possibilities, appropriate motivations would be difficult to surface, and if they did, frustration would reign. Those who were reared in a setting that was not exposed to education and its benefits, most likely did not acquire a positive attitude toward education.

Individual strength, socially, emotionally and physically, were important determinants on how well a child was able to deal with the ills of poverty and gain an education against all odds. However, many became caught in deep-rooted illiteracy and were unable to help themselves as problems accumulated. The life style and culture of these people probably hid the reality of poverty for such a long time that they accepted it as a way of existence. Illiteracy was so ingrained that parents saw nothing wrong with their children living the same way they had, and continued isolation from communities did not help the situation. These people were poor and this often meant that they had no reading or writing materials. Some children did not want to go to school because they were embarrassed by the clothes they wore, or not having pencil and paper. When a child was absent more than usual, it became difficult to catch up with studies, however compulsory attendance did not exist and school personnel could not enforce rules. Children who lacked a background of basic developmental skills could not keep up with the rest of the class, fell behind in their studies, and as a result, eventually dropped out of school.

During the 1930's, eastern Kentucky schools experienced other barriers toward developing an effective educational program. Rural children were receiving seven months of school, while in city systems, such as Louisville and Lexington, students were getting nine months of education. Monies collected in rural eastern Kentucky were very meager, as the tax base was practically non-existent. Collected revenue in this region could not match the affluent north central urban areas, which were able to draw tremendous taxes from concentrated wealth in their communities to support education. Teacher salaries were much better in cities and metropolitan areas than in rural eastern Kentucky. Educational systems in the north central region where facilities were built by the W.P.A., also benefited more than poverty-stricken Appalachia. Advantages that students from Louisville and Lexington had over the youth from small mountain villages and towns became more evident, as their schools ranked higher academically.

Another deterrent for educational growth in Appalachia was that as soon as teachers taught a couple of years in the mountains, they were offered or sought better jobs in higher paying areas. There were others who felt suited for something else and left the teaching profession altogether. Of all the states in our nation, Kentucky had the greatest percentage of college graduates teaching outside its borders. For example, in one county of West Virginia seventy percent of the teaching personnel came from the "blue grass" state. In addition, many Kentucky-born teachers were found throughout the state of Ohio, Illinois, Indiana and Michigan, as well as New York, Tennessee and New Jersey. The major reason for educators migrating out of Kentucky was that they were able to double or triple their salaries and work under better conditions. An added problem in Appalachia was the lack of teaching jobs, thus, the migration of school teachers set precedent for a trend that would continue many years thereafter.

The School Trustee

A major obstacle to educational progress that started during the early 20th century was the "school trustee" structure, which continued through the Depression years. Under State law, school trustees were elected by the constituency, which created undemocratic conditions in the schools and frustration among educators. A trustee was capable of control that would lead to damaging effects on schools for years. There were many problems that this structure imposed on the educational system, creating ineffectiveness, inequality of employment practices, and teacher instability. Politically it conflicted with basic principles of democratically-run schools. This extent of control by the trustee structure brought about significant constraints for administrators, Boards of Education and teachers. The dichotomy between this political position and educational responsibility was a serious weakness that created difficulties for school systems to improve.

These people, by their very nature of being politically rather than educationally oriented, were easy prey for coal corporations who included them in their domain of control, like they had done with other local and county government officials. Trustees, along with certain school superintendents were pawns of power brokers. The system became increasingly corrupt, and there were allegations that some individuals did not qualify for those positions they occupied. A trustee was elected by the local community, but did not "run on a political party ticket." However, the saying goes that these elections were more corrupt than if political sides would have been chosen. Many problems relating to elections of trustees created discontent among the populace. Depending on the community, not all issues were the same, such as backing a candidate by one church versus another or the "wets" against the "drys." Even feuding of one clan against another entered into the election scene of a trustee, and teachers found themselves drawn into power struggles, which caused feelings of being suppressed in carrying out their daily school work. They had been placed in an untenable position, if a candidate for trustee won the election and did not approve of their work. There were ways to get rid of teachers, and a simple unprofessional approach was to find fault, organize a group of people and sign a petition to have the educator ousted.

Election of a trustee was so volatile that the force of hostility came to a point where people were killed or injured without thought. In one community election of local school trustees a woman tried to register to vote for her candidate, when folks from the opposite side objected, anticipating a voting violation. Shouting led to violence that erupted from both sides, and six people died. Thus, election of the school trustee became the most involved and vocal event in many communities, and peace was non-existent during that period.

The school trustee system created a "self anointed" leadership role for certain people, who were illiterate and tried to tell faculty how and what to teach. Educators had even been evaluated by individuals who never finished school. Therefore, effective leadership of administrators and supervisors became an impossibility. It was not difficult to document trustee impropriety and violation of teachers' civil liberties. Individuals not from the immediate area were forced out of their jobs, and local teachers had to resort to flattery or educationally undesirable practices to maintain their positions. With the trustee in political control of the school system, other more essential aspects of education were increasingly neglected. The local district trustees dictated to the superintendent and Board of Education members how schools should be run, and in certain communities these "good ole boys" were supported by voters who were bought in various ways. Others benefited through the trustee structure by getting jobs or gaining business contracts with the school district. Some of these persons were outspoken toward critics of the trustee structure, knowing that their benefits would cease if the system was discontinued.

Jesse Stuart — Battles Injustice

It is undeniable that many good educators performed their tasks and also defended against uncontrolled judgments from certain powerful trustees with deceitful intentions. Jesse Stuart, eastern Kentucky born educator who experienced injustices, wrote about this period in his book "The Thread That Runs So True." He made the reader aware of the unfairness that people endured, and expressed through his writings their needs and described the surroundings. Jesse provided his reader with first hand knowledge of the mountaineer's virtues and vices. He was concerned for others and wanted to help his people overcome the ills and hardships they faced. Jesse Stuart demonstrated with striking brilliance honesty, sincerity and committment as a school superintendent and friend to his fellow workers and students. When trustees, often uneducated or unable to write their own names, came to visit his schools and gave educators instructions on how to teach, Jesse fought against this injustice and stood up against many other unrighteous actions.

In retrospect, it is difficult to understand the rationale by the Commonwealth to have superimposed such dominance of power for one group of people. Whether the State realized the implications of their action or not, violations of basic constitutional rights occurred. Elections as well as functions of school trustees were laced with low political ethics and human behavior, that led Jesse Stuart to rebel against this type of conduct with fervor.

Someone once said, wherever there are eastern Kentuckians, stories will be told. Jesse Stuart, who was born in a log cabin August 8, 1906, recorded many life experiences. Through his storytelling and writing about hillfolk, he provided authentic portrayals of their ills, sorrows, hardships, close family ties, and traditions. For many years he wrote stories, essays, and poems, making him a unique legend, whose "pen was a mighty weapon." In this respect, his literature describes proud Appalachians, who did not complain about their "lot" in life. Jesse's contribution by writing about their plight and distinct culture, awakened readers throughout the country.

When I first met Jesse Stuart in the 1950's, he had been on a lecture tour, covering Ohio and all points east. I remember reading his "Taps For Private Tussie" in undergraduate school, and had been impressed by his own struggles as a novice teacher and experienced administrator in "The Thread That Runs So True." One could tell in his lecture that Jesse Stuart was proud of his native State. He spoke about his people with a classic directness. Jesse lived among them, and saw each day mountaineers trying to exist on their meager income, witnessing the disastrous way of life that hung over these individuals. The audience and I knew what he meant by referring to his people as being undernourished, ill housed and lacking the many basics of life.

It was years later in eastern Kentucky that I met Jesse again. At that time he had written many more books and was one of Appalachia's prolific writers. I mentioned to Jesse enjoying his story about helping a local man get his true worth for the coal he had been selling to a mining company. Because of the man's lack of education, this company had been taking advantage by not reimbursing him for the actual weight of coal. With Jesse Stuart's guidance and a simple bit of advice the man was able to use a measuring technique to estimate the correct tonnage of his truck load of coal. As a result, the coal company had come across an illiterate man who was taught by an educator, forcing them into "playing fair." I asked Jesse jokingly "if the coal company rode him out of town on a rail?" He chuckled and said," I am still here." There are many people today that wish he was still alive. Jessie Stuart died in 1984, and a monument is dedicated to him as poet, author, and educator in Greenup County, where he was born. The legacy of this sincere and honest person, who loved his fellow Kentuckians, shall always be remembered.

Summation

For people of Appalachia, the 1930's were not only marked by the Great Depression, but oppression as well. Bold and reckless control by coal moguls continued, as they accumulated political power that became a deterrent to progress. Prosperity of the 1920's, which other parts of our nation enjoyed, was not shared by eastern Kentuckians. Arrival of the Depression in 1930 created very little change for mountaineers, as hard times had already been experienced by miners since 1926, when increased use of fuel oil and natural gas forced coal prices to drop, causing job losses. People in other parts of the country were more surprised and shocked than Appalachians when the Depression set in, because rising prosperity and economic waste that they had experienced came to an abrupt end. As the nation's economy took a downturn, the crisis in all of America became more severe. Tarpaper-covered shacks were no longer limited to Appalachia. Farmers of eastern Kentucky, joined by others throughout the country vented their anger in frustration, because food products were selling for much less as the Depression began. What occurred in a few short years, was total economic collapse.

FDR's many government programs, included making much needed jobs in public work projects available, and proved to help slow down the economic decline, as well as restore dignity and self-respect to many people. However, economic and social reform hardly took place in Appalachia. It was not effective enough at the regional level because of limited opportunities for expansion toward a diversified industrial base. The fact that eastern Kentucky's total structure collapsed left people in hopeless situations, for even small workplaces went out of business and lifetime aspirations of many were crushed. However, our federal government, under Franklin Delano Roosevelt, rectified inadequacies of unemployment by encouraging people to take advantage of New Deal projects and gain pride in making a living. This was achieved through various "alphabet soup" programs, such as PWA, WPA, CCC, TVA, and NYA.

Even though America began to emerge successfully from the Depression, poverty still lingered in Appalachia as the 1930's ended.

Chapter IV

1940 — 1959

War, Prosperity, Poverty

In 1940 our country was experiencing a renaissance of economic recovery, along with a sense of optimism. This was encouraged by Franklin Delano Roosevelt's driving force to overcome poverty. The New Deal's emphasis on the common man became a symbol of hope, and it was evident that Roosevelt would coin many programs for "the people." Projects such as Art for the People, People's Concerts, and People's Theatres were examples of esprit de corps that uplifted the citizenry throughout our country. This symbol even became a byword in the literary field with such giants as Carl Sandburg, who wrote the book of poetry called "The People, Yes." Movies, stage plays, and radio were all concentrating on the people.

Important changes came about as a result of this optimism in America. A transition was evident, when many workers were returning to employment, and industry retooled itself to help provide armaments for allied forces in Europe. Even though our nation remained neutral, fear of war was lurking over the horizon. Nevertheless, citizens felt the ecstasy of their worth and status. Our country's wealth, energies and resources were devoted to health, welfare and overall benefit of the people. Poor and middle class citizens had opportunities for better education, improved housing and community services, upgraded social security through a more

74

comprehensive program, as well as expanded health care.

Proliferation of private industry throughout the nation had very little effect on Appalachia, since the region continued its dependency on a single industry. Limitations of a non-diversified industrial base brought to eastern Kentucky less stability than the rest of America. Even though the coal industry's second boom occurred from 1940 until after World War II, the region still had many needs in areas of health, education, and welfare, while the political structure remained status quo, because of control by a few elite. Improvements were limited, with the exception of federal government sponsored New Deal projects.

If it were not for the Works Projects Administration, Civilian Conservation Corps and National Youth Administration, the Depression would have had a more devastating effect on the young people of Appalachia. The Civilian Conservation Corps specifically gave young men ages 18 to 25 an opportunity to work and train in varied conservation projects, which were supervised by the Agriculture and Interior Departments. This program started in the mid-thirties and carried over until the early part of 1942. Each youth registered for an initial six month period, with maximum reenlistment of up to two years. Young men who lived in camps received $30 a month, of which the government forwarded $25 to their families. The multitude of conservation activities included wildlife protection, erosion control, and development of national parks. Dam construction and reforestation projects were also part of the broad work experiences. Planting millions of seedlings made this undertaking one of the most worthwhile contributions of American conservation, and of all trees planted at that time, seventy-five percent were contributed by the Civilian Conservation Corps.

Appalachia benefited from the CCC program in many different ways, as young men had the opportunity to work, build character and achieve self-discipline. The healthy outdoor atmosphere made their working conditions much more desirable, and they took pride in this well planned conservation approach that developed good environmental conditions, benefiting not only the region but our nation for many years thereafter. CCC camps were also advantageous to nearby towns and villages, since the money that was spent in these communities helped fuel local economy. People showed great appreciation for what this project gave to their region, and they were impressed by work ethics of the youth, along with the results and benefits. The camps functioned in orderly fashion based upon an army regimented structure and style, which encouraged self-discipline and strengthened character for CCC volunteers.

On December 7, 1941, Appalachians, along with other Americans were enjoying their Sunday noontime meal, when Japan attacked Pearl Harbor, placing the United States in an unwanted position of declaring war on the Axis powers, which included Germany and Italy. Throughout America, assembly lines in war plants of our cities revved up with 3 work shifts, operating 24 hours a day, 7 days a week. Appalachia's coal miners were working up to 16-hours per shift each day, and with the addition of automation, coal production was greater than at any time in the history of this industry despite fewer miners. Through financial assistance from the government some corporations benefited by mechanizing and upgrading their operations to improve the "war effort."

When the attack occurred, Appalachia's young men in the tradition of loyal Kentuckians volunteered to serve in the armed forces. Their actions preceded the drafting of soldiers and became a rallying cry for others throughout the nation. The war had a tremendous impact on young mountaineers, whose commitment to the United States has always been without question. Volunteers were outnumbering draftees, and in some hamlets and hollows there was competition to determine which group or clan would out-do the other to join the armed forces. Also, it was a known fact that having enlisted instead of being drafted made a mountaineer more proud of serving his country, and as the old saying goes, "a man was not a soldier unless he joined up." Mountain people exhibited a little flag in the front window of their shanties, and each star indicated how many family members served in the war. Families whose sons were killed, displayed flags with a gold star. In certain situations a light burned constantly, signifying their contribution to the war, and this symbol of patriotism became a tradition throughout our nation.

The pride that people of Appalachia had in this country was still evident years later. When President Will Hayes of Alice Lloyd College and I got together for a meeting with Mayor Willie Dawahare of Hazard in the 1960's, Will mentioned to Mr. Dawahare that we had just come from a local restaurant, where a World War II Norman Rockwell poster was hanging on the wall: the Four Freedoms — Speech, Worship, Want, and Fear. Printed by the Office of War Information, it exemplified patriotism during that conflict, and I will never forget when Willie Dawahare smilingly stated that in the Hazard area one would find many more of these displayed. As Mayor Dawahare was talking, he pointed to a poster in his office that showed one of the four scenes — the common man standing among a group of fellow citizens, which Rockwell so aptly designated as "Freedom of Speech." Having lived in other parts of this great country and viewing attitudes and actions of many different groups of people, I can say with sincerity that the negative conditions and situations which confronted Appalachians, did not change their loyalty and devotion to the United States. Even the intriguing examination of these people by such authors as Caudill, Harrington and Flynt, brought out the mountaineers' strong desire to be free, individualistic and independent, yet committed to their country, which one cannot help but admire.

As World War II moved toward an end, our nation was shocked by the death of Franklin Delano Roosevelt in 1944. His legacy to the American people consisted of many good deeds, but the one that stays in my mind the most was expressed in Arthur Schlesinger's book "The Coming New Deal," by referring to Harry Hopkins' explanation that people had faith in F.D.R., because he was a great spiritual figure, whose indestructible idealism gave Americans hope. Roosevelt was a man of values which were founded on a strong family and religious orientation, and came to light through the many social programs he championed for the people.

F.D.R. contributed in many ways to America and called for our country to build from the bottom up, with its foundation resting on the "common man's" shoulders. He was the kind of leader many people were able to identify with. His desire was to rebuild this nation by creating opportunities for the needy to overcome poverty. It showed in his concern and understanding that he wanted a fulfilling future for Americans after the War. Franklin Roosevelt had a vision and hoped all people, poor and middle class, would have a better life, by providing national health insurance, employment, and other improved social programs. These dreams were never carried out because this great man died, and too many distractions existed in our society at that time. As a result, the importance of his prophetic long range plans was soon forgotten by many Americans. Today, almost half a century later, our nation is grappling with these exact issues that are extremely important to the survival of our society.

Diversions occurred right after Roosevelt's death and can be attributed to the fact that for many years our nation became accustomed to rock solid leadership of a humanitarian, whose demands always had best intentions for the people. Above all, our country had a sense of direction, however this unfortunately ended as the war was nearing its final days. Many segments of our society were concerned about their own future. Power brokers that had been held in check, now flexed their muscles for control of their domains. Industry was retooling itself for a post-war era with anticipation of a recession, similar to the period after World War I. Unions were projecting themselves into the political arena as representatives of the worker and special interest groups began to influence the everyday scene of society. Lobbyists in Washington added to an exploding population of political and social self-servers, who previously never had been that powerful in our nation's capital, as "grabbing a piece of the pie" was the motto for each and every day.

The common man, whether coming home from the service or leaving assembly lines of closed war plants, was in a quandary. Veterans had needs and fears for their future, as well as concerns about jobs. Since

World War II began, the employment picture in America had changed and included the female population as equal partners. The new scene of America's life style was so inconsistent, moving in different directions, that the media along with writers of books and articles labeled the post World War II era as "tumultuous."

As the nation's greatest productive era was winding down mechanization increased at a greater rate, replacing workers in coal mines of eastern Kentucky. Adding to this predicament, strip mining had shown growth in production. Since the technique required fewer miners than underground work, there was a noticeable drop in jobs, and in the late 1940's due to increased unemployment, people started migrating to other parts of the country. Appalachia was continually showing a loss of population, as the rest of our nation grew. Thousands of farmers and miners left the region to seek employment in places such as Cincinnati, Cleveland, Detroit, Chicago, and Gary, Indiana. Those that remained in eastern Kentucky were doomed to a life of economic and social problems. During the late 1940's and 1950's, the topic of poverty was virtually nonexistent in newspapers, magazines, or books, and very few people in America were aware of Appalachia's disastrous economic and social conditions. Industrial expansion benefited most of the nation, while this region's single-direction-economy underwent crucial periods of adjustment.

Social conditions, such as poor health and lack of health care, illiteracy, inferior education, inadequate housing and living standards had always existed in Appalachia and did not go away. In the late forties and early fifties, sociologists were befuddled that government was unprepared to deal with the issue of poverty. Some felt, they did not have sufficient data to provide analysis of the cause and effect of deteriorating conditions. Government lacked research information, and even those studying economic and social problems tied to poverty were short of answers. The result indicated that whatever had been known or available was "minuscule," and one noted statistician complained, it was "deplorable" not to have appropriate information to get a grip on this situation. Lack of understanding the needs of Appalachia's poor lasted through the late 1950's, as the rest of our country continued in a period of prosperity and contentment. Family income increased in the mid-fifties by almost 40 percent, but the welfare system of the United States provided very little help to poor people in comparison to European countries, such as England and Germany. The neglect of poverty and ignoring welfare exposed a lack of readiness on the part of Americans.

As prosperity came to many, forgotten were the Depression years of deprivation and suffering. However, various movements in our society began to stir. A young senator from Massachusetts, John F. Kennedy, was aware how the totality of poverty had been affecting Appalachians. In 1958 and 59 he supported programs for the poor, such as Medicare, Federal Aid to Education, manpower training, and extension of public assistance. John Kenneth Galbraith wrote in 1958 about poverty and its economic and social conditions in our society of prosperity. His book, "The Affluent Society" identified "insular poverty" as pertaining to those poor people living in rural areas. The reason they were poverty-stricken, categorized as "case poor," was because of lack in education and inaccessibility to health care. Kennedy, campaigning for the presidency, became an important ally to the people of Appalachia. He understood their misery and suffering, but also knew that they needed help.

In 1959, the State of Kentucky elected its first governor from the eastern mountain region, Bert T. Combs. The impact this man had will stay forever in the hearts and minds of Appalachians. With Bert Combs in office, expectations began to rise and the start of political movement made eastern Kentuckians aware of actions that could be taken. This dynamic leader brought about changes that benefited the mountaineers, and his election as governor preceded the anticipation for a new federal government leadership in 1960 that would listen to Appalachians. Bert Combs was not only their voice, but his actions and good deeds for all people of Kentucky were significant, long lasting, and visible to the federal government.

Coal Mining

During the war, change taking place in coal mining was determined when young strong men of Appalachia left for the armed forces. Elderly miners, who had been around since coal was discovered in 1912, as well as other hillfolk, outsiders, and rejected "4 F's" were called to work with the physically disabled in the mines. With the W.P.A.'s dismantling of its operation, some men were transferred to help in coal mining. In early 1942 the War Manpower Commission was established to improve problems created by the drafting of young men, however, some of those Appalachians that did not qualify for the service had decided to leave and pursue work in Chicago, Detroit, and Cleveland war plants rather than go back into the mines. There were other eastern Kentucky men who no longer wanted to stay in the region, and left for other parts of the country to join the assembly lines as welders, riveters, mechanics, painters and carpenters. Many of them would never return to the mountains, because financially they were now able to determine their own destiny. By 1944, eleven and a half million men and women served in the war, and the increasing need to provide workers for the mining industry forced our government to discharge servicemen prematurely.

In spite of miners leaving the region for better paying jobs and improved working conditions in other areas of the country, the war years brought a second coal boom to Appalachia. In many respects, this era had a greater impact on the economy in a shorter period than the early 1900 boom, as production of large coal corporations nearly quadrupled. WPA construction projects during the Depression provided new gravel roads, built alongside thousands of acres of coal land that previously had never been touched. The local "gentry" realized the advantage of mining coal that existed on the fringes of these roads. Hence, "truck mines" were established as fathers, sons, clans, and everyone who had the opportunity made a living in this ingenious way. They hired independent truckers to haul their coal to a local "sizing tipple," where it was then sorted and broken down. Miners who had been earning 6 to 8 dollars a day in previous years were now doubling and tripling their income by operating truck mines. Others, such as lawyers, doctors, and businessmen, invested in small abandoned underground mines, revitalizing them to meet the demands of war, and coal corporations were no longer talking "millions" but "billions" of dollars in income. Even the "small man" found himself earning a decent living, and in certain situations some individuals were operating up to three truck mines at one time.

Ironically, big coal corporations who anticipated a depression after World War II, continued their devious methods of controlling coal towns and camps. They ceased to keep up with the maintenance of their communities, and in a selfish way, with approval of the "bosses," carried on with their negative attitude toward upgrading living conditions in mining camps and towns. Ignoring to re-invest even a minimal amount of their profits into these communities, as physical surroundings and housing began to break apart and deteriorate, created incomprehensible living situations. Along with this continued neglect, coal companies kept on ravaging the land. A study of ownership in eastern Kentucky showed that altogether there were about 35 individuals and major corporations owning approximately 90 percent of mineral rights in the region. The future implications of this domination by those selected few were yet to show the full impact of greed, indifference, and disregard for mountains and people.

The Union and John L. Lewis

Events taking place in the United States during the 1940's had a profound effect on miners of Appalachia. John L. Lewis established himself in a more powerful position, as the U.M.W.U. increased to over 500,000 members and became the strongest union in the nation. Coal had to be produced at all cost during World War II, because American industry needed to fuel its furnaces in providing arms for fighting the war, and this gave miners their much sought after advantage in collective bargaining. As a result, the Union gained concessions and won its long battle for better wages, hours and benefits. Federal government as well as state authorities, who in the past were not sympathetic toward strikes, now backed the United Mine Workers Union. Serf-like existence of miners and tyrannical control by coal barons began to change, and the Union was regarded not only as a collective bargaining organization but also became the "change agent."

The coal companies had met their biggest challenge and were no longer able to control miners. However, along with power to negotiate for better conditions, John L. Lewis and the U.M.W.U. encountered a transition period of the coal industry that would have a devastating effect on miners. With the introduction of machinery, some miners went on unemployment as their jobs were eliminated. Coal companies thrived even after the war, producing more coal with fewer workers. Starting in the late 1940's, the Union's collective bargaining deteriorated due to job losses and because of many bitter battles that giant coal corporations never forgot. Their highly paid lawyers would not acquiesce to John L. Lewis' demands to do something about the employment situation. By 1950, the industry was beginning to show interest toward further mechanization, as Lewis tried in vain to protect workers from falling by the wayside. He recognized and understood that the inevitable disappearance of miners' jobs would ultimately disenfranchise the United Mine Workers Union in Appalachia.

Coal Corporations Continue Control

The end of World War II did not provide a depression as anticipated, and coal mines continued to blossom throughout the 1950's. Nationally, corporations as well as the coal industry were unhappy with controls that Roosevelt's Administration had imposed during the war, and their major target was the Office of Price Administration. Big business, in the guise of the National Association of America and Chamber of Commerce, prodded citizens into believing that government policies should be changed. Yet business profits had been frozen because of O.P.A.'s intention to curb inflation, and proved to be an effective tool in curtailing price increase, therefore having a positive influence on the economy of not "going belly up" after World War II. However, fear instilled in people by spurious efforts of power moguls formed a mood in our country that led Congress to dismantle the O.P.A., as business and industry claimed that cheap-priced, high quality goods would further enhance the lifestyle of America's burgeoning middle class. Coal corporations of course experienced another benefit from the elimination of the O.P.A. Its control of stabilizing prices during the war kept coal industry's profits from skyrocketing. However, by dismantling the O.P.A., power brokers were now able to raise the price, and since coal was still very much in demand, it increased fifty percent per ton.

Continued Decline of Farming

As World War II began, the condition of farming in Appalachia was one of chronic struggle and uncertainty. Even with improved living standards in the rest of our country during and after the War, small farmers in eastern Kentucky failed to improve materialistically. The married veteran who left his family behind in the mountains as he went off to war, experienced a deteriorating scenario upon his return. Before going into the service many Appalachian farmers and their families lived in poverty. During the war, most wives with children were unable to work, simply because no jobs had been available, or they needed to stay home and take care of the young. Their only means of income was the husband's service check, which could not sustain family life. When World War II ended, many soldiers came home to conditions that did not improve, instead they had become worse. Bewilderment and despair in the eyes of their loved ones led to painful decisions.

Numerous World War II veterans and their families were falling into poverty, thus being forced to leave the rural scene of Appalachia. Many lost farms through bankruptcy, while others sold their properties for less than what they were worth. Some just gave the land to extended family members, packed their belongings into beat-up cars or small trucks and moved to other states looking for work. For poverty-stricken farmers, migration from Appalachia was a continuation of the past, however, this exodus jammed roads to Ohio, Michigan, Illinois, and other parts of our country. Movies have been made about these occurrences, and one such film featured Jane Fonda in an adaptation of Harriet Arnow's "The Dollmaker," for which she won the Emmy, by portraying a determined impoverished Kentucky farm woman. The love that Appalachian parents have for their children, in spite of poverty and unemployment, is exemplified in this family's struggle, when they leave home and move north to find work. Gertie Nevels, played by Fonda, was a mother of five, who followed her husband to Detroit. They were overwhelmed by difficult adjustments and tragedy; however, the strength and courage to keep the family from falling apart is an inspiring story of human spirit, which many eastern Kentuckians experienced in real life. Like some Appalachians, she, her husband and their five children eventually moved back home.

There were also people who stayed in their new surroundings, but never lost their love for Appalachia and relatives. One such person is Bob Butler, who migrated to Cincinnati, Ohio in the late 1940's. Bob tells that on weekends there were more out-of-state cars on Appalachian roads than Kentucky-registered cars. Children always came to visit their "daddies, mommies, granddaddies and grannies," as well as other relatives. Bob, born and raised in the rural area of McDowell, exemplifies the spirit of eastern Kentuckians who never forgot their roots, and went "back home" whenever they could. Even his son Dave, who is a medical professional in Florida, keeps up with this tradition, visiting Kentucky as often as possible.

Farming Conditions Worsen In 1950's

Appalachian farmers' incomes in the 1950's were pitifully lower than the standard poverty level of our nation. During this period, a Department of Agriculture research project released significant findings, pertaining to the extent of rural poverty. The study indicated that in 1955, nationally 1.5 million farmers had an annual income of one thousand dollars or less, and seventy-five percent of small Appalachian farmers matched this description. In previous years, such information would have met with the wrath of many people, especially politicians. However, our society was becoming financially more successful, and conservative in its nature of looking at life regarding the poor of our nation. The middle class was enjoying the fruits of their labor and rich people were gaining greater wealth. Overall, the attitude of being concerned about others was changing toward a society that emphasized "individualism". Even the federal government's endeavors to help poor rural farmers were a sign of "tokenism." Through the Agricultural Extension Service, technical assistance was provided to counsel on new farming possibilities, and if all else failed, training for employment was offered. U.S. Senator Paul H. Douglas submitted to Congress a bill that would help small farmers by providing financial assistance to low-income families. Ironically, this bill died by "pocket-veto" from the President.

During the 1950's, federal government action favored large corporate commercial farmers who were able to acquire financial aid. However, the same government requirements and standards made it difficult for a small farmer to receive equal benefits. Despite denial, it appeared that a deliberate policy of agriculture depopulation was encouraged. The awful truth about small farms' deteriorating conditions inevitably carried over into the sixties. American agricultural policy favoring the upper income farmer became a reality of unfair proportions. Not only had the government completely ignored small poor farmers of Appalachia and other parts of the country, but did so with reckless abandonment. Policy measures were developed that placed economic control in the hands of a special privileged group, which contributed directly to the despair and deprivation of small rural farmers.

Health and Health Care During World War II

When World War II ascended upon our nation, health care in Appalachia and other parts of America was dramatically affected. Enlistment and drafting of medical personnel threw new burdens on Appalachian health care services, whose numbers were already inadequate. Health services of the region continued to diminish, because our country needed physicians, dentists, nurses and other health workers in the armed forces. Improvements that were attempted prior to the war experienced a setback, and health conditions in eastern Kentucky took a critical turn for the worse due to shortages of medical personnel.

During the war, replacement of physicians from medical schools bypassed Appalachia. Physicians and health personnel remaining in the region found themselves running ragged, covering a greater amount of territory. Counties without professional health care depended on the humanitarian efforts of devoted and overworked physicians and nurses, who traveled from county to county. Worst of all, the health condition of poor people did not improve, because access to services was not available, and in many areas, transportation to medical facilities had been lacking. Hospitals depended on general practitioners to cover specialists' duties. These medical facilities were short staffed, and it was not unusual for patients to be transported to Lexington and Louisville for a major operation. This, along with other concerns for health care services contributed to the mortality rate increase during World War II. Lack of knowledge to maintain good health resulted in children suffering from many diseases that could have been prevented. General living conditions of the poor were unsanitary and dehumanizing, as the ravages of time had created wear and tear and dilapidation to dwellings.

After a disastrous depression, the majority of Appalachians were trying to adjust to the stresses of war. Many lived without the family patriarch, who was away in the service. Mental health care became an urgent need for poor families. Daily health care necessities, such as soap, toothbrush and paste, decent clothing and furnishings, were not available for them. To help meet these personal needs, the private sector of communities, like churches or nonprofit organizations, would dedicate time by visiting families, showing them basic ways to maintain good health habits.

Terrible working conditions in the mines during World War II, along with lack of accessibility to health care took its toll on miners. With a concerted war effort, the coal industry was functioning 24 hours a day and pressure had been put on workers to produce more coal, which created greater potential for hazards, injuries, and death in the mines. During this period, documented data of mining injury and death had prompted a change of attitude toward prevention. The greater numbers, frequencies and dimensions of mining fatalities and accidents that were considered "random and unavoidable", began to be viewed as predictable and preventable.

Health and Health Care After World War II

On December 26, 1945, Appalachia's worst post war disaster occurred in Bell County. Twenty-four miners died in an underground fire and explosion. Shortly thereafter, another mine tragedy happened in Centralia, Illinois, killing 111 men. With living and working conditions deteriorating, it was evident that safety, medical services and housing had to improve. The United Mine Workers Union was calling for a federal safety code, and when the government did not respond to their concerns, miners had no alternative but to threaten with a strike. A nationwide walkout appeared imminent, however, the government "seized" the mines, immediately requesting a study of coal communities in Appalachia.

In 1947, the United States Bureau of Medicine, which was responsible for the research, issued a scathing report that medical facilities, services and sanitary conditions of Appalachia were the worst in the nation. The report shocked Americans and made them aware that people lived in squalor and hazardous substandard dwellings, as poor sanitation led to the spread of infectious diseases. It further elaborated that one had to personally view the scenes of Appalachia in order to fully realize the situation, because photographs could not reflect the true picture of abandonment, dejection, and deprivation. Unpainted houses of "board-and-batten" revealed unmentionable deteriorating conditions. Roofs were either caving in or broken, and porches fell apart with steps bending to unpredictable angles. The report cited that outhouses left human waste exposed to saturate the air with terrible and nauseating odors, and the stench of rubbish permeated yards and surroundings. Disease spread throughout the region, and in certain instances led to death.

After release of the 1947 Report, condemning conditions in Appalachian mining communities, the United Mine Workers Union

Welfare and Retirement Fund was established. The income for this fund had been based on levy per ton of coal that was mined, bringing millions of dollars into the U.M.W.U. treasury. It was the first such plan that coal miners ever had, which included a rehabilitation program to help the sick and injured, along with free medical care for workers and their families. This plan went beyond other industrial union benefit programs, by providing a boost for miners on pension, giving free medical care to them and their families, along with allocating death benefits and maintenance assistance to widows and orphans.

The principle behind this program was probably one of the most energetic and practical approaches to improving the health status of miners and their families. It included the raising of medical standards in Appalachia in order to attract additional qualified doctors and improve health care facilities to reach national norm levels. In spite of their past frustration and problems with health care, miners rejoiced and looked forward to having the "best that medicine could offer". Union members were told that they would have the most efficient hospitals, doctors, nursing care, and "everything" necessary to relieve pain and suffering, as well as restoring health.

Unfortunately, greed prevailed on the part of some doctors and hospitals when contracts called for an increase in physicians' fees, fattening their pockets, along with added incentives if a patient's stay in a medical facility was extended. Hospitals had been financially benefiting more than twofold from the U.M.W.U. fund, but their facilities were still drastically inadequate and needed improvement, as called for by the U.S. Navy Report. The Union "coffers" were overflowing with income and purse strings loosened a little too much for the medical profession. Opportunities of taking financial advantage became inviting, and lack of honesty by health care services left a negative impact on miners and their families. Dilapidated hospitals overcharged for services, and were stacked with patients who should have had outpatient care. Right from the beginning, it seemed that the U.M.W.U. Board of Trustees was not experienced in dispensing funds appropriately, and failed to effectively monitor the overall program, as hospitals' incomes increased.

This triggered reaction from critics and inflamed sensitivity by the medical profession because of potential consequences that such a health care program would bring about. The American Medical Association objected and claimed that the union-funded program was another example of "socialized medicine." However, ignoring critics of the deplorable medical situation, some coal camp doctors were able to continue financial gain from the "welfare fund gravy train." They were filling their small hospitals with patients, warranted or unwarranted, dispensed medicine or performed unnecessary operations, and did everything that brought in money. Operations relating to tonsils, adenoids and appendices were performed on people, as if "they were going through the turnstiles of a sporting event".

Trustees of the Miners Fund finally concluded that if the Union was paying for good medicine, they should receive it. In 1952, U.M.W.U. decided to build ten modern hospitals in mining regions of Kentucky, Virginia, and West Virginia. Six of these medical facilities were located in eastern Kentucky at Whitesburg, McDowell, Pikeville, Middlesboro, Hazard and Harlan. They were called Miners Memorial Hospitals, in memory of those who had died or were injured while working in the mines. In 1956, with national acclaim for many modern architectural features, the hospitals opened their doors to miners and families. Changes that took place in planning these facilities bore little resemblance to their counterparts of the early twentieth-century. The new hospitals accommodated expanded services, such as a laboratory, examination areas, x-ray diagnosis and treatment center, emergency and operating rooms, along with the most modern equipment of that era. These facilities were also able to provide for patients with communicable disease, and accommodate maternity, nursery, and children's wards. Miners finally had their own "state of the art" medical facilities.

Education

A major sore spot that continued to plague Appalachia during and after World War II, was the deterioration of schools. Except for W.P.A. school projects in the county seats and a few villages, educational facilities were in disrepair and overall depressing conditions. Driving on gravel backroads, one could see tar paper pasted over boards on one side of a shack, and a small 6 by 6 foot front porch hanging at a 40 degree angle on no foundation. This might have looked like a shanty, but instead it was a one-room school house. One cannot imagine the kind of privies students had to use; they were outdoor shacks infested by snakes, rodents, and other unwelcome varmints. Children faced indignity at its lowest level. A pot bellied stove in the school room served as the only heat source, and winds of the cold battled to find a way through many cracks of loosely nailed together slats.

Most eastern Kentucky schools were built in the second decade of the 20th century. When union supported communities called for better schools and improved teacher salaries, reformers departed from the non-direction of coal-baron-controlled predecessors. More taxes had to be collected from coal companies to resolve their lax payments, and this was the objective of reformers. Complaints were numerous that coal corporations were not carrying their level of financial responsibility. This became a constant condition of frustration that led to disillusionment of the reformers. In certain instances, even with reform as a driving force, tax collectors obligated themselves to coal owners. There was some dispute about the role these public servants were playing, for coal companies were very persuasive and succeeded in avoiding their obligation to the community.

Harry Caudill, in his book, "A Night Comes to the Cumberlands," cited how the necessary taxes to finance schools were not collected and why. The misconception was ingrained in people's minds that equitable taxes would destroy the coal industry. Incredible as it may seem, the citizens were told by political powers that financing of decent schools would ruin the industry, and people accepted these explanations. They were led to believe that coal companies would go out of business if they had to pay taxes for all the houses and properties they owned, therefore miners would have no more jobs. Caudill called this nonsense and absurd, and further criticized the coal companies for charging rent at hefty prices, without paying taxes on those properties. The result was that the financing of decent schools never reached Appalachian communities.

In 1946 and 48, the Kentucky Education Association urged the legislature to guarantee a minimum teacher salary of one hundred dollars a month. Political powers on the regional and state level reacted with an attitude of disregard and unconcern, even though teachers' salaries were considered to be at the poverty level in many districts. Inferior working conditions left school districts susceptible to mediocre education, limited access to very important services, subordination of educators to authorities of the schools, and insecurity in teaching positions. In essence, schools were suffering from a myriad of deterrents: politically, economically and socially, which led to frustration among teachers. Despite all their disappointments, the education reform forces tried to persistently fight against indifferent attitudes, but reluctantly pulled back because of a hopeless situation.

By the 1950's, most school facilities and little one-room school houses felt the brunt of year in and year out neglect. Since educational experiences were progressing at a snail's pace, the harmful combination of a politically controlled school system, misguided administrators, and underqualified teachers influenced the scene. However, before going any further, it should be pointed out that there had been dedicated, highly trained administrators and teachers, who were good-hearted humanitarians and left an impact on the children. If it were not for these individuals, who had concern and commitment, there would have been many more students faltering and quitting school. Overall, the poor level of education had a depressing effect on children of Appalachia.

Since the 1930's, reformers attempted to improve the educational system of eastern Kentucky, yet mediocrity persisted. For years, inequality of education between Appalachian school districts and vanguard systems of Jefferson and Fayette Counties had been a constant comparison for frustrated state legislators and leaders. Any mention of problems pertaining to Kentucky's educational system immediately conjured up an image of those wretched conditions in rural mountain schools. The challenge of educating children of poverty in eastern Kentucky was recognized as a difficult task. For a child whose impoverished family struggled under the burdens of just getting by, staying in school was the only hope for a better future. Yet, despite the opportunity to get an education, these students were hindered from performing effectively in their pursuit of learning, because of economic hardship and accompanying social disadvantages.

As a result of these continuous conditions, the State legislature passed a significant reform in 1954, which affected education. The "Kentucky Educational Foundation Act" required that a minimum quality program be established for each school district. It was designed to provide equal public school educational opportunities throughout the commonwealth of Kentucky. All under-financed and backward school districts were to elevate their standards to the level of wealthy counties, such as Jefferson and Fayette. The law had shown promise, and in certain parts of the state, enthusiasm and acceptance by the people prevailed. However, Appalachia's school districts were hopelessly bogged down through self-perpetuating and irresponsible administrative actions. The relationship between teachers, superintendents and school boards became strained, jaded and showed distrust. Teachers were frustrated over low salaries, inferior working conditions, lack of school supplies and materials, along with the overall apathy of students. These concerns had been often ignored by authoritarian superintendents, and their position was so politically oriented since the 1930's that it became a major deterrent for those who wanted to enforce educational reform. School boards also provided ways and means to strengthen a superintendent's control, and in certain instances, this position became politically the most powerful in a county.

As poor educational conditions continued to exist, some eastern Kentuckians were very concerned for their children and wanted them educated not only in elementary and secondary schools, but through college. These people were determined and proud and did not want their offspring to encounter a future of living in poverty. Persistency paid off, and the children knew that education was their only opportunity for advancement in life. Whether parent-motivated or through self-determination, for decades some of eastern Kentucky's brightest and most ambitious young people left Appalachia to enrich other communities and states.

Important developments took place during the 40's and 50's that revolutionized the American employment market, but never found its way to Appalachia. Emphasis was being placed on the educated person in workplaces. However, the region had been isolated for generations by different kinds of barriers and was not fortunate enough to share in the growth and prosperity of our country. Those college students who grew up with poverty and its resultant ills, found it difficult to return to their homes. Need for retaining intelligent young minds of Appalachia was never greater than during this period. The rest of America had gained an industrial competitive edge that made it impossible for these youth to stay on in the mountains. Upon graduation from college, many young people could not get jobs that were related to their special line of work due to the lack of diversified industries in Appalachia. Business opportunities, whether small or large, were non-existing and venture possibilities limited. This left a vacuum for "young blood" to generate new directions for the region, as future leadership had only a small chance for growth.

Impact of Humanitarian Leadership

Fortunately for some communities, not all young brilliant and potential leaders left the highlands for other parts of the country. The impact that certain educators had on their students made a difference for some, and they came back to eastern Kentucky serving their local communities. Individual leaders in education, such as Alice Lloyd, had to be creative and encouraging to those Appalachians whose leadership qualities needed nurturing for their role in mountain society. Former students who returned and helped the less fortunate through their service and commitment beyond the call of duty, had never forgotten that their benefactors gave them the opportunity to be successful.

Denzil Barker, M.D.

One such beneficiary of Alice Lloyd's humanitarian efforts was Dr. Denzil Barker, a pleasant and unassuming gentleman, proud owner of a Phi Beta Kappa Key, and a Rhodes scholar nominee from the State of Kentucky. When Denzil started in medicine he was considered a novice, however, soon demonstrated being in a league by himself. Integrity, compassion, and understanding were strengths that enhanced his outstanding professional work. Dr. Barker came back to practice medicine in Hindman, Kentucky, after World War II, as his benefactor had wished. Born and brought up in humble beginnings, he never forgot his fortunate boyhood circumstances that led him to success through Alice Lloyd's determination and drive.

Denzil was an outstanding athlete and wanted to be a famous baseball player. Apparently he had the tools and was good enough to play professionally. I remember in the sixties that some of his hillfolk friends spoke guardedly "mountain style" and stated, "Dr. Denzil Barker would have been a great major league ballplayer." He did not pursue this career but became a medical man, and thanks to Alice Lloyd's perseverance and faith in him, he came back to serve the poor of Appalachia. Dr. Barker was always concerned about the importance of medicine for people of poverty and knew, if they did not receive health care, many would face an even grimmer future. Denzil did not become a major league ballplayer, but he sure was "The Natural," who left an impact on his people in the field of medicine.

Dan Martin, Attorney

Dan Martin was another eastern Kentucky gentleman whose life was enriched and broadened by much encouragement from Alice Lloyd and her devoted assistant June Buchanan. When Dan was a young boy, his mother knew that she could not financially afford an education for him. Mrs. Martin wanted her son to have a chance in life, so she walked many miles to Caney Creek Community Center for a meeting with Alice Lloyd and June Buchanan. When Mrs. Martin met both ladies, she knew that Dan's future would be assured. Making a secret agreement, she turned her son over to Mrs. Lloyd at an early age to be tutored. Dan became a ward of Alice Lloyd and June Buchanan and was educated from elementary through secondary levels and college. He went on to law school with blessings and financial assistance from Alice Lloyd.

After World War II, Dan Martin returned to eastern Kentucky, opened his practice in Hindman, and became a successful lawyer, working for the poor of Appalachia. Dan never knew about his mother's arrangement with Alice Lloyd. However, after Mrs. Martin passed away he was cleaning out her house and came across a bible. In it was the document that Alice Lloyd returned to Mrs. Martin, after Dan received his law degree. Mrs. Lloyd's mission had been accomplished, and a loving mother's wish for her child to have a better life was fulfilled. Dan Martin's success in helping people of the hills is well known. As a former board member and legal advisor to Alice Lloyd College, Dan highly encouraged countless students over many decades to attain their professional goals, and hoped that some would return to help the less fortunate.

As one looks back, many other Alice Lloyd graduates excelled and achieved success in their professional future, which was largely due to sacrifices of parents. What these parents had in common was the all-consuming love for their children. By ordinary college requirements, standards and criteria for success, Appalachian college students had to work even harder to overcome deficiencies of their limited educational background and other obstacles. They had to have strong self-determination and drive. Parents, often illiterate, recognized the importance of education and demanded extreme efforts from their children. The pride that parents had in their children's success could not be measured, and it did not matter how much they gave up, because this meant an avenue for a better future and escape from poverty.

Religion

Religion in this part of Kentucky had many interpretations, but the fact remains that those people who are religious and have a solid foundation of faith, are able to carry themselves through most difficult times. Since the settlers first came to this region, religion has played an important part in these people's lives as isolation and poverty led to the need for great inner strength in order to triumph over helplessness. Through religion, people were provided with values that included individual worth and human meaning.

Hillfolk probably are no different than other people in the way they respond to organized religion. The religious were always involved in church and community functions, working hard to help the needy. Belief in their Christian heritage "to do good unto others" always stayed with them, even through their years of suffering. In many instances, religion brought stability and a sense of belonging to their community, its people, and the family. However, the conditions under which religion had to serve people in Appalachia as compared to outside affluent communities, presented a monumental task.

After World War II and continuing into the 1950's, poverty brought about a feeling of resignation and lack of self esteem, which led to a sense of fatalism in Appalachia's needy. Unpredictability of economic and social conditions hindered their endeavor to succeed, creating an increase in alcoholism, abuse, and depression, which even led to suicide. As some economists declared, these people were not just "statistically poor," but "painfully poor." Their physical and mental problems increased and some gave up hope, living drab and unfulfilled lives with no comforts. Since mental health care was practically non-existent in this region, a pastor's roll went beyond that of a spiritual leader. Even though some churches were not strong enough for people to "lean" on, there were congregations where the pastor provided whatever help he could. If the resolve of a spiritual leadership and congregation was strong, the needy were able to survive.

Some churches in Appalachia had focused inwardly; however, the influence of those pastors who were concerned about the total community was an important asset of their leadership role. They wanted to reach outward by doing good deeds for all people, especially the poor. During the 1940's and 50's, churches changed in many ways since their beginning in Appalachia. It is true that preachers in the past were self-ordained, however during this period, influence of religious institutions like the Southern Baptist Theological Seminary became a major factor for educated ministers to work in Appalachia. Their goals generally dealt with developing the ministry to meet needs of the community and make it a better place to live. In examining the pastor's role, one cannot help but admire the determination and meaningful contributions of these concerned religious people, in spite of the many burdens presented to them. They were able to restore respect for fellow Appalachians by revealing the naked truth about many struggles of the needy. Their well-grounded realism provided practical leadership for communities.

As outside miners moved into Appalachia after the turn of the century, they led the way for missionaries to follow. Those immigrants that came from Italy, Poland, Germany and other European countries, opened the door for a small group of Catholic, Lutheran, Methodist and Presbyterian churches. With the development of mission churches in this region, ministries were targeting all types of people wherever possible. During the 1950's, I visited the communities of Prestonsburg, Pikeville, Hazard, Whitesburg and Harlan, and noted that churches were feeding the hungry, nursing the sick, providing clothing and giving guidance to unfortunate and bewildered adults and children. In certain instances, even filthy, infested places that people lived in were cleaned up by church groups. The only hope poor people had was that the religious would be able to help them overcome hunger and misery. At first, some of the long standing people of these communities were suspicious of new mission groups, but they soon saw that the humanitarian actions were sincere, practical and beneficial to the poor.

Father Ralph W. Beiting

Humanitarians probably had the greatest positive influence on needy people of Appalachia since individual crusades took place. They became role models and because of their kindness and charity, children liked to emulate them. One person that comes to mind is a man of religion, Father Ralph W. Beiting. It was over 35 years ago that I visited a

93

friend in Berea, Kentucky, and my memory of the occasion is still vivid, because the conversation all evening revolved around the good deeds of Father Beiting, a local missionary priest. Since he had been working with poor people, Father Ralph Beiting's story is so striking and entwined in leadership action that it needs to be told.

One of eleven children and a native Kentuckian, he was born to Ralph and Martha Beiting, and knew from his early days as a young seminarian that he wanted to work with the poor of Appalachia. When Father Ralph Beiting started his first mission parish in 1950, he began carrying out that vision. His goal was not only to serve as spiritual leader for Catholics in the area, but also help poor people regardless of their religious background. He set out to gather food, clothing, and household goods that eased their burden. At first, Father Beiting relied entirely on contributions of his family and friends from northern Kentucky, trekking endlessly and gathering much needed replenishings for the survival of these poor. This approach led him to question the long range implications, and he realized their needs were so enormous that help from others, along with new approaches, warranted expansion of services.

As a result, he began to focus on finding ways for the needy to care for themselves, become independent, and effectively work with others in the community. With this concept as the basis for action, Reverend Beiting and his associate pastor Father Herman Kamlage, started a camp for needy youths of poor families in the counties that he served. As his work expanded, so did the newly founded Christian Appalachian Project, and Father Beiting organized volunteers who were also concerned about the less fortunate. Many obstacles had to be overcome, but this did not deter him and the CAP organization in helping to bring about change for the poor of Appalachia. A key for success was Father Beiting's ability in leading volunteers and showing needy people the importance of self-help in order to overcome impoverishment.

In the late 1950's, Appalachia's fragile economy did not experience growth, and CAP became incorporated as a non-profit organization in bringing greater opportunities to the needy. Father Beiting and people who worked with the organization, began to expand services leading toward employment, which encouraged the poor to help themselves through educational and other human development programs. Creative ventures were added to help those individuals who had the ability and initiative of achieving in small business projects. By showing through example, Father Beiting has encouraged poor people to succeed. Today, many of these business ventures have expanded and flourish in Appalachia.

Father Beiting is known to many eastern Kentuckians as a man of God, who is concerned about poor people's conditions and provides opportunities for hope, giving them a sense of purpose. In his book, "God

Can Move Mountains," he wrote about a visit to one of the backcountry hollows outside the town of Martin, meeting with an 83 year old man who was poor. This elderly person had been living in seclusion for ten years, and the only people knowing that he existed were his brother and sister who lived 2 hours away. Reverend Beiting told of the man's living conditions and the kind of squalor and filth no human being should experience. It is to the credit of Father Beiting and his good followers of the inter-denominational Christian Appalachian Project that a small house was built, which gave this man of poverty a new lease on life.

From the start, Appalachians' perspective about Father Beiting's humanistic dimensions was evident in the help he gave each individual. Overall, religious belief of the people was not Father Beiting's concern; he just wanted to alleviate their suffering. Thus, he initiated an organization that would blossom into one of the most dynamic humanitarian endeavors for helping Appalachia's needy.

Summation

If one had driven through the coal fields of eastern Kentucky during this period, unimaginable, discouraging and hopeless forms of impoverishment would have been visible. In the late 1950's, writers of books and newspapers brought attention to social consciousness. Dark forebodings stirred many intellects and young college students to reexamine the problems of poverty. It was during the late 40's and 50's that rural poverty spilled over to metropolitan areas of America, as Appalachians migrated to northern cities, hoping for a better life. Instead they found new obstacles and different kinds of problems. Some ended up in ghettos which were exposed to the "affluent" people who had to travel daily through these blighted areas. Appalachians who could not get jobs in their new urban surroundings, saw their conditions worsen and eventually returned to the mountains.

Even though government research and studies cited that poverty in eastern Kentucky declined in the 50's, they were mixed messages and did not show the total picture. Data failed to bring out the fact that this period experienced the greatest migration of Appalachians, but despite this exodus, poverty was still 30 percent higher than in other parts of our nation. Also, there were some clear reasons why government's description of impoverishment was open for debate, which encouraged disparaging remarks by critics. Concerns of how government determined the poverty level led to variations of interpretation, and as a result, this "relative, inexact term" has become a "bone of contention" with critics. Some went so far as to say that it was easier for poor people to exist in rural situations because they could grow their own food and live on less income. These kinds of statements are made to satisfy those who do not want to know what poverty is all about. However, in order to understand impoverishment, one must realize that it consists of a vast and complex variety of uncontrollable conditions.

A major concern for those who knew about the situation of poor people in rural areas was that the many services one took for granted in urban living were very limited or non-existent in eastern Kentucky. Health care centers, education, transportation, housing and general living situations, along with other community services, were lacking for the rural poor. Economically depressed farms and mining towns of Appalachia continued to propagate many conditions of poverty, and this region's single major industry made it much more difficult for people to gain a foothold on a decent way of life. The need for expansion toward a diversified industrial economy bypassed the Cumberland plateau country, and increased paucity of employment opportunities not only affected the poor, but also potential future leaders of Appalachia. Many home-grown, college-educated eastern Kentuckians were forced to migrate to other parts of the country that benefited from their contributions. In the late 50's, poverty was so intractable in Appalachia that the poor were locked in a stranglehold without any possibility for change in the near future.

Chapter V

1960 — 1979

A Time for Action

The sixties in our country exemplified challenge, leading to many questions of how to focus on social issues in an era of causes, which would bring about change. There were monumental victories, such as a new found freedom for those Americans who were subjugated to second class citizenship for hundreds of years. President John F. Kennedy in his inaugural speech referred to "a new generation of Americans," and encouraged them to take action by challenging, "Ask not what your country can do for you, but what you can do for your country." To many Appalachians this was not an idle message, for these magical words gave them renewed hope by the new leadership, calling for a summons to fight impoverishment. Presidents Kennedy and Lyndon B. Johnson gave poverty their priority in the sixties, and many people in Appalachia became enthusiastic about the opportunity for change. Bert T. Combs, Governor of Kentucky, who worked effectively and cooperatively with the federal administration, was able to confront the state's many problems, bringing hope through action. It was at a time when civil rights came about and black people of our nation were fighting inequality, which affected their lives. This was viewed with sincerity by the mountain folk and others throughout the nation, who believed that every human being should be free. It led mountaineers during the sixties and seventies to heights which previously could not have been achieved, due to oppression of individuality and beliefs. They felt it was time for taking a stand to preserve their land that was stripped and left damaged by the coal corporations.

During the early sixties certain events occurred, which played an important part in J.F.K.'s decision to fight poverty. Kennedy's astute observation during his presidential campaign of 1959 left him with great concern about deprivation and degradation that the poor had to endure. Governor Combs also discussed in his meetings with President Kennedy much needed initiatives to improve living standards in Appalachia. In 1963, the book "A Night Comes to the Cumberlands," written by Harry Caudill, enlightened many people, including the administration, about failure of man toward his land, and how humans have had to pay with their lives of wanton spoils. Caudill, a native eastern Kentuckian, told it the way it was: a depressed Appalachia, with destitution brought on by wretched conditions. He called attention to the rising need for teaching the poor to help themselves, and championed new ideas for reform. Harry Caudill's book presents one of the most perceptive views on poverty in eastern Kentucky. Other literature, such as the 1962 writing of Michael Harrington's "The Other America: Poverty in the United States," also had great influence on the Kennedy Administration. Harrington's challenge called for full-fledged mobilization to end impoverishment, with the belief that government should be an instrument for positive change.

As a result of the conditions, President Kennedy immediately set in motion federal projects to alleviate suffering which was becoming increasingly worse. During his first months in office J.F.K. initiated anti-poverty action, designed to help all depressed states of the Appalachian range. The Area Redevelopment Administration was started in 1961 to halt economic downturn and social disintegration in Appalachia, thus three-hundred million dollars were appropriated to those states. This action had called for private business initiative to stimulate and design economic programs, while the Accelerated Public Works Act of 1962, provided nine-hundred million dollars in public funds. Kennedy's attack on poverty continued with enactment of the Manpower Development and Training Act (MDTA), which was based on the assumption that this approach would encourage people to help themselves, and cut short their dependency on welfare. MDTA proved to be so popular with Congress that it led to establishment of the Job Corps in 1964.

Even though certain federal initiatives proved to have a positive affect, Governor Bert Combs discussed with President Kennedy that greater emphasis had to be placed on eradicating impoverishment through proliferation of alternatives that would respond more effectively to human needs. J.F.K. promised Combs that he would do more for eastern Kentucky, and had on his drawing board a financial plan, which was supposed to help strengthen the fight against poverty. Prior to taking action in providing funds for Appalachia, Kennedy had favored Vice-President Johnson with a visit to the state of Texas. J.F.K. never returned to Washington, D.C., to fulfill his promise, due to his premature death in Dallas. However, despite this great tragedy in the history of our country, Lyndon B. Johnson carried out President Kennedy's dream to fight poverty.

Many of John F. Kennedy's plans served as the basis for L.B.J.'s "War on Poverty" in 1964. Research and studies were conducted to gather necessary information about the needs and number of people living in poverty throughout the United States, and results provided estimates to determine new classifications. A family of four with an income of less than 3,000 dollars annually, was considered living below the "poverty line." President Johnson announced in 1964 that 20 percent of the American population belonged in this category. However, in eastern Kentucky counties like Knott, Floyd, and Letcher, pockets existed where almost 65 percent of the population fit this classification. Later, under President Johnson, federal programs provided funds to restore forests, build roads, and retrain workers who had lost their jobs in coal mining, lumber, and farming industries.

Johnson concerned himself with developing social programs, mainly employment-related opportunities for the needy. As Senator and President, he gave particular emphasis on education, by introducing Head Start, which was of great importance for the future of poor children. In a 1964 speech, he asked that educators play an important role to uplift the people from impoverishment. L.B.J. wanted education to serve as the foundation for indigents to help themselves move up from poverty by taking advantage of the many government programs. This included youth training, job training for adults, work study programs for those in school, aid to rural farmers and small businesses, loans to industry for hiring unemployed persons, volunteers to assist the needy, and the Community Action Program to help poor people plan and direct projects for their own development. However, a major deterrent toward producing an effective anti-poverty program was a combination of lacking patience, money and long range goals for the job corps. This program's hastily put together plan had curtailed an accountable approach to implementation and efficient evaluation. The amount of infighting and disagreements at the top level limited any effective movement of providing long-term jobs for the needy.

Joining the long line of anti-poverty programs were Food Stamps, Medicare (for the elderly), and Medicaid (health insurance for people who were indigent). The strong leadership that came from Appalachia to push for development of such humanitarian initiatives included Bert T. Combs and Congressman Carl Dewey Perkins from Hindman, Kentucky. Even after leaving office as Governor, Combs had played an increasingly prominent role as one of the original architects for Johnson's "Great Society" Appalachian projects. Carl Perkins had served as chairman of the powerful House Education and Labor Committee and was responsible for steering President Johnson's anti-poverty program successfully through Congress. He achieved implementation of Federal Aid to Education, Head Start, school lunch programs, job training, and other projects, critical for helping the poor.

Having had the opportunity to observe firsthand some of the War on Poverty programs, it is more than fair to say that certain ones were and still are a success, despite being maligned by critics through the years. The one social program that stands out as President Johnson's greatest long term contribution is Medicare. In fact, many authorities rank it second only to F.D.R.'s Social Security initiative during the Depression. Medicare came about in the 60's, after at least two decades of controversial and unwarranted denouncements by congressmen and the elite of our country, criticizing that the concept was a form of "socialized medicine." However, after serving all those years in Congress, President Johnson knew it was time to finally convince his backers in Senate and the House of Representatives that Medicare would make a difference in lives of the elderly and long-term disabled persons.

Despite the constant bashing from conservative forces, results have shown that Medicare has contributed immensely to the quality of life. Prior to Medicare the elderly and disabled of Appalachia as well as the total country were living in vulnerable situations, brought on by increased hospital costs, which a large segment of these people were unable to pay. Too many Appalachians lived in poverty and could not absorb health insurance payments. Others, because of pre-existing conditions, were faced with being refused health insurance. Many elderly and disabled found it difficult to recover financially after requiring hospital care, and President Johnson knew that this was part of the continuing cycle of poverty, affecting a helpless segment of our population. As a result, Johnson seized a much needed opportunity to initiate the Medicare health insurance program, which was funded through Social Security contributions, premiums, and general revenue from the federal government.

Head Start, another favorite long lasting social program, was under great scrutiny from the beginning, but its amazing success through the years is a tribute to idealism, dedication and concern of many people. One unfortunate aspect of the Head Start Program in Appalachia was that in certain counties poor children, who should have had the opportunities offered through this program, were bypassed by local political factions. Children, whose parents lived above the poverty level were benefiting and took away classroom seats from the needy. Head Start had always been vulnerable to criticism, and its educational program constantly came under fire from "early childhood" educators, social analysts and psychologists, who personally felt that this endeavor was not worthwhile and wished it would go away. Not knowing all the program's benefits they unceremoniously, and in certain instances with malice, proclaimed its failure. Another obstacle was the uncertainty of funding from year to year, and frustrated personnel felt insecure with this type of situation hanging over their heads, which led to constant questioning about continuation. Nevertheless, research and parent response about children's success far outweighed the problems, as Head Start has left a positive impact on early childhood education.

Over the years, both major political parties in our country have embraced this popular program that has not only helped children to succeed in school, but also offers comprehensive health and social services to a child's family. Regardless of differing viewpoints by the Democrats and Republicans as to how Head Start should be run, there is an obvious need that the federal government must provide funds. After all, this is considered one of the "shining lights" of government sponsored initiatives.

Aggressive action by the Johnson Administration projects moved a large percentage of the population above poverty level, and within a decade approximately 14 million people had reached that goal, because American families were gaining steady increases in income. Another reason for this was that married women were leaving their domestic lifestyle for a workplace, and two paychecks became the norm for families. However, Appalachian environment was not conducive to producing these types of opportunities for eastern Kentuckians, which the rest of America was enjoying. Since mountaineers mainly worked for a single industry that was changing to automation, jobs and income declined. Women were still at home, unable to get some kind of work, and the continued high fertility rate, along with illiteracy added to their existing problems. Full-time or part-time jobs were not available. Even low-income families, who managed to stay out of poverty, had declining salaries during recession years.

The War on Poverty provided a measure of success to those eastern Kentuckians participating in its projects. However, there were some mountain folk, who by the nature of their pride and independence, refused to accept "hand outs" because they felt not being that bad off. Their cultural background projected an attitude of non-acceptance in government support even though income was meager. These people had been self-sufficient for years and felt they could survive without aid, and valuing each other's self-respect meant everything to them, since their community expected this type of attitude.

As I look back at the implementation of War on Poverty, it was apparent that most Appalachian people were committed to "attack this dreaded enemy." The mountain folk had felt ignored in the past, and finally, with President Johnson's concern, they were eager to make War on Poverty a success. Alice Lloyd College was no exception, for it had played a leadership role in alleviating impoverishment by giving people a chance to help themselves through education. I remember the first VISTA Conference, which was held at Alice Lloyd College in 1964, bringing together nationally known educators, leaders of law, business, politics, and government specialists from all parts of our nation, to expand upon and develop a sense of direction for this new poverty project. Kentuckians and outsiders who developed the planning phase had a common cause — fighting poverty. However, camaraderie and vision of these people did not carry over to the everyday operation of VISTA. It became increasingly clear that what was needed in many instances entailed organized social services to meet the infinite variety of poor people's needs, which were by-products of poverty. Also, volunteers in the "field" should have gained more knowledge of understanding the cultural differences and background of Appalachia's needy.

Unfortunately, War on Poverty never met the expectations of many workers, politicians, and policy makers. For example, in 1964 President Johnson stated that "for the first time in the history of human race, a great nation...is able and willing to make a commitment to eradicate poverty." Instead, it became one of the greatest soul searching acts of American political decision-making, for it was a testament to a broken dream. Accountability was ignored in managing certain projects, which appeared poorly prepared and hastily launched on a crash basis.

One of the most telling frustrations was that War on Poverty had too many distractions in its implementation. Critics complained that this was an expensive scandal ridden program, with some founded and unfounded truths. Others seemed to feel that certain projects were too revolutionary for the government to undertake. There were politicians, "kingpins" of big business, and influential people, who considered War On Poverty to be very socialistic, using "federal funds to undermine free enterprise." Many problems that existed, whether nationally, regionally, or locally, deterred the true receivers from benefiting — poor people. The bureaucratic structure was out of sync with the original purposes of War on Poverty. Misappropriation of funds, political infighting to control regions and localities, along with forms of violence in job corps centers and communities became a hindrance to its success. The result was a loosely connected cannon spraying havoc, instead of spreading good deeds throughout the countryside of our nation. Everybody was blaming everyone else for its failure. However, there were exceptions, where individuals or groups showed "modest success" in the implementation of their respective programs serving a purpose for the needy.

As our country progressed through the sixties and seventies, showing growth in the economy, Appalachia remained in an unchanged position. Lack of concern from Americans toward conditions of the needy was discouraging, and attitudes of some people were that the poor would be with us for quite some time. Certain individuals viewed the indigent with disdain, while others considered poverty to be an unappealing backdrop. The lack of understanding and concern for the less fortunate was not new to people of Appalachia. This led Americans on November 4, 1979, to elect a conservative administration for the 1980's, which in turn removed some War on Poverty projects without a solid plan to effectively serve the less fortunate.

Through the years, lack of knowledge about eastern Kentucky has played an important part in unfair judgment of its people. Many comparisons of this region to other places were based on misconceptions, because their ills were not as visible as in urban settings. Little did outsiders realize that physical barriers played a role in deterring and slowing growth. This worked both ways, first it kept progress from reaching hollows, hamlets and towns, and in turn blocked the economic and social ills from being viewed by the rest of our nation. In the 1960's and 70's, accessibility in and out of Appalachia existed, but most of this region was still remote and invisible to others.

Individual Contributions

In the 60's and 70's, new elements were introduced into the traditional framework of Appalachian life, which must be considered when talking about changes that came about during the War on Poverty years. Most writers for newspapers, magazines and books chose to emphasize the hopelessness of this region, rather than give examples of people striving to improve lives of the poor. Having lived in eastern Kentucky at that time, I would like to offer a perspective on the dedication of certain people who made changes in many areas of social development, ranging from education to health care. There were others, who were making inroads in economic development. All these people were intense and passionate in their convictions and advocacy on socioeconomic issues, leaving little doubt of their intention to provide solutions for persons in crisis.

Changing Appalachia was and is a formidable task, however these individuals knew, in order to overcome complex and tenacious problems, they had to have personal integrity and face sacrifice. They succeeded in serving as pillars of strength for their less fortunate fellow eastern Kentuckians. In spite of many obstacles, this breed of leadership was beginning to develop a new direction for change. In short, they were accountable in building a foundation for the poor of Appalachia to improve their human condition, individual worth and dignity. People such as Dr. Grady Stumbo and Benny Ray Bailey came to the forefront in health care services by opening the Eastern Kentucky Community Health Clinic in Hindman, and through Mrs. Eula Hall's leadership, the Mud Creek Health Clinic came into existence. Among other leaders throughout the region was Lois Baker, who worked to establish the Mountain Health Clinic in Whitesburg. Their knowledge, understanding, and actions to help the less fortunate of eastern Kentucky would have a positive impact on health care service for years to come.

In industry, one of the most successful stories of the 70's was the start of an Appalachian high tech computer service corporation, headed by dynamic leader Ken James. This business brought new hope to the people of London and its area, by providing jobs and demanding skilled workers. In the mid 60's, Father Ralph Beiting and the Christian Appalachian Project were expanding a human development program and small businesses opened up, creating a demand for jobs. New educational programs were initiated to meet different needs of people. The CAP "Attic Stores," which are a success story in their own right, were developed by Father Beiting and started out as used clothing stores, blossoming into large retail businesses, combining grocery, boutique, and antique shops. Toward the late 1960's, Brothers of Charity from Philadelphia, Pennsylvania, came to assist the people of David in buying this unique mining town from the Princess Elkhorn Coal Company that had shut down its operation. Catholic nuns and VISTA volunteers also moved to the community, addressing many problems of the area, and working with people to uplift themselves by establishing economic opportunities. Today, David is known for its ongoing battle against poverty, and assisting people to become productive citizens through different programs under the leadership of Sister Ida Marie Deville. One program, the "David Appalachian Crafts," has brought national attention to this historic and unique coal-mining community.

In the field of education, Dan Greene, a graduate of Fordham University in New York City, came to Floyd County in 1972 to start an independent school in David, giving dropouts and undereducated youth a second chance at learning. Through the years this school would flourish and graduate thousands of students, who were written off by public schools of the area. Today, Dan Greene and David School are recognized nationally for bringing opportunities of change to poor youth. Even senior citizens got involved in helping these children. Mrs. Molena Tunnell, an elderly VISTA volunteer from San Angelo, Texas, decided that she wanted to come to Appalachia and work with the Library Service

Home Start program in Corbin. A retired librarian, Mrs. Tunnell brought caring, concern and help to isolated children of the area, whose parents in many instances could not read or write. She worked with children and parents at home, or would drive them to the local library, to provide learning experiences.

People of all ages who were dedicated in fighting the ills of poverty came forward to guide the less fortunate. It is regretful that very seldom their good deeds have been told, for there were many who repeatedly showed either through public service or the private sector that they had great leadership quality. Unfortunately, it is impossible to write about all of them, however, I would like to mention some of eastern Kentucky's outstanding individuals during this period.

Bertram Thomas Combs

One such person of leadership, greatness and giving was Kentucky's most prominent citizen, Governor Bert T. Combs. He was a truly remarkable man, from Appalachia, who overcame many odds, committed himself to help the commonwealth's citizens, and lived long enough to experience the fulfillment of his work. Bert Combs was a warm and caring individual, who demanded the best from those working with him. Acumen, tenacity and graciousness were characteristics that Governor Combs carried with him throughout his life. He was elected Governor of Kentucky from 1959 through 1963, with one of the largest pluralities, and became known as a most progressive leader, who had a positive and lasting impact on the people. Under his orders in 1960, Kentucky established the Commission on Human Rights. Combs' desire to do things for "betterment of the people" made him work endlessly, pursuing ways to overcome many obstacles. Finally in 1963, he bypassed the State Legislature and signed an executive order, prohibiting employment discrimination by businesses who sold goods to the State of Kentucky. Included in this executive order were persons, companies and groups that had contract work with the State Government. During his term in office, Governor Combs established a "spirit of doing," and the State of Kentucky showed remarkable growth, especially in metropolitan Louisville and Lexington, where new highways and superhighways were built. He also engineered passage of a state sales tax to provide funds for veterans' benefits. His concern for education, especially in poor districts, led to the inclusion of schools, along with roads and parks in benefiting from taxes.

Before Bert Combs took office, the countryside in many areas of the Commonwealth, specifically Appalachia, was inundated with ugly trash and junk. During this period of change, he had encouraged the clean up of stranded, broken down old cars and trucks, along with garbage that littered the sides of roads. In 1960, one of the state's main themes was: "Make Kentucky a cleaner greener land," and many people responded favorably through action. Thanks to Governor Bert Combs' effectiveness and vision, Appalachia as well as the whole state benefited from the results, ultimately making it an inviting place to live. Building a diverse park system has also led the state to being a very attractive tourist destination, and it was in the sixties that Bert Combs had envisioned this direction. Under his leadership, Appalachia was beginning to benefit from these parks, and the vigorous effort of Governor Combs and his administration paid off, because Kentucky became the first state to win a national "Keep America Beautiful Award." Today, tourism has become one of the biggest industries in this state, giving it an economic boost. However, Combs expressed great concern that Appalachia had not yet reached its potential, and saw expansion of tourism as a necessity for this region's survival.

After leaving office as governor, Bert Combs served on the United States Sixth Circuit Court of Appeals. He received many acknowledgments for his sincere work, and was awarded a special honor as recipient of the Second Annual Joseph Kennedy Foundation Medal. On one occasion, Ralph Lewis and I drove to Prestonsburg to meet Bert Combs at the local airport, which he was instrumental in building, discussing matters regarding education. Ralph had been one of his press staff members before coming to Alice Lloyd College. A major concern for Bert Combs was that schools from eastern Kentucky were financially "being short-changed." We talked about working conditions in schools, ineffective methods of teaching, and overall inadequate education for children. At a subsequent meeting, Bert Combs was concerned that schools needed to keep up with the change of advancement in technology. He always searched for ways that would lead to solutions of educational problems not only in mountain regions, but the total state.

The greatest contribution Bert T. Combs has given his fellow Kentuckians occurred in 1989. A most closely observed case, held before Kentucky's Supreme Court in Frankfort, gathered a large crowd to hear the brilliant, eloquent and successful presentation by Attorney Bert T. Combs. He worked gratis as the lead attorney, representing sixty-six property-poor Kentucky school districts that challenged the way public schools were funded. The subject of inequality in financing education was an event that started trekking its way from a complaint filed November 1985 in the Franklin Circuit Court, "challenging the equity and adequacy of funds provided for education of young Kentuckians." In 1988, Judge Ray Corns issued a judgment in favor of the plaintiffs. The decision by the Supreme Court in June 1989 led to education reform of enormous future implications, and in 1990, schools began implementing the Kentucky Education Reform Act. Benefits of this program have yet to come to fruition, however it is certain that Bert Combs' leadership and caring for equality in education has brought a chance for children in all of Kentucky to succeed. Even though Bert T. Combs is no longer with us, his contributions have left a legacy of leadership from which future generations will benefit.

His daughter, Lois Weinberg, in her own right a fine educator, and today chairperson with the Pritchard Commission of the Kentucky Education Reform Act, told me about her father's drive and energy. She mentioned that Bert Combs in his later years did not let age deter his eagerness to take on a good battle. He believed that a person should not get old and cease to function. What I found very amazing about this man was that he undertook with confidence and vitality such a challenging and precedent setting lawsuit, at his age.

Harry Caudill

For almost three decades, I have been an ardent admirer of Harry Caudill's writings. As others will attest, from Washington, D.C. to Appalachia, Harry Caudill had one of the most poignant and strongest voices of eastern Kentucky. He was a native mountaineer who lived most of his life in Whitesburg, Kentucky. Harry came to lecture at Alice Lloyd College right after his book "A Night Comes to the Cumberlands" was receiving accolades nationally. The message that he always carried to the outside world of uninformed people, dealt with what Appalachia was all about — poverty and the accompanying facts, such as unemployment, health care needs, illiteracy, inadequate schooling, poor living conditions, and oppression. He also had a unique ability of exposing the greed and callousness of the coal barons.

Harry Caudill wrote comprehensively and accurately about Appalachians, their struggles with the coal industry, political bosses who stifled in many instances their own people, and "law and order" agencies that served at the beck and call of corporate elite. He described with great detail the unspeakable acts of cold blooded beatings, jailing of miners, and fabricated evidence that characterized law enforcement in some eastern Kentucky communities. His work succeeded in making people throughout America aware of what had happened to Appalachia. Harry Caudill's details about the plight of his fellow hillfolk was a rude awakening for the reader, and he emphasized that people themselves must work toward helping their own cause. His observation of antiquated school systems and power of school boards and superintendents were not just an historical presentation, but a judgment of their corruptness.

He stood up for coal miners and their hardships of organizing in Harlan County. They had hoped to right the balance of power with coal companies, but experienced frustration from the miners' union. Harry wrote of their own union schemes, looting of pension funds and exploiting the membership. Caudill was proud of his heritage and talked about ancestors' settling in eastern Kentucky in 1792. He treasured stories and tales of his family, as well as amusing anecdotes from his clients. Harry Caudill's background as a lawyer, University of Kentucky Professor, and author were a good mix for expounding on the "current conditions" of Appalachia before congressional committee hearings. When Harry talked about conditions of Appalachia in Washington, D.C., he always left his audience with the following: "Come, look for yourselves." Many reporters, politicians, social workers, educators, humanitarians and common citizens wanted to help, and accepted his invitation. On December 1, 1990, Harry Caudill passed away at age 68, but left a legacy of comfort and pride in his people through his writings, touting a call for betterment of eastern Kentucky. Caudill was one of the most influential figures in Appalachian history and will always be remembered by those who knew him. Jim Bergman, Administrator at Alice Lloyd College said, "Harry was the kind of man who told it like it was. He would not hold back any punches." Eula Hall, in her own right a leader of the hillfolk, said this about her dear friend: "Harry made more Americans aware about the plight of Appalachians than anyone else. His leadership will be missed by those who need help."

In the bleakness of this depressed region, Harry Caudill stood as "tall" as Black Mountain. With a pen, he showed all of America that Appalachians were his people. He wrote about the loyalty that hillfolk had for this country and the pains of their poverty, which affected him deeply. For a man to be considered at the same level of greatness as John Steinbeck, Upton Sinclair and William Agee, Harry Caudill's contributions to his fellow highlanders are without reservation. While living in the Washington, D.C., area in the late sixties, I had an opportunity to experience one of Harry's presentations to a congressional committee at the invitation of Carl Perkins. It was obvious that not all congressmen or government people liked Harry Caudill's frankness and openness, because they did not want to hear the unwelcome truth. The fact remains that his powerful words affected the course of Appalachia's history.

Carl Dewey Perkins

When I first met Carl Dewey Perkins in the 1960's, he had already established himself as a leader of social legislation that is still the basis for aid to poor people in Appalachia, as well as all of America. Carl Perkins had been a congressman since 1949. He was a legislative leader and champion of many great society programs during Lyndon Johnson's administration and a force behind much of the legislation that our nation produced during this era of social consciousness. Perkins earned respect and love of eastern Kentuckians as a congressman for over thirty-five years. Born in Hindman, Kentucky, he lived there until his death on August 3, 1984. Carl Perkins was a representative of and for the people and their leader, whose generosity and thoughtfulness brought necessary social change through government aid. His education started in Knott County, where he attended elementary and secondary school. He was a student at Caney Junior College (now Alice Lloyd College), where Alice Lloyd had impressed upon Carl and his class mates the importance of honesty, sincerity, and respectful leadership.

One reason for this congressman's success in public service was the ability to lead. Perkin's concern, caring, and communication with people, representing them throughout his political life, was consistent during good or difficult times. He was a successful advocate for federal aid to education, school lunch programs, job training and coal mine safety. These initiatives that Carl championed for the people are an example of his many broad accomplishments. He knew firsthand problems and issues of Kentuckians, and felt that his role was to help them have a better life. Congressman Perkins had a strong belief and trust in the role of government to assist people. He laid groundwork for legislation based upon needs of the poor. Carl Perkins made a determined effort to overcome the many problems of coal miners, whether they were work-related or concerned about their personal health and care. His influence on government, as representative of and for the people, will be realized for a long time.

Coal Mining — Hazardous Conditions Continue

During these two decades there was great concern that coal corporations were operating with great abandon of federal safety rules and regulations and their callous disregard of human carnage in the mines. Even the most effective mine operations had astoundingly high accidents and violations. The death rate of miners in underground work was eight times that of workers in the second highest hazardous occupation. One young gentleman whom I met in Leslie County during this time presented a very vivid picture of his life as a miner, and stated to me "you don't know when you go into the mines in the morning, whether you will see daylight again." Work had not been steady for him, and he, his wife and child were living with her parents. He was hoping one day to build a home, but every time money was put aside, a family member would get sick and they had to pay for care, since health insurance was unaffordable. This miner then turned to the topic of disasters, which are always on the mind of workers. He had seen things that caused him to think about leaving the mining workforce, and if there had been any other job available, he would have taken it. His anxieties and fears were understandable, for this young man was relating to a tragedy that involved some friends.

This incident occurred in 1970, when a group of men went underground to work in the Finley Coal Company's mines #15 and #16 on Hurricane Creek in Leslie County. Around noontime, one man came out to fetch some supplies. As he reached the tunnel exit, there was a strong shake in the earth, and a tremendous rush of heat, smoke and dust came hurdling out, lifting this stunned miner in the air and throwing him fifty feet away. Inside the mine, thirty-eight miners were dead.

Over the years, very little progress had been made in overcoming mine disasters. The indifference toward human suffering that prevailed throughout the Appalachian mining industry has been one of tragedy, leaving many workers frustrated and antagonistic toward coal corporations. Miners had to have great strength and resolve to face each day being confronted constantly with life and death situations. It was sad to see the resignation of this young miner from Leslie County, realizing that there were no alternatives for him and many others in achieving a better way of life.

Strip Mining

During this period in Appalachian history, economic problems continued to effect mountaineers' social conditions. Starting with the late fifties, damaging changes occurred that continually benefited a few, and turned the countryside into an environmental wasteland. When strip mining came about, it changed the nature of coal production in eastern Kentucky. Mineral rights that the forefathers had deeded to coal companies and land speculators would create further frustration and despair. Problems with coal corporations were no longer limited to miners, but affected the total region of eastern Kentucky. Land was taken over by the "spoilers," and topsoil of properties was stripped away by mechanized equipment. Strip mining created pollution of streams and rivers, leaving damaged earth with pockmark ugliness. Sludge and mud slides became abominable after a rainstorm, flushing and toppling shanties off their pinnings into nothingness. Certain areas reminded one of lava flowing down a mountainside, after a volcano eruption. Beautiful trees in their almost unaltered natural environment were pushed aside by huge tractors and shovels. Topsoil was never seen again on thousands of acres of land.

In the beginning of 1960, approximately twenty-five percent coal extraction was done by strip mining. However, in the 1970's, strip and auger mining combined spiraled to about seventy percent of eastern Kentucky's coal production. Throughout Appalachia, without regard to where families lived, the people were pawns of strip mining owners. Coal companies avoided reclamation projects, which required replacing topsoil, and made no distinction as to what land should be strip-mined, for as possessor of the mineral rights, this gave them the privilege to do as they pleased.

As these unfair practices were occurring, mines supplied coal cheaply to the Tennessee Valley Authority as well as neighboring states. Ironically, through strip mining of eastern Kentucky land, T.V.A. provided electricity at low cost to other communities at the expense of hillfolk. T.V.A. in its demands for coal in order to run power plants, created a monstrous condition not only for the land of eastern Kentucky, but for people that always lived there, who ultimately were uprooted. Large areas of counties, such as Knott, Harlan, Pike and Letcher, were stripped and gutted. In 1964, Knott County's small landowners organized the "Appalachia Group to Save the Land and People." Their purpose was to fight coal companies with whatever means they had. By standing up to coal owners, they went to court, and if it meant to defend against bulldozers, they did so with their bodies and guns. Their patience had finally run out.

Widow Combs

One person to fight a coal company's strip mining of her land in Knott County was a little old frail woman, known as Widow Combs. Mrs. Combs had lived on her 20 acre farm for over forty years. This property had been owned by the Combs family ever since settlers came to Knott County. Unfortunately, mineral rights were signed over to coal speculators at the turn of the 20th century. In 1965, it was a sad sight to see this dejected and frustrated woman sitting on a boulder, trying to defy a bulldozer that was plowing away the top soil within inches of her body. She had courage and perseverance to stand up to the coal bosses. Finally, in total frustration, she sat down in front of the bulldozer, which led to a standoff. The confrontation culminated when sheriff's deputies were told to remove Mrs. Combs from the premises, because she had been holding up the strip mining process. Consequently, widow Combs was taken to the local county jail for protecting her land, and the law had served its purpose for a coal company. Activists in the area came to Widow Combs' defense and she was released from jail. This injustice was the rallying cry for many people, who united in vocal opposition to strip mining.

Activist Movement

Throughout the years, the control that mineral rights owners had over other people's properties left Appalachians fending for themselves when their land was no longer needed for strip mining. The backing of coal companies through court decisions and a listless government favoring some unconscionable strip mining corporations, left landowners with nothing but insecurity and hopelessness, sacrificed by the courts for economic growth of a few. As coal companies continued to abrade the face of eastern Kentucky land, they carried on brazen and devious actions, which were further fueled by federal government inability to control the industry's misdeeds. It became difficult for people of Appalachia to insist on their right that coal companies restore strip-mined land to its original condition or make it conducive for useful purpose.

The continued frustrations that Appalachians were experiencing finally took a toll and led people to take matters in their own hands. With individuals throughout this region sharing the same cause, a strong activist movement emerged, consisting of common folk from a wide spectrum of the population. Miners, farmers, unemployed, disabled, heroines, and retired senior citizens were joined by ministers and preachers, newspaper publishers, writers, songwriters and others, who had been opposing the desecration of land. It is only fair to acknowledge those people who developed a strong sense of social consciousness and solidarity for their fellow Appalachians: Joe Begley of Blackey; J.T. Begley, Blackey; Wendell Berry, University of Kentucky; Harry Caudill from Whitesburg, Jim Cornett, Whitesburg; Tillman Bell, Bell County; Tom Duff, Harlan County; Edith and Jake Easterling, Poorbottom; Bessie Smith Gayheart, Knott County; Dan Gibson, Knott County; Tom Gish, Whitesburg; Sara Ogan Gunning, Knox County; Eula Hall, Floyd County; Jim Hamilton, Poorbottom; Gurney Norman, Perry County; Mike Paxton, Pikeville; Jean Ritchie, Viper; Everette Tharpe, Perry County; George Tucker, Perry County; Warren Wright, Letcher County. To those activists that are not included in this book I apologize, for there were so many and they all deserve to be recognized for their good deeds.

The horrors of strip mining disasters, farce of land reclamation, and inaction brought attention to different types of activists who expressed themselves in various ways, and people like Harry Caudill came to the forefront. He provided the stimulating pen to fight social injustice along with other unique writers. From the beginning, eastern Kentuckians have been prolific writers of music, expressing a variety of social issues like unfairness and injustice, telling about conflicts, work, of heroes and lamentation. Writers of activist movements conveyed in an assortment of songs the indignation of conditions, as well as attitudes and feelings of Appalachians, whose time had come to fight against destruction of their land. Bringing attention to Americans was the husband and wife team of Ray and Candy Carawan, who came to Appalachia in the 1970's. Giving tribute in their book, "A Voice From The Mountains," they wrote about the people, and collected songs that were composed by some famous and lesser known hillfolk.

Other eastern Kentuckians wrote songs about what used to be, this region's natural beauty, or exploitation of land that led to misery for its people. They brilliantly captured in words and music stories relating to the black lung disease, death in mines, and preachers fighting strip mining. I will always remember the lyrics and music by people such as Jean Ritchie, Gurney Norman, and Hazel Dickens. There were many more songs written about Appalachia, reminding one of cemeteries in backyards, where crosses stood silently, divulging the suffering of the poor. Slopes of hillsides that used to be are now land slides, because coal was taken out of the region and shipped elsewhere, with profits never benefiting these people. They wrote about how land was stripped, "stolen by friendly faces for only twenty-five cents an acre," and complained that "Those evil individuals took away their land." The writings captured true life experiences, revealing shortcomings of this most dangerous occupation and sympathizing with miners, for coal mining did not justify giving up or risking one's life.

In the 1960's, scare of communism was greater than one can imagine. This happened during a time when strikes occurred, and the law automatically was unfavorable to miners. The local and state police, along with county sheriffs and coal company henchmen, would use any method to prevent people from striking or shutting down the mines. In 1965, Tom Paxton wrote words and music to a very fitting song that exemplified what was going on. He extolled how a sheriff harassed and degraded a striker, made false accusations, beat him and threw the man in jail. This sheriff was the coal company's man and became a wealthy mine owner himself through scheming and corrupt actions. The only way to end the injustice of his kingdom of power was to vote him out of town.

On one occasion, I met leading activist Sara Ogan Gunning, a

113

woman of strong character, whose father and husband had worked in the mines. She had written many songs, but I remember one in particular that she used to sing: "Dreadful Memories." This song tells about the loss of a baby that had starved to death in the early 30's. Conditions in Appalachia that led to early death reminded one of the unbelievable hurt and unfairness poor people faced every day of their lives. She wrote about the inequities of living in a mining town, where the company store charged customers three times as much as one in a nearby village. Yet, if a miner went to the village store to shop and coal company officials found out, he was fired from his job. Mrs. Gunning, who had been prolific in composing many songs about miners and their concerns, is an example of the strong role that women of Appalachia have played in fighting for better social conditions.

The "best music to the ears" of some miners and their families was probably the action taken by a group of unemployed coal workers in January of 1964. Coal companies were cutting back on jobs, and with no work available families went hungry. As a result, a group of miners decided to take their concerns to the federal government and chartered a bus to Washington, D.C. The campaign was twofold: making the nation aware of economic conditions in eastern Kentucky and getting federal relief for people that lost their jobs because of automation. These unemployed miners talked to persons at various levels in administrative, congressional, and executive offices, or wherever possible. They met with high government people and the outcome was successful. Miners who were unemployed in eastern Kentucky counties finally got a token of financial help.

It should be understood that this action did not provide a quick fix, nor was it a magic potion for overcoming increasing unemployment of miners. As was expected, lack of job opportunities for the region led to intense desire for successful implementation of the War on Poverty jobs program. The willingness of people to work hard was never in question, but hopes of a long-term commitment to achieve job stability of miners did not materialize. Eastern Kentucky could not offer an environment of success for its miners, because there was no atmosphere for growth, encouragement or new horizons. Yet, Appalachia's writers through their desire for change influenced the people, by telling what they saw around them.

The tradition of Appalachians to write about their hardships and commitment to the land they love so dearly, carried forth through the sixties up to the present time. Songs about coal miners are like an old soldier: they are never forgotten. Even today, a famous and well-liked song "Coal Miner's Daughter," performed by Butcher Hollow's Loretta Lynn, projects inner feelings and human kindness of hillfolk, who have been able to survive in spite of their many hardships.

Migration Continues

In the 1960's, migration of people from eastern Kentucky was continuing, but at a lesser rate than during the 1950's, when 250,000 Appalachians moved to urban centers, mainly in northern states. Generally, hillfolk left due to continuous deterioration of economic and social conditions. The migration out of Kentucky took place on account of the coal industry becoming more involved in strip mining and utilizing heavy equipment to increase production, despite less manpower. With unemployment growing daily, miners were forced to face reality that there were no other jobs or industries in the region. However, families had to survive, which led them to ponder their future, and if they stayed, it would mean to exist on surplus food distributed by the U.S. Department of Agriculture, along with other forms of government assistance. A decision to leave meant that the head of the household would try to find work in Detroit, Chicago, or other places north, east, west or south. If "Daddy" returned one weekend with a job in hand, the family dutifully packed their belongings and moved to the city of destination.

In many cases, Appalachian families became virtually over-whelmed by incredible adjustments to urban community life. The drama of an impoverished eastern Kentucky family that migrated elsewhere was portrayed in every possible way. Some people encountered one setback after another, as shattering tragedies struck their families. They had to develop strength, courage, and determination to keep themselves and their loved ones going. Others that struggled, feeling lonely, longing for their land and relatives, eventually returned to the mountains. The distinctive-ness of hillfolk culture also played an important part in deciding to return home, as their singular direction of mountaineer life made it quite difficult in adjusting to a pluralistic society and its diverse conditions.

Some migrants' fatalistic attitude of life also presented a conflict of inner-self, as they delved into urban experiences. The demands to exist in a city brought on many challenges that they never experienced in Appalachia. Cities were a melting pot of people, where some valued their personal role over other human beings, regardless of consequences. The struggle of urban survival and the fast pace of living did not sit well with migrants. Back home, value of the community was automatically an extension of their own family, and they abhorred the urban way of exis-tence. They did not feel the sense of closeness that was experienced in Appalachia, which bonded them with their kinfolk. The city had too many contradictions that were devastating and difficult to cope with. Also, strong beliefs and convictions of independence hurt their cause, since they did not like to ask for needed improvements of their life situation. The tradition of being proud and not request help from organizations, whether private non-profit or public, made it difficult for them to benefit from opportunities that were available for needy people in urban settings.

For many Appalachian migrants, illiteracy was a major drawback to access and mobility in the labor market of urban communities. Once they reached the metropolitan areas, eastern Kentuckians looking for work in industrial places found that unemployment was three-fold and competition for any kind of occupation much greater. The only jobs illiterates could apply for were the ones that did not require skills, but even those were scarce. If a person was unable to read simple instructions or warning signs in a workplace, they were not hired. Illiteracy came back to haunt those who did not know basic reading, writing and numeric skills. Converting American industry technologically was an undertaking that continued to present insurmountable barriers for the non-skilled worker. The employment outlook for basic skill deficient workers began to develop a downtrend that would continue to the present time. Companies or corporations hiring these people for low level occupations were less likely to provide training for them. Government research cited that during the 1960's and 70's, there were too many workers available for low level jobs. Companies did not think it was necessary to educate or take time to train the illiterate. Employers hoped to replace unskilled workers with people who were being retrained and educated in basic skills programs by trade schools and community colleges.

As the 1970's were coming to a close, the trend for employing highly skilled workers became more evident, and an extensive amount of adults were going back to school, to qualify for technologically advanced jobs. For some Appalachian migrants, illiteracy's barrier was overcome by gaining an education, to fulfill job requirements that were called for by the advances in industry. These people finally found themselves making a decent living, working hard to make sure that their children would have greater chances for a different and better life. They realized that education was a vital weapon in attacking poverty, which gave them the opportunity to become productive citizens.

There is another story about migration from Appalachia during this period. Even highly educated young adults confronted many obstacles of finding employment in the highlands. I understood how these people felt, and what they must have endured in leaving their families and the region. Many students who graduated from institutions of higher education, often left Appalachia to enrich other communities and states. It was not difficult to sympathize with their decision to leave for better opportunities. The continuing need of a diversified economic base for the region and consistent lack of job opportunities through many decades, made one wonder whether education was an advantage or disadvantage for Appalachia. If economic development of eastern Kentucky failed to materialize, the stigma of repetitive patterns of poverty and its consequences would never cease. Indeed, if the learned population continues to disappear, melting into the rest of our nation, it would be a great loss for Appalachia. To have educated youth of eastern Kentucky for the future solved one of many problems, yet to educate them for carrying their knowledge elsewhere, was and is unfortunate. Failure to heighten this region with bright young minds has been tragic, because these individuals could have enhanced the future of Appalachia.

When educated young people left to enrich the overall culture of the United States, it created a vacuum of leadership quality in eastern Kentucky that hindered growth for years. Some went on to become scientists at high places of employment in government and the private sector. Others contributed to influential communities throughout the country as educators, doctors and medical personnel, corporate and business leaders, engineers, lawyers, and public servants. In fact, a unique contribution to the United States during the 1960's were four native-born Appalachian Kentuckians serving in the Senate, representing Arizona, Iowa, Tennessee and Kentucky.

Union Decline

A most telling tragedy during the 1960's was the impact of events made by U.M.W.U.'s hierarchy, in funneling money from the miners' fund into suspicious union accounts. Eastern Kentucky miners were hurting due to Union inflicted actions by the leadership and certain fund trustees, whose deceptive intentions went unnoticed by the highlanders, as their hard-earned work entitlements dwindled away. Britt Hume in his book "Death and the Mines," tells how certain suspicious actions had taken place and conspiracies between the Union and big corporations, led to maneuvering welfare fund royalties, which not only effected the miners but also small coal operators. The so-called "sweetheart deals" came "to light too late" for Appalachian miners to realize that they had not only been hoodwinked by the large coal companies for their failure to pay royalties, but with full knowledge of the Union's leadership, who in turn terminated benefits to employees. The tragedy is that conspiracy by the Union succeeded, because eastern Kentucky miners had vented their anger toward big corporation management, blaming them for their lost benefits. As Hume had written, if miners would have understood the forces at work that created the turmoil, they might have aimed their frustration and displeasure in the "right" direction.

As the seventies began and the coal industry was enjoying an upsurge in profit, the cutting of jobs continued, as big corporations were increasing productivity through automation. During the late 1970's, coal mining experienced a boom because of an energy shortage, and ironically more coal was produced through mechanized equipment with fewer men. Strip mining had reached its peak, and Kentucky became one of the leading producers of coal in the nation. However, with greater unemployment the union role in Appalachia diminished. Too many miners did not forget the fact that "they were sacrificed" by the union, as one former coal worker told me recently. Compounding the increasing problems, the United Mine Workers Union was in deep trouble, and its president was in jail for a terrible crime, relating to the murder of opposing labor leader Joseph Yablonski, his wife and daughter.

Corruption of the coal miners' union, promises to its workers that were never kept, along with reneging on pension and health benefits created antagonism and disgust toward the U.M.W.U. The Union had fewer members from eastern Kentucky, and its influence deteriorated not only in Appalachia, but throughout the country. Action by the Union in selling the Regional Miners Hospitals, which were only six years in existence, created anti-union sentiment up to the present day. Union mismanagement, lack of accountability, graft, and corruption led to financial trouble and dissolution of hospital benefits, which were direly needed by the miners. Income received from coal companies to benefit the U.M.W.U. fund, was handled by people with questionable motives, who lacked expertise to manage a health organization. The existence of the coal miners' union came about, because workers were not treated fairly by management in regard to working and living conditions. However, the intransigence and corruptness of the Union hurt its own cause and ultimately sacrificed the Appalachian coal miner.

Farming

Between the 60's and 70's, small farmers of Appalachia were no better off than rest of the hillfolk. Individual farmers could no longer make a living off their land and were forced to leave. The cost of machinery, along with needing more land in order to show an income, made it impossible for already poor farmers to improve their lot, and approximately fifteen percent ceased to do business from 1960 through the 1970's. During this period, the size of an average farm in the United States had more than doubled. Appalachia was no different. The small man had to sell his property to bigger combines, and expansion encouraged by continued government policy provided benefits for large farms.

However, this action continually threatened the existence of small producers. Another factor leading to the demise of family farms during this period was that agriculture had more competition than other industries. The small farmer was automatically pushed out of business if farm prices went down. In an industry where one had to produce more to stay in business, the small farmer's limited land prevented him from doing so due to physical barriers. He could only grow so much on a little piece of property. Ironically, increased production also led to lower prices, subsequently in many instances there was no profit and farmers went out of business. Government programs, aiming to provide assistance for Appalachia, failed to accommodate small producers.

Adjustments that these farmers had to make during that time were accompanied by great sociological changes. The future appeared inevitable, and many had to look beyond Appalachia for making a living. For those inhabitants that felt they could no longer endure poverty and its many ills, crossing the mental threshold of leaving was not that difficult, as they deserted their farms in favor of work in urban America. The truth of the matter suggests that opportunities for broadening ones horizons appealed considerably to many farmers. Further, their continued adherence to a meager and subsidized way of living was no longer acceptable. Agriculture and rural life did have important and unique characteristics that held these people here, but the expansive problem of poverty left them no other choice but to leave.

Health and Health Care

One day in the early 1960's, I was traveling from Wayland to Pippa Passes on route 588, which winds along Caney Creek. At some point, I noticed two weather beaten shacks, a single-width trailer, and children playing in an open area on a few acres of bottom land. Standing by the roadside was a young man, waving his hand. He had a brown weathered face, disheveled hair, smiling, with half his teeth missing. He asked for a ride and his destination was the tiny Pippa Passes' hamlet general store. As we drove, I pointed out a boy on his knees, digging coal from a pit in the mountain side. It was a scene common throughout Appalachia in those days. Stakes, no wider than 2x4's and cut from trees, held up the ceiling of the dugout, so that families could retrieve coal for heating and cooking purposes. The young man riding with me told how his brother was killed ten years earlier, trying to get coal in a similar way. Apparently, a slab fell on his brother and crushed him. According to his account of this incident, the family was not able to get in touch with a doctor by phone. He had been on the other side of the county, covering

119

another emergency call. Being able to get in touch with the only doctor available for 17,000 people was a task of insurmountable frustration. It was not easy in those days to get to a telephone or contact the doctor by beeper. This tragedy occurred in the 50's, not the 1990's.

As we drove along, he explained further the anguish of his brother's death. He and the family realized that his brother would die, because there was no doctor or medical service available. They were powerless and knew it, yet looked at their loved one's fate as "God's will." The fatalistic attitude of these mountain people made it possible to accept ills or deaths as a way of life. It may be incomprehensible to outsiders, however having lived in Appalachia, I understood this appraisal of an unfortunate and sad experience. This was the way they lived, abiding by the hand they were dealt. In fact, fatalism has been with Appalachians ever since their forefathers arrived, and reconciling helped them overcome hard times.

This was just an example of the myriad of problems rural people faced during that time. Access to health care, especially doctors, had always been filled with roadblocks. It was clear, whatever methods of measuring medical services were used, the historical situation of doctors in Appalachia has been one of chronic shortage and uncertainty. Moreover, despite increase of medical services in the rest of our nation, the relative position of health care had failed to improve the health status of Appalachia. During the 60's and 70's, doctors were covering more than one county, trying to offer the best possible medical care. It was ironic that medical schools were graduating enough physicians, and training programs were providing more specialists than necessary for urban settings, yet, expectations for more young doctors to meet the health needs of Appalachia were not realized. In fact, there were very few doctors who had made a commitment to serve as general practitioners in rural regions. This was also the beginning of a period, when medical schools trained too many physicians in specialties, rather than emphasizing the need for general practitioners.

Specialists in the 1960's and 70's selected medical facilities that accommodated their line of work, which were usually located in large urban communities. Major factors for doctors being enticed to metropolitan areas as specialists included: shorter working days than those of a rural physician; and surgeons, anesthesiologists, ophthalmologists, cardiologists, etc., were able to charge almost twofold the general practitioners' rate. In rural Appalachia, doctors often absorbed the office visit charge of a person in poverty. I heard, where on one occasion a local doctor took care of a patient over an extended period of time. The man was unemployed for years and his government assistance had run out. Even though the physician did not charge him, the patient was embarrassed of not being able to meet his obligations. The physician, of course, did not want him to pay.

However, this man came to the office one day and left a note, asking the doctor to look out his back door. As soon as the physician looked outside, he saw the patient's payment — a cow.

Loss Of Union-Run Regional Hospitals

With the United Mine Workers Union pulling out of Kentucky in the 1960's, a few union locals remained in Pike, Harlan, and Letcher counties. Elsewhere, workers were employed in non-union coal mining, which paid much less than unionized operations. Not only were their pay checks smaller, but their health benefits were completely taken away. The United Mine Workers Union of America ceased to own the Regional Miners Hospitals. Trying to avoid closing the Regional Hospitals, a Board of Missions of the Presbyterian Church intervened and purchased these facilities as non-profit hospitals. Even though they continued to operate, the quality of service and staff took a downturn. Administrators and physicians who had developed, organized and managed the Regional Miners Hospitals did not stay around to work with the new organization.

Black Lung Disease

With health cards taken away, medical services reduced, and Miners Hospitals no longer available, the physical condition of many workers who had contracted the black lung disease was deteriorating. On top of this, miners were confronted with federal bureaucracy, which created problems of insurmountable obstacles. The government was lacking in providing effective criteria to determine black lung benefits for miners, and not only were the guidelines inadequate, but physicians, in many cases, did not have the professional background in treating this disease. While research was limited at that time, it was left up to physicians' discretion to determine the illness. Since they had no experience in diagnosing pneumoconiosis, detrimental decisions were made as to the validity of each man's condition. Misdiagnosis did not help the morale of miners and their families. Many had worked in mines for years and were finding themselves smothering to death with this disease.

In their battle with doctors and government, miners were looked upon by critics as though they tried to get something for nothing. They were unable to work because of symptoms such as headaches, shortness of breath, and pains in joints. In certain cases, memory loss struck miners, who at first complained about dizzy spells or shortness of breath when getting out of bed in the morning. Doctors and government personnel questioned whether psychiatric services were needed. They were attributing the deterioration of some miners' mental state to stress, rather than to deplorable environmental working hazards, such as being unable to breathe fresh air. A major problem with some doctors was that they were not able to determine if the individuals' condition was related to working in the mines. They could not come to terms that if symptoms were showing, the degree of disability should be the only issue of concern. An unfortunate situation was the lack of knowledge for interpreting x-rays. The truth doctors had to face was that many did not have enough expertise of tackling this major health problem in miners.

In Pike County during the early 60's, a group of activists, led by Jim Hamilton, organized coal miners who were turned down for black lung benefits. Others, such as Eula Hall, at that time President of the Kentucky Black Lung Association, and Bill Worthington, past president, fought hard to get adequate black lung compensation for miners. After all, it was impossible for a person to get away from coal dust in a mine shaft. It is everywhere and gets into everything. As one miner friend put it, "you just can't step over to a window and open it to breathe clean air." Since the beginning of mining in Appalachia, the staggering rise in black lung disease began to reach a preponderance of older workers. Medical people who have studied this problem cannot disagree that if a person works under these conditions over an extended number of years, the disease eventually kills.

Poor Health Conditions Continue

For years, much concern existed regarding the poor health condition of people in Appalachia The health status of the 1960's seemed as though time stood still in this region. However, other parts of our country had become more conscious toward increasing life expectancy, while Appalachia's people were still worried about babies surviving beyond birth. Even though great strides were made since Mary Breckinridge arrived in Kentucky to develop the Frontier Nursing Service, high infant mortality was a major hurdle. Appalachians continually experienced premature death rates that were higher than the national norm, and conditions such as malnutrition, disease, and poor health still prevailed. People continued to live in shacks and old cabins with no running water or electricity; hand clothes washers were commonplace, situated on broken down porches. In order to get water for washing and drinking purposes, buckets were filled from a nearby spring that was polluted by runoff from the strip mining industry. If one was lucky to have a well that was not contaminated, neighbors were invited to share the good fortune. However, even those were beginning to become polluted. The waste from outdoor privies was still creating disease and illness, and lack of sanitation promoted deteriorating health conditions.

Many children were exposed to nutritional diseases, brought on by poor diet and lack of food. In poverty-stricken families the most common disease was malnutrition. This weakens people and, especially in children, leads to premature death through pneumonia, influenza, and other illnesses. For years, the children of Appalachia experienced a high mortality rate from malnutrition and resulting diseases. If they did not die young, they grew up with physical disorders that were constantly life threatening. In eastern Kentucky, education relating to good health was lacking in school and community, as well as at home. The overall poor health conditions of Appalachians presented frustrating experiences to the family doctor. His goal of treating patients dealt with physical, emotional, and social needs as well as medical. The necessity for comprehensive care was never more evident as doctors were finding themselves overwhelmed with a greater variety of urgent cases.

Community Health Centers

As various government programs got underway in the 1960's, new directions for improving health care services were showing signs of effectiveness. The Neighborhood Health Center program was launched in 1965, under the direction of Sergeant Shriver and the Office of Economic Opportunity. This became a sincere federal government effort to reform the financing and delivery of health care for the less fortunate. Eight "demonstration" health centers were built throughout the U.S. by public and non-profit private groups. These programs, sponsored by the O.E.O. with community action organizations that included hospitals and public health departments were to benefit residents of high poverty areas. In the eyes of government specialists, it was a program that proved its effectiveness more so than any existing services in health care, and offered a combination of good medical delivery and genuine humanitarianism, rarely seen in such areas.

By 1967, Congress amended the Economic Opportunity Act to earmark fifty million dollars for the establishment of thirty-three centers. Medicaid, "third party payers," maternal and child agencies, and other programs provided money for the new centers. This became a smooth integrated process through state and federal legislation. Results from implementation of these centers were encouraging, and additional clinics began to develop each subsequent year, with Public Health Service taking over the responsibility of coordinating the overall organization. In the

123

early 1970's, official transfer for administration of this program shifted from the O.E.O. to Health, Education and Welfare. Today, over 1500 clinics exist in the United States, known as Community Health Centers, and results indicate that they have succeeded beyond all expectations.

With the initiation of Community Health Centers, people were able to come out of their cocoons. Infant mortality showed a decline, low birth weight improved, diseases such as rheumatic fever and middle ear infections were drastically reduced. Improvement of prenatal care was a unique endeavor, because Appalachian women had been very private in the past and shied away from exposing themselves to medical analysis. Children also became a prime target for the centers to help overcome common diseases like measles, whooping cough, tetanus, and diphtheria. Long neglected illnesses and disabilities were taken care of at earlier stages. The Special Supplemental Food Program for Women, Infants and Children (WIC) was enacted by Congress in 1972 due to documented research, which cited that inadequate nutrition in infants, children and women was leading to premature death and mental or physical disability. Purpose of this program included nutritional education to low income and high risk women, who were pregnant or breast feeding. Even though WIC had a difficult start in its implementation phase, it grew steadily during the seventies, successfully serving this important health care need.

The Selective Service found in 1966 that 15 percent of eighteen year olds examined for military service were rejected because of physical deficiencies, such as dental, eye and ear problems, along with social and emotional disorders. Consequently, the Early and Periodic Screening, Diagnosis and Treatment (EPSDT) program was added to Medicaid for meeting the health needs of children and at the same time establish cost-effective preventive services. Medicaid was introduced in 1966 for poor families who were without care or on charity. This program uses a combination of federal and commonwealth funds and is administered by the state to pay medical bills for the poor. Since implementation of this program, Medicaid reported good news concerning children — their health was improving. Other positive effects regarding Medicaid coverage for poor children showed higher immunization rates.

The purpose of establishing community health centers was to meet long overdue needs of the poor. Rural Appalachians in many back country areas, where medical facilities or primary care were not available, began to view community health centers as their "savior." Before the existence of these centers, mothers who did not receive any prenatal care very seldom notified proper health personnel regarding the birth of a baby. However, with the development of health centers, mother and family assessment, along with information on services available, were provided to meet their health and social needs. Centers further counseled families on nutrition, family planning, and child care services. In certain situations, health care professionals developed "outreach" clinics in tiny back country hamlets or villages. Vaccines were given to prevent many childhood diseases, which increased during the 60's and 70's. A cornerstone of these centers was the emphasis on preventive medicine. It was also the beginning of addressing a current health crisis, common in Appalachia, where married women's fertility rate and teenage pregnancies were still the highest in the nation. These centers were equipped to handle routine care, such as Pap smears, uncomplicated pregnancies, immunizations, and routine physicals. They were also equipped to treat the common as well as uncommon ailments. Above all, these centers were aimed at providing comprehensive medical care, whether preventive or curative.

Even though health clinics were giving generally satisfactory service, a few obstacles had to be overcome. One major concern was the need for doctors to participate in these community centers. Those that had been employed in clinics were scarce and overworked. Also, not many doctors committed themselves to work in an environment serving the poor, where hours are long and income much less. By having their own practice, they were able to earn more money. Nationally, overall shortages of primary care physicians had been increasing, leading government in the late 1960's to promote federal support for a new training program, emphasizing family practice. A second strategy was to employ nurse practitioners, clinical nurse specialists, and nurse midwives. They were called "advanced practice nurses" and provided care of comparable quality to that of doctors. Despite the shortage of these nurses, they had to substitute for the doctor and handled a good percentage of primary care for children and adults. Research developed over two decades cited findings in the 1993 summer issue of the "Yale Journal on Regulation" that nationally some advanced nurses were covering up to ninety percent of primary care services. However, the Yale report noted that certain implications, such as financial, legal and professional barriers would prevent nurses from replacing physicians.

Mental Health Needs

An area of concern during the 1960's and 70's, was poverty's impact on the Appalachian family's social climate, which was painfully obvious. Those people that lived under these conditions were very susceptible to mental illness. A federal lawsuit in the 60's charged mental hospitals to be unsafe and inhumane, violating rights of patients. Hospitals throughout the nation closed, but a most unfortunate consequence was that effective guidelines were lacking as to appropriate targeting of alternatives for mental patients. The courts in their decision left regions like Appalachia in a quandary. Psychiatric hospitals were located hundreds of miles away, and local medical help was limited for those people with mental illness, who required long term care or frequent hospitalization. Families and friends were the ultimate salvation for these people, because a qualified psychiatrist was only available in Lexington or Louisville, at least a five hour drive. As a result, the mentally ill had to be cared for at home. Doctors were able to treat other physical conditions, but when it came to helping certain mental disorders, they had to refer the patient to a psychiatrist.

Denial of accepting mental illness in general was a traditional characteristic of the Appalachian family. In some very small and remote areas, religious snake believers tried to apply some form of faith healing act to rid the unfortunate of their affliction; but this was very rare. Home remedies were not applicable to this kind of condition, and in many instances a family would keep the person hidden, living an agonizing life without proper medical help. Children were no exclusion, and often suffered from diagnosable mental illnesses. Some had developmental impairment, which limited their ability to think, learn, form social attachments, or communicate effectively. Other children, because of poverty surroundings, experienced severe emotional disturbances, such as depression and pervasive anxiety. Social conditions of each generation that lived in poverty placed incomprehensible stress on a family and resulted in drinking, abuse, even suicide, worsening of health habits, until it reached a point where the people lived in squalor and seclusion. Instead of becoming a wholesome human being, these circumstances led to a regressive form of existence.

The tragedy for these people was that community mental health programs did not have enough staff to satisfy their needs. Alcohol rehabilitation services were equally necessary but not accessible, because of distance to the nearest treatment center and cost for services. An alternative was the county jail as a dumping ground, and in certain cases, mentally ill and alcoholics were finding themselves locked up together. Breaking the law was the only way that people could receive treatment for chronic illnesses, unless they had family that would care for them. A case comes to mind, where love of the family made a difference for an individual to overcome mental despair. They felt helpless when confronted by the mental condition of one member, who began to show signs of strange behavior. As days wore on into weeks, and weeks into months, the conduct of this person became more erratic and antisocial. After hiding in the home for days on end, the individual finally came outside, walked around the community talking strangely to people.

Hillfolk were very polite in nature and accepted odd mannerism, because they had seen this out in the open before. One day everything snapped and this person came babbling and dancing down a mountain path, singing a song to the hills. With no immediate psychiatric help available, the individual refused to see a doctor, but was convinced to go to the closest mental hospital, which was six hours away in Louisville. For more than a year, no one in the family knew what to do with this individual. The ultimate salvation was the family's caring and willingness to overcome this situation. Eventually, that person was able to function in society again. However, this was an exception, because generally lack of suitable alternative mental health service for a patient would bring neglect, frustration, and despair. One of the loving graces of Appalachians is that they show compassion and understanding for the mentally ill. There was no mental health assistance available at that time, yet family and friends of these small communities had to bear the burden. It has always been their fatalistic attitude that those with emotional handicaps are also "children of God," therefore have to be cared for, no matter what the consequences might be.

Education

Ever increasing demands of society during the 60's and 70's were continually challenging educators to search for improvement of schools. Accountability was the topic of concern for educators, politicians and citizens not only nationally, but also in Kentucky. Research studies were conducted, and seminars, conferences, along with conventions, keyed in on the effectiveness of the educational system. However, solutions for the Commonwealth's many problems were few and vague. In eastern Kentucky, schools were at a disadvantage to participate in the challenge for finding meaningful solutions to problems involving improvement of education. These were school districts primarily under a political structure of control that made it virtually impossible to break with tradition. However, teachers and some administrators, not satisfied with conditions that existed, were eager to participate in improving their roles and the overall educational process.

Many obstacles impeded these dedicated educators, and negative attitudes of people toward schools also had to be dispelled. A need existed in every school district to strive for higher levels of educational performance, for if schools failed to do this, Appalachia and other weak areas of the state would continue to provide mediocre education. The key therefore was development of a proper climate for improvement. State government at that time believed, if educators were given opportunities, they would be spurred toward new and creative solutions of educational problems. Thus, Kentucky's long trek to find ways of financing the school districts began. The major goal for subsequent legislation during the 60's and 70's affected educational funding of schools. Starting in 1960 under Governor Bert Combs' direction, the legislature levied a 3 percent general sales tax and devoted 65 percent of the proceeds to the Educational Foundation.

Landmarks, such as the 1965 decision by the Court of Appeals, required 100 percent full value assessment of property for taxation purposes. This led to a Special Session of the General Assembly, calling for an enactment of a "rollback" law to offset any increase in the property taxes collected. In 1966, authorization was given to include three permissive taxes for schools. Even though action was taken by each General Assembly in subsequent years, funding continued to be a struggle. Improving Kentucky schools required tackling a wide range of complicated issues, such as authoritarian and political control by certain school superintendents and boards of education, low teacher salaries, unqualified staff and faculty along with nepotism. Schools were without books, except texts, which in certain cases had been outdated. In 1963, antiquated school systems still existed in the United States, of which nearly forty percent of all one- and two-room schoolhouses operated in Kentucky. Most of them were located in the poverty stricken eastern rural region of the state. As a result, Kentucky became one of the last states to join a national trend and consolidate school systems.

New School Facilities

It was not until the 1970's, when one and two-room schoolhouses disappeared from the scene of eastern Kentucky, and the need to improve education in Appalachia was very evident. The start of school consolidation, planning for new facilities, expansion of curriculum and services, by districts with help from the State Department of Education, reached a peak of activity. Modern facilities, previously unknown in some parts of Appalachia, were constructed at a record pace. Selling state supported county bonds helped to finance these new school buildings. Old wooden structures had been either torn down or in some instances used for community centers and other public services. New facilities, generally single-story brick-and cement buildings, were simple, architecturally plain and inexpensive compared to national standards of school plant construction. However, Appalachians viewed these schools as "palaces" of the community. A major goal for centrally locating the community school was not only to provide classrooms, but also after-class activities, as well as functions and meetings for adults of surrounding areas. The commonwealth also endowed the local populace with buses, bought from new state funds, to provide transportation for children.

Teachers

Teachers' salaries during this time showed a slight increase, even though Kentucky had one of the lowest schedules in the nation. In the 60's and 70's, there was discontent and activism from teachers. The Kentucky Education Association had created some stirring of individual districts, such as Pike County which led to further action by the state organization. On February 23, 1970, K.E.A. called a statewide strike in order to force the state legislature to increase an already approved annual salary schedule by three hundred dollars. At that time, the wage scale averaged seven thousand five hundred a year, with beginning teachers starting at five-thousand dollars. The teachers, after refusal from the state, went on strike. Some 24,000 of the 32,000 educators stayed out of school on February 24, which forced 118 of the 193 school districts to close. On March 3, teachers ended a week long statewide strike and returned to class. However, K.E.A. continued to pressure the state legislature through an intensive advertising campaign. On October 30, 1970, an Appeals Court in Frankfort rejected the teachers' Union arguments and ruled that public employees had no right to strike. This decision by the court, while reducing the intensity of K.E.A. pressure for better wages, did not assure that educators would discontinue their battle for salary and educational improvement. Quite the contrary, they were gaining strategic bargaining power and a strong voice for change in schools.

Control Of Schools Hinder Progress

During the 70's, activism to improve education in eastern Kentucky continued. However, one must consider that the state played a hesitant role, which critics analyzed as a "soft approach" toward the local school districts to initiate change. Politically, the state's authority stopped at the front door of a school system. A problem that not only the state but also local communities often faced, was political control of an authoritarian administration and school board, whose only concern was to satisfy their own desires, instead of improving educational results. Selfishness led to greed, and nepotism at the school district level was an important factor for the state wanting to make changes. Other avenues that detoured improvement of education included bloated school bureaucracies and appointment of political cronies, who were not even qualified to serve, administer, or teach.

Local school districts avoided hiring outside teachers, and if a faculty member spoke up, disagreeing with certain issues, this individual would be blackballed not only within that district, but throughout the region. Recommendations from the State Department of Education, regarding new and experienced teachers from elsewhere to local school districts, in certain instances were ignored. Reason for this was that the State had not been able to penetrate the local level, for necessary changes to take place.

Family Conditions Affect Education Of Child

During the 1960's and 70's, eastern Kentucky faced a dual crisis involving the family and student. On one hand most students did not learn what they needed to know for leading a happy and productive life. At the same time, their parents had lived with many disadvantages. The 1960 census indicated that twenty-four percent of the adult population of the state was illiterate, and eastern Kentucky reached fifty percent in some back country areas. The family with its many conditions of impoverishment lacked self-confidence and motivation. All this of course failed to nurture children, and drove family life further into hopelessness. Student interest in school declined, with a sense of abandonment toward any form of educational success.

On top of this, school districts had encountered obstacles of trying to maintain fiscal responsibility through a state funding system that did not prove beneficial in helping to meet educational needs of the students. State funds given to each school district had been based on the Average Daily Attendance Formula (ADA), instead of number of children enrolled. A major problem of the Average Daily Attendance Rolls showed that absenteeism was widespread. Parents in many instances did not adhere to the importance of educating their children, and apathy became a difficult problem for local schools to deal with. The district lacked personnel to search for the children and when found, parents provided excuses. Problems intensified as the district's fund for enrollment dwindled, especially when students did not attend school. Educators were caught in a dilemma, as efforts to overcome their problems became secondary to the re-election of board members and re-hiring of a school superintendent. They had to tread lightly with constituents instead of focusing on educating the child. When the truancy problem persisted, court action took place. This type of situation was minuscule, and generally a judge would lightly admonish parents for not making their child or children aware of education's advantages. Judges, of course, were hesitant to treat parents harshly, realizing the importance of getting their constituent's vote in the next election.

It was during this period that much had been written about hungry children in Appalachia and the United States. Malnutrition became a major concern that had to be dealt with by providing meals for disadvantaged children. School districts were publicly advertising that aid from the state and federal government was available, and children would learn better with "food in their stomach." Finally, the importance of education and its advantages became a battle cry for teachers, administrators and other personnel in each community. Advertising available meals in school was a major reason that truancy declined through the years, because breakfast and lunch provided by the school cafeterias, along with milk in the morning, appealed to those parents, whose children were under-nourished and looked forward to these assured meals.

Higher Education

In eastern Kentucky, high school graduates wishing to attend college were few. An average of five out of 70 boys and girls matriculated to college, and in many instances were without a solid foundation of secondary education. This occurred during a time when the community college movement in Kentucky was just stirring. These two-year institutions were built in a few selected areas of eastern Appalachia, with the majority springing up in Louisville, Lexington and the western region. In Floyd County, Prestonsburg Community College of the University of Kentucky system was very active enrolling students in a transfer and two-year degree program. Led by President Henry Campbell, his staff and faculty played an important role in the community, providing a comprehensive program for youth and adults, who never before had the chance to go to college. Special programs also expanded opportunities for future employment.

Since the start of community colleges in Kentucky, these institutions showed tremendous growth during the 1960's and 70's. Today community colleges have become the fastest growing institution in Kentucky's educational system. Opportunities provided by two-year colleges meant that a greater number of people have been able to gain post-secondary education. As time goes on, these institutions will have greater importance for communities. An intrinsic value of such colleges is the comprehensiveness of curriculum offerings for the wide diversification of attending students. From the earliest days of the community college movement in our country, this institution has been an innovative and dynamic force for educational change. The characterization of Kentucky's community colleges as a positive educational experience since development in the 60's, continues to leave a strong impact on Appalachia's people.

Alice Lloyd College Student Of The 1960's

There are many reasons why I count myself fortunate in having served as Academic Dean at Alice Lloyd College. It gave me the opportunity to work with devoted, concerned and caring educators in aiding students who came from a background of poverty. It also provided great satisfaction to see these young people fulfill the College's hope for their success; more so, because they came from the most depressed region of America — Appalachia.

The purpose of this part of my book is to give a general picture of some problems that staff and faculty members had to face, while teaching and administering at the college level in the heart of Appalachia. Working with students who came from a background afflicted with many disadvantages presented challenges, which other colleges would have hesitated to deal with. One can say with pride that Alice Lloyd College satisfied the needs of its students. Of course, when we look back and think of this institution and its uniqueness, we have to redefine traditional ideas of "college and college work."

Creativity and innovation of the faculty had not been tied to a uniformity of teaching, which was called for by many colleges during this period. It was a time when American higher education was aiming for reform. Alice Lloyd College developed effective change in its educational programs through pedagogy, rather than personality and politics, and provided the best possible optimum learning situations for its students. Inner motivation and self-discipline were key goals in education. The proper learning environment had to draw on the elements of individual differences, and education was geared toward active learning rather than passive. Giving students the freedom to learn and develop self-discipline was a means of preparing them for dealing with a complex and technologically demanding society.

The role of this College was diverse. Bewildering it was, when I remember the challenges that were before us. Students that came to Alice Lloyd College knew, the only way to lift themselves in the social and economic scale was through education. The College felt, that due to their social, economic, and cultural background and inadequate K through 12 program of study, it could not afford to merely bring each student to the discipline, but had to bring the discipline to each student. Alice Lloyd College obligated itself to give the best possible opportunity for full development of individual capabilities. To do this, it was necessary to understand the student's motivation. Ideally, the prime factor should be centered on a thirst for knowledge. However, we had to recognize that these young adults came to us with many background deficiencies, even though their past academic achievements were respectable.

Because secondary school programs were considered dismal and lacking in Appalachia, the College took an approach to develop and enhance positive learning experiences for incoming students by providing an advanced placement program. Freshmen entered the College during summer school with special orientation on continued success in changing over to collegiate level learning. The advantage of this head start academic experience was truly beneficial. An intensive eight-week advanced summer study program included academics, necessary study skills, learning habits, improving social skills, and upgrading their value system. Student services did an excellent job in planning and implementing the advanced placement program. I was impressed with the Dean of Students, Bill Hughes and his staff, including Thelmarie Thornsberry, in coordinating this transitional period for incoming freshmen. There were two aspects of information about students that were necessary to help them overcome difficulties they encountered in college. First, we had to assemble reliable, accurate data about each student on a much broader scope than was being done in colleges during the 1960's. Secondly, this information needed to be transferred to the instructional staff in such a manner that made it useful for them.

We knew that Alice Lloyd College students represented a challenge, based upon their backgrounds. They came from areas of Appalachia where many people were functionally illiterate or close to it. The students were very bright, but never had an opportunity to show their potential. Thus, our professors were asked to work in a climate where they had to know as much as possible about the students and their problems, in order to assist them in successfully completing programs of study. The College had to possess measures beyond traditional ways in describing the student. We therefore developed additional and more effective means of evaluating and testing. A challenge for our staff was to investigate ways in which students functioned and how their patterns of abilities differed. Any assessment of the student's characteristics included an examination of as many variables as possible. It was important to have data on such matters as range of abilities, family background, social attitudes, intellectual disposition, peer group influence, and a host of other factors that usually were not accessible to faculty members. Any information on a young person's value system, orientation toward a career, personality patterns, motivation, influence of background, etc., was important.

A major reason why Alice Lloyd College students were able to achieve success, was because the teaching-learning process in almost every classroom contained individualized instruction as the center of focus by faculty. In addition, our staff was applying principles of group dynamics to their respective areas of study to better understand the Appalachian student in relation to the classroom group, thereby improving learning individually and collectively. Humanitarian attitudes and democratic values may have accounted for our interest to see the Appalachian youth succeed. We knew that the extra attention given to students everyday, would directly or indirectly guide them through successful learning experiences that mirrored concepts of confidence, caring, concern, and communication. Our effort to help them understand other cultures in our society was an important ingredient in their learning experience. Many students would be moving on to professional schools outside of Appalachia to become doctors, lawyers, engineers, and educators, therefore, it was pertinent to have knowledge and reasoned judgment of the "outside world."

Though our faculty was significant in constituting the teacher-learner relationship, students supplied the other half of the success formula and were responsible for outcomes of this mutual interaction. They brought to the classroom Appalachian culture, social-emotional needs, conflicts, interests, fears, feelings, and interpersonal abilities, along with strong values. However, learning was far from being a passive transmission of thoughts and processes. It involved acquisition of knowledge, to be sure; but it also required intellectual skills, such as generating hypotheses and exploration, heightening sensitivities, extension of perspectives, deepening of perceptions, and rendering of judgments. This meant development of complicated intellectual and creative capacities, hopefully motivated by zest and enthusiasm. It was also our wish for each student to emerge in an individual style of learning, which a discerning faculty helped to cultivate.

The myth outsiders had about Appalachian's lack of desire and willingness to enhance their future proved to be wrong, for these young minds were eager for knowledge and understanding of society in order to develop full potential. From our viewpoint, a most important function of the College was to enable students, through voluntary participation in classroom activities, to find and understand their place in the group, and develop a sense of belonging. To achieve this, our faculty organized classes in such a way that it helped each student gain better understanding of their role and responsibility in the learning process. This consisted of a series of effective goals, such as teacher-student planning and socialized meetings. Group discussion was a chief technique of teaching and learning, and each student had the opportunity to actualize their potential. Discipline became self-discipline, as the individual's integration of behavior developed into a desirable attitude, as defined by the group.

When dealing with college students from Appalachia, we found that traditional methods of rewards and punishment by credits and grades were increasingly less effective. Lectures and recitations did not meet enthusiastic response of students, who were determined to achieve an understanding of the world they lived in. Accumulating a large amount of more or less related facts was not the goal of Appalachia's youth. Conditions demanded a re-examination about the psychology of motivation, particularly as it applied to classroom instruction and curriculum change. This was no easy task, for in education, changes are often unwelcome and more difficult, because the approach to teaching-learning was not merely changing the students' past structured experiences, but from our point of view, changed the behavior of people in groups. To have the desired effect, we had to apply our understanding to the dynamics of combining individualized instruction, group formation and collective action.

In spite of many obstacles, the Alice Lloyd College student succeeded and moved on to greater heights in education. I felt encouraged, and liked what I saw in the scholarship of students. Their growth and maturity were remarkable and they absorbed many of the diverse challenges presented to them. These were much greater than one can imagine, for the students had many strikes against them because of their background. Despite this and high demands from the College, they were able to carry themselves into society as respectable leaders and effective citizens.

The founder of Alice Lloyd College, would be proud to see the accomplishments of this institution and its student body that represent a broader spectrum of Appalachian youth not only from eastern Kentucky, but also West Virginia, Virginia, Tennessee, and Ohio. Encouragement and drive that Alice Lloyd imparted on her students in educating them for positions of leadership and service to the mountain people, had become the foundation for this institution's objectives. She and the presidents that followed her, William S. Hayes, Jerry C. Davis, and the present Chief Executive M. Fred Mullinax and his dedicated staff, led by Wallace Campbell, Jim Bergman, Christine Stumbo and Thelmarie Thornsberry, have all emphasized that education should be democratic and humanitarian, a process that does not stop with graduation. The goal of Alice Lloyd College is to encourage and expand this type of role beyond community life, to produce leaders for Appalachia with strong beliefs and objectives, who possess high moral and ethical values, and a sense of serving others.

Too many institutions of higher learning had moved away from an ideology that emphasized leadership, which incorporates democratic and humanitarian qualities. In positions of influence, greater focus on quality of leadership is needed. Research has cited that to measure the overall impact of higher education is a difficult task. However, when an institution such as Alice Lloyd College is so close to the community and has served as an educational springboard for humanitarian leadership, one does not require extensive research to determine its effectiveness.

This kind of leadership, necessary for change, was and is firmly entrenched in the minds of Alice Lloyd College graduates, as they moved toward a new direction for the future. The aim of leadership to overcome poverty has been based on social good rather than personal gains. Another objective of this College is to serve the community and region through appropriate outreach programs, emphasizing that mountain people learn how to help themselves. The College's role in planning for the future has served as an aid in maintaining solid values, and encouraged high personal standards. Appalachia needs men and women with those kinds of skills that include social understanding, which in turn will bring people together in overcoming their conditions of poverty. Motivating students to become humanitarian leaders may have been difficult and unrealistic for some institutions to achieve. However, to Alice Lloyd College, the goal was for students to become leaders with understanding and rationality.

Results were very evident in the 1960's and 70's, as some college graduates were beginning to assert themselves in positions of influence. Many people, through selfless contributions, made it possible for young Appalachians to embark on careers in helping others. There were two people I respected and admired for their influence on many of today's leaders: Will Hayes and June Buchanan.

Dr. William S. Hayes

Will Hayes became President of Alice Lloyd College in the early 1960's, after having served as its Academic Dean. He immediately embarked on a vigorous and courageous program of development and modernization, starting with the renovation of old standing buildings and the addition of needed facilities. Will Hayes traveled extensively throughout our nation, selling the cause of the College, and people were amazed about its innovative approach to educating the youth of Appalachia. I remember one occasion while accompanying Will on a trip to the east coast. My role was to make donors and supporters aware of the purpose, objectives, and strengths of the academic program. We dispelled the myth that people had about what type of student our College elected to educate. They were surprised to hear about the many young people with potential for leadership.

Dr. Hayes was a social reformer, who believed that education is the most important tool to help transform poor Appalachian families and their children. He felt that through education, many of the social and economic ills these people experienced could be overcome. Will Hayes also had confidence that acquisition of knowledge cultivated interaction of the student with his or her surroundings. He had been a strong believer that learning as a process affected behavior and social attitudes, as well as intellectual skills. Dr. Hayes was the type of person who did not hesitate to congratulate and encourage students on a job well done. Even though he advocated tailoring the curriculum to needs of the time, he believed in intellectual discipline.

During the 1960's, activism played an important part in accomplishing social change for Appalachia. The most effective leaders at local levels were not elected officials. Contrary to the supposed powers of town halls, common men and women were providing direction for citizen influence and participation. Will Hayes and I had the opportunity to attend various Appalachian regional meetings and conferences that brought out the leadership qualities of ordinary mountain people. Even though Will had to deal with action on the national level, he was always cognizant to realize opportunities for significant change in Appalachia. His conviction that the College should also use its influence to affect social change, led Will to host the first VISTA conference on campus. Bringing together recognized educational people, government policy makers, other national social leaders and workers, provided an excellent opportunity for input into the planning phase of this program. It was Will Hayes' hope that VISTA would have a far reaching impact nationally, but above all, for Appalachians.

Dr. Hayes had a dream that Alice Lloyd College needed to commit itself in preserving the history of Appalachia from the time of its settlers. He envisioned that the College would serve as depository for the legacy of this region's people, their cultural heritage, expressed in writing or orally recorded, for future use and research. People such as librarian Charlotte Madden, who endlessly worked to preserve the many deeds of Alice Lloyd and other eastern Kentuckians, helped to develop the beginning phase of a priceless historical archive of information, to better understand the past of Appalachia. The archive contains a combination of Appalachian history, folklore, and folk history. Stories of and by old-timers give great insight and valuable data of the people and its region. Through the efforts of Laurel Shackleford and Bill Weinberg, the archive includes the Appalachian Oral History Projects, along with photographs, which provide a rich source of documentary information of folk sayings, customs and anecdotes of eastern Kentucky life.

Will Hayes did not come from Appalachia, but he was a man who had understanding for the people of the mountains. It was difficult to follow in the footsteps of Alice Lloyd, since people of Appalachia, in their loyalty and dedication to her, were not that quick to accept an outsider who replaced this most revered giver of opportunities. Dr. Hayes worked with dedication and enthusiasm to build a growing college and community in spite of many distractions and deterrents. Will was a person of great inner strength and acknowledged that each individual had goodness in their heart. He continued his journey through life with each learning experience, whether success or failure, challenging every new encounter as a humanitarian leader. The impact of the late Dr. William S. Hayes' presidency effected many Appalachian lives more than they may realize.

June Buchanan

I remember my first day as Dean at Alice Lloyd College, when faculty, administrators and students were adapting to the opening summer session of the new academic year. As the sun went down and darkness began to ascend over the campus, I saw June Buchanan through a maze of students heading toward her office, to meet with various individuals from the community. When I approached her, she smiled and acknowledged me. I noticed a lady and three children standing on the porch leading to June's office. Each child was given a warm pat by her, and she went on to talk with the mother. I was impressed to see this inspiring person so humbly assisting them by giving food, goods and clothes. The mountain woman, herself humble, could not thank June enough for the good fortune that she and Caney Creek Center had provided. I felt honored being in the presence of a great lady with individuality and stature.

June Buchanan had worked with Alice Lloyd for over forty years. She stood out as a woman of elegance, who was educated at Wellesley College, but gave up a life that had everything, in order to work with Alice Lloyd. Alongside her mentor, June carried on with sincere dedication to help the needy. She had a good heart, and it was her greatest joy to make mountain people happy.

On another occasion, I had the pleasure of June Buchanan visiting my office. She mentioned hearing about the College faculty enjoying the open and relaxed meetings and asked if I wouldn't mind having her sit in on the next session. I extended an open invitation to attend all meetings. She didn't have to, but June became a regular member of our faculty gatherings. After half a dozen sessions, she came up to me and paid a compliment, which was so sincere that I will always remember June Buchanan with great fondness. She was not a woman who hesitated to express her feelings, and her candor was with a touch of class. Born and raised in upstate New York, educated at one of America's most elegant women's colleges, she became enthralled and committed to the great work of Alice Geddes Lloyd. Instead of just visiting, she spent the rest of her life in Appalachia as successor to Alice Lloyd, and continued to blaze a trail of educational endeavor that to this day amazes many outsiders. Not only did these women educate young people for leadership roles in Appalachia, but they also were responsible for starting many schools in the mountains for underprivileged eastern Kentuckians.

June Buchanan received many awards during her lifetime, such as the Arent's Medal from Syracuse University, describing her greatness as a teacher, author, administrator, and dedicated humanitarian to the people of Appalachia. She believed firmly, as did Alice Lloyd, that even though opportunities were given to Appalachians, the will of self-help was necessary for them to succeed. In the many conversations I had with June, she proved to be an advocate of traditional education that included a strong value system. Developing a sense of responsibility in her students was June Buchanan's forte. It helped them gain confidence in themselves, while progressing through life as citizens, family providers and professionals. In the spring of 1965, June told me that she wanted to spend the rest of her life at Alice Lloyd College. She was never to leave, for in 1987, June Buchanan died and was buried alongside her dear friend Alice, overlooking the College campus. June Buchanan is gone now, however, her legacy of unwavering dedication for the Appalachian people will continue to live on in the Alice Lloyd College graduates of yesterday, today and tomorrow.

Foundation For New Leadership

It was during the 1970's, when a few concerned citizens came together and started to plan long-term goals and objectives that would lead to a greater core of participants from the region's infrastructure. The continued stifling of economic growth in Appalachia led to the formation of ideas and conclusions by these individuals. They felt, what eastern Kentucky needed was not the stop-gap solutions of relief or recovery, but strong private involvement of people, who were committed to help make Appalachia a better place to live. They had experienced "War on Poverty" programs and saw the government's investments in social action that tried to stimulate people by changing their situations; but there was one major problem — the economic picture of Appalachia had not improved. These astute citizens knew that something needed to be done to bring change that would have an everlasting affect. It was their conviction that strong leadership from the region would be needed in order to improve the economic and social conditions, which continually affected the people and led Appalachia into greater depths of poverty.

This new group was committed to long-range endeavors, having a positive impact on people. They had lived through many different government ideologies which had been forced upon them. Having grown up in Appalachia, they wanted to understand all the alternatives for the future and be able to make right decisions. They were concerned that the region would remain a "welfare state." Their focus centered on permanent improvement for Appalachia and to have a loose-knit, yet cohesive group of concerned citizens, who would work cooperatively to precipitate action for change. Regardless of political affiliation, they came together to discover common interests and bonds for creating individual and group initiatives of economic and social development over the coming years. Thus, Appalachia was on the threshold of new leadership, consisting of a diverse and eclectic group of individuals.

One of the major objectives of this group was to build a concept of regionalism, because they felt that positive actions affecting one area, would help others in keeping the infrastructure of eastern Kentucky up-to-date. The main purpose was not to reinvent government but to improve Appalachia's future, using their talents and independence without political pressure to develop strategical opportunities which would lead to an economically and socially improved region. These concerned citizens had strong foundations in ethics and values. To a large extent, they came from educated backgrounds that espoused democratic leadership and qualities of humanitarian goodness. They were aware of the need to develop an economic base for this region, which would be built on values of community and individuality. Their goal was primarily for a democratic region at work. It should be noted, what some of these new leaders started in the 70's, is felt by the people of Appalachia today. The reaffirmation and reinvigoration by these individuals to improve life in eastern Kentucky deserves to be recognized.

Eastern Kentucky Leadership Organization

In the 1970's, a physician, an administrator and an attorney, all with selfless determination and long-term initiatives for the people, met to discuss and develop a strategy for development of the Eastern Kentucky Leadership Organization. The physician was Dr. Grady Stumbo, Health Administrator Benny Ray Bailey, and Bill Weinberg, Attorney and former History Professor at Alice Lloyd College. In developing this organization, the concern was that there should be a fusion of people with different backgrounds, regardless of their political or organization affiliations, to come together by encouraging growth and change for the benefit of Appalachia's future. The Eastern Kentucky Leadership Group would serve as a springboard of ideas and knowledge for the region's economic growth, along with providing services through certain offshoot organizations for individuals and groups that needed special skills or "know how" in starting businesses. They would also provide the community with leadership and coordination capabilities to assist groups in long range planning, and join with business and individuals in attacking unsolved problems. Another objective of this organization has been to seek out, identify, propose solutions, and gain support in providing responses to the large variety of community needs. Results of this positive and aggressive posture of community leadership would eventually have an impact on the region in coming decades.

Summation

During this era, the government offered poor people of Appalachia and the country a sweeping reform of programs to fight poverty. Sometimes it seemed that things were going from "bad to worse," however, occasionally there was a reason for people to be encouraged by actions of individuals or groups. War on Poverty was disliked by certain people and anti-feelings of cynicism and pessimism existed. However, policy makers learned a great deal about programs and actions that were effective. Even more important, they were able to understand the people of poverty. A factor, realized too late in this program, was that people had to have desire to make the most of what they had. The emphasis "to help the poor help themselves" was never more evident than at this period.

At the same time, there were powerful actions taken by individuals and groups from the Cumberland plateau of eastern Kentucky that left a strong impact for the future. Most notable was the role of women as a driving force behind the activist movement in areas such as welfare, justice, education and health care. Their presence in the forefront of activity, reflected a growing influence on Appalachia. This was not new for hillfolk, because in the early 20th century, women were providing leadership for the poor downtrodden people in areas of health, education and social services. I remember some of the elderly talking about how they fought side by side with their husbands in the 1930's against unfairness and injustice in mining and general living conditions. The 60's and 70's were the start of women's organizations in this nation, and the fight for their rights began. Women of Appalachia have always been concerned about all people, especially the family. Their objectives dealt with the "nitty gritty" of rights and justice for all, as well as improvement in socioeconomic conditions.

Two major social forces were aimed at making fundamental changes in education during this period. The first was accountability, which centers on procedures of stated objectives in education and the attainment of these objectives. The second, humanism, involves values, attitudes and high-quality educational services, which should be equally available and accessible to all people as their basic right. These forces inspired thoughts for a new direction that eventually would have a profound effect on education in Kentucky by the late 1980's and early 1990's.

141

It meant that school systems should assist the individual and society, with proper focus placed on the output of their services for each person and the community. Clearly, this is in conflict with the approach of education that had prevailed for many years.

Finally, Appalachia had suffered shocking and difficult changes to its society, as repetitive blows were released toward private and social belief structures, which left many people unsure of themselves and the future. The U.S. government's displacement of families, uprooting them from their homesteads to construct dams and lakes that benefited metropolitan areas outside Appalachia, led to clashes of beliefs and tradition. Change was occurring, yet many of these people were trying to maintain the humanistic posture of their culture that extended back to the beginning of this region. When electric power, telephone, and cable lines were cutting their way over hills and valleys, people and land were no longer isolated. The 1960's and 70's were a period of frustration, malaise, and power struggles that would lead to significant implications for the eastern Kentucky landowner during coming years. Above all, it was a time of beginnings, establishing many new possibilities for leaders and activists of the 80's and 90's.

Photograph courtesy of Alice Lloyd College Library Archives.

Photograph courtesy of Alice Lloyd College Library Archives.

Photograph courtesy of Alice Lloyd College Library Archives.

Photograph courtesy of Alice Lloyd
College Library Archives.

Photograph by Lorraine Corsale,
courtesy of the
Christian Appalachian Project.

Photograph courtesy of the Christian Appalachian Project.

Hazard City Hall. Photograph courtesy of the City of Hazard.

The Hazard Pavillion. Photograph courtesy of the City of Hazard.

Hazard Appalachian Regional Hospital. Photograph courtesy of the City of Hazard.

Perry County Central High School. Photograph courtesy of the City of Hazard.

Hazard Community College. Photograph courtesy of Evelyn Bernitt.

Chapter VI

1980 — To the Present

Working Toward Change

The 1980's and early 90's can be viewed as a time in American history filled with distrust, confusion, and discontent, as disparity and double standards prevailed between the have and have nots. Our nation was dominated by greed, huge corporate takeovers, and fraudulent conditions, which were created by certain individuals in the financial community. Corrupt politicians and some persons in law and order had been part of the deceit during this period. America was controlled by a corporate few, where C.E.O.'s robbed people by collecting outrageous and inflated salaries. On the other hand, workers were let go from their jobs to justify profits and income of these top brass. Society had been told that prosperity was within reach, while the Administration showed interests toward a sophisticated business elite with laissez-faire utopia attitudes, as more middle class citizens were ending up in poverty. This led to disheartenment, futility and indignity of many people, because economic conditions had been deceptively spawned by power brokers who were allowed to get out of hand.

Government's inaction made it possible for a number of persons in our country to ruefully use a "me-first" attitude in climbing the ladder of financial success. Unfortunately, the Administration provided opportunities to rich people and left nothing but a bitter struggle for the less fortunate. Federal policies enacted during the 1980's, such as income tax breaks, benefited those in high salary brackets, whereas the middle class and poor had been misled to believe that benefits were intended for them.

143

The wealthy were reaping bigger incomes, while everybody else was struggling. A study by the House Ways and Means Committee showed that federal taxes were higher per family income among the middle class and poor, while the rich paid out a lesser portion. The administration's policy toward rich people was evident, according to a 1990 report by the non-profit Washington-based Center on Budget and Policy Priorities. Their information, gathered from Congressional Budget Office data, cited that our nation's wealthiest one percent increased their income by 87 percent during the 1980's. At the same time, earnings of the poorest people, who represented twenty percent of the population, dropped by 5.2 percent.

Since record keeping began by our government in the 1950's, there was never a wider gap between rich and poor than during the 80's and early 90's. On July 29, 1990, the Buffalo, *New York Evening News* stated it would take the combined income of all 100 million poor Americans to equal that of the 2.5 million wealthiest people in our country. Further studies showed that prior to the late seventies, the United States had a stable income tax system that was well accepted by its populace. However, with implementation of the 1981 Tax Act and subsequent revisions, tax burdens began to fall more heavily on the middle class and poor, but earnings for the wealthy skyrocketed. At no other time in American history has a tax program had such a negative effect on the middle class and poor of our society than during the 1980's.

A strange contradiction in our country was the persuasion for people to "buy now, pay later," without regard to implications of credit, and this misconception made them overspend beyond their means. Critics cited that credit buying in the 1980's created a false sense of growth, while our Administration proudly made the country aware that these were "the best of times." The events during this period of conflicting conditions and mixed messages provided unmistakable evidence that business and industry showed growth until the late 80's, when people's savings started to crumble and credit promoted greater debt. Individuals with already little means were finding themselves in default of carrying out their financial obligations, as America was experiencing an incredible amount of bankruptcy filing in the courts. During the 1980's, the middle class and poor were persuaded and manipulated into believing that tax programs of previous years would not suffice in this decade. Unfortunately, the Administration had assumed that lower taxes, deregulation, and low inflation would help fuel economic growth. Instead it brought little, if any, positive action for change. Proclamations and statements that the downturn was temporary did not sit well with those people who were direly effected by this crisis.

Another shocking truth during the eighties was that billions of dollars had been funneled into the coffers of corporations, which were supposed to create opportunities for employment. The results of this intent became a paradox, because lack of corporate action and manipulation of government money did not provide job opportunities for the needy. Our economy encouraged excessive situations that not only burdened the country, but created hopelessness for the common man. The late 80's began to show a tremendous array of problems for American workers, and an alarming high rate of persons were unemployed as job-cutting became a daily occurrence for large corporations. Poverty was setting in for too many, nevertheless, each year financial statistics indicated economic growth, obviously benefiting those in high income brackets. The Administration was indifferent to various issues confronting the people, and as our country was going to be exposed to a recession, the Persian Gulf Conflict with Iraq started. Questions about domestic problems of the 1990's were put on hold, as priority was given to war.

After the Persian Gulf Conflict and Cold War with Eastern Europe, there have been few celebrations for Americans. Today, economic decline and social ills of our nation are the greatest concerns to our citizens. Some authorities believe that this period, even though it was not a depression, has been a severe recession. However, the poor of Appalachia have experienced this kind of situation for decades, which has led to a prevailing sense of dejection and frustration. Certain patterns that occurred for many years in Appalachia have surfaced all over our country. No longer are boundaries dividing the poor from the rest of society, because more people throughout this nation are forced to a life of impoverishment.

When looking at the picture of poverty and its many ills, we search for solutions that will satisfy needs of not only eastern Kentucky but all America. Economic and social problems that have continually existed in this region for generations, have now festered throughout the nation. Every fiber of our society is faced with this, day in and day out, as the ills are presenting a challenge of how well Americans can deal with these problems. In doing so, we must remember Appalachia's ongoing struggles, by giving attention and responding to its needs.

The reality of life in the 90's is that poverty in urban America overshadows rural conditions. Urban ghettos are visible to the beholder every day, by witnessing homeless in the streets, unemployment, disease, lack of health care or insurance, and starvation. Adding to decay and destitution in cities and surroundings, our nation's industrial base was restructured by decline in productivity, competitiveness, and companies either went out of business or moved to other countries. This led to loss of many jobs, which affected middle and low income employees. However, those people working in high paying positions were not relegated to lower salaries, whereas income of the average wage earner declined, creating even greater disparity for the middle class and poor of our country. With white and blue collar workers taking home smaller paychecks, economic distress has plagued the workforce, and a disturbing employment picture shows that our total country is experiencing the "Appalachian poverty syndrome." Approximately seventeen million people are unemployed, underemployed, or on involuntary part-time work, while others have become discouraged and stopped looking for jobs.

A nationwide network of food banks, called Second Harvest, released a study in March 1994 on hunger, citing that nearly 26 million Americans rely on food pantries, soup kitchens and emergency feeding programs. Yet, thousands of people are still turned away each day, because shelves are bare. If it were not for many private organizations that care and help the needy throughout this country, there would be catastrophic proportions of suffering. The homeless are provided with beds wherever possible, but too many are still living in open squalor. What we are experiencing is an economic and social discontent, where all the worst case scenarios are played out and poor people are the sufferers. Our government's failure to stop economic and social deterioration in the late 80's and early 90's left a legacy of a cumbersome bureaucratic structure. Unable to improve the ills of regions such as Appalachia, the Administration shifted fiscal responsibility of many programs onto state and local government.

This sweeping change by the federal government in cutting aid made it more difficult for states to recover from the economic recession. Kentucky was further burdened through its own strained and out-of-date tax structure, developed in an earlier decade. Compounding this problem is the fact that the U.S. tax system needs to be overhauled, or else our country will be pushed into a greater uncontrollable situation of income disparities. Consequences of the present system are the misguided policies that were largely responsible for industry and jobs moving to other countries. Echoing the sentiments of critical observers, there is a need for government to replace our current tax system with a new initiative.

Concurrent with passing down responsibilities to states and counties was the Administration's efforts to downsize the Appalachian Regional Commission. With a conservative leadership in government during the eighties, A.R.C. funding was cut to one third of the late 70's administration. A.R.C. was created by Lyndon B. Johnson during the 1960's "Great Society" era and has since served 13 Appalachian states, from Mississippi to New York. Its many funding efforts have included education, health and health care, water and sewage projects, as well as highway improvement. The Appalachian Regional Commission had given eastern Kentucky a most significant boost during the eighties, by funding about 70 percent of the approximately 100 million dollars to build eighty miles of state highway 15, intersecting with east and west route 80 at Hazard, Kentucky. Even though A.R.C.'s work is not finished and forces have

146

pushed for its end, credit should be given to this agency for recognizing eastern Kentucky's economic and social crisis and searching for solutions to problems that have deterred this region's progress for generations.

The vulnerability of county and local governments' fiscal responsibility in eastern Kentucky during this time was very evident, as the economic crisis and federal policy change practically forced communities to cease functioning. Financial condition of local government was so weak that it affected all aspects of community life. Villages and towns had to operate with limited income which became a constraint on the amount of services they could offer. Lack of control over resources hindered a community's movement toward any form of growth. During 1992, a touch of humor and ingenuity occurred when Lynch, a community of 1,100 people, found itself with a forty-thousand dollar deficit, and the mayor's wife opened a thrift shop in City Hall, organizing bingo games in order to raise money for covering the financial accounting loss. This was not an uncommon approach taken by small impoverished mountain communities. Often Appalachian villages, towns and county governments were in a situation of having a budget deficit and had to let employees go, or place them on part-time schedules. Others did not receive a salary increase and hiring practices ceased, because there just were no local or county jobs available.

Many communities and counties could not dip into cash reserves like other parts of the country. For years, eastern Kentucky governments have been functioning on a day-to-day basis trying to make ends meet, with revenue getting more difficult to come by. Also, callous disregard by federal government in the eighties and early nineties created a domino affect on communities. Fueled by declining federal funds, the State tightened its budget, added new laws and mandates, along with capping taxes. However, the costs of running county and local governments along with providing services to constituents continued to increase, which created red ink ledgers.

For example, the region's counties are being drained financially by trying to maintain collection, storage and processing of waste materials. Over decades, liquid waste took the natural process and solid waste materials were hauled into open gullies or abandoned pits, bringing deterioration to areas of Appalachia with the need for clean up. When 49 environmentally unsound landfills were closed by the State in 1992, eastern Kentucky counties had been left with too few places to ship garbage. Some were even forced in hauling waste to areas over a hundred miles away. Financial burdens of these counties increased further by landfill dumping fees, extended transportation and labor costs.

Too often in the past, Appalachian political leaders were content not to face the issue of waste materials, and consequently costs today are much greater than they would have been had attention been given to this problem at that time. Necessary changes for environmentally improving collection, storage and processing of waste materials are taking place, but it is more difficult, because past governments did not prepare for them in a sensible way. This is just a microcosm of Appalachia's struggles, but it should be told so that the reader can gain a greater understanding of the varied issues that confront local government.

A Story of Frustration

For generations, the way of life in Appalachia has always been a struggle, and today many people find themselves worse off than twenty years ago. With the economic decline of the late 1980's, "tight money policies" were created and some families had to face great frustration in trying to stay above the poverty level, even when husband and wife work. In order to pay bills and taxes, credit and credit cards have become a false substitute in sustaining and holding off eventual bankruptcy or foreclosure of their homes. There are others who just can't get credit because a financial status is non-existing. Being placed in such a dilemma leaves a person with fear and hopelessness, not knowing what to do. Unable to meet property tax obligations, some of the poor had no other choice but to sell their vehicle. It is inconceivable to imagine a family without a car, but it has happened, and without some form of transportation, especially in rural settings, emotional problems become more severe.

Throughout life, people experience situations that have a profound effect on them. One such incident occurred when I visited Prestonsburg, Kentucky, in July of 1989. A man in his late thirties approached me and asked if I was interested in buying his car. He sounded depressed and was trying to get enough money together to pay his house tax bill. Seeing a human being so desperate and in a degrading position makes one realize that poverty, as it occurs in Appalachia, rarely exists for just one simple reason. This man had a job, but apparently was not earning enough to support his wife and four children. Married over fifteen years, all he had to show for his effort was the broken down 1976 car and a very small two-bedroom dwelling. He had been able to save five hundred dollars for a down payment on his home in 1980, making seven thousand dollars a year, while the average Appalachian family income was just below that figure. However, according to the Census Bureau, his earnings were considered below the national poverty level, and in 1989, the situation had not improved.

Like this gentleman, many people are working, but the structure of Appalachia's economic situation restricts them to limited jobs.

However, even these fail to provide workers with adequate means of supporting themselves and their families, yet the fact remains that they are unable to pay bills and taxes. This is one of many stories, and one cannot stress enough that varied ills of poverty exist. Unfair conditions, which are characteristics of impoverishment, as well as consequences of its effects must be considered when assessing today's situation. In general, upward mobility for Appalachians will require economic, social and political elements that work interdependently, to effectively overcome this problem.

The Family — The Father

In isolated Appalachian communities, a tradition of family self-sufficiency developed over many generations. The father, whose main responsibility was to provide for his family, worked 12 to 14 hours a day, six days a week, and he either dug coal, hauled timber, or planted crops. His major concern was to make enough money to feed and sustain the lives of his loved ones. It did not matter in the past if the family's patriarch had no schooling or lived in a forlorn dwelling without plumbing and other necessities; his self-dependency was strong, which carried him and the family through life.

The role of a father as breadwinner for his family has always been entrenched in Appalachia's culture, but is today without question, under great strain. Jobs in the region's male dominated economy of mining, logging and farming have given way to automation, diminishing the need for workers, leaving a growing number of unemployed and broken-spirited men. They have tried to find other work, and in many instances were discouraged by the lack of employment opportunities. Jobs are still not available, and compounding this problem is that some men lack education. Another dilemma confronting the unemployed is black lung disease, which disqualifies a person automatically from pursuing other types of work. It is a grim reminder that working in the mines not only afflicted those strong men's health, but it also put a stranglehold on their future which they cannot control. The result is that joblessness and disability has changed the role of a father. Improved living conditions are unpredictable, and instability of income and lack of direction has increased social problems that appear to be bottomless.

The Changing Role of Mothers

In poverty-stricken families, where illiteracy is prevalent, the traditional role of a woman as homemaker, taking care of children, farming the small plot of land and raising chickens, is not enough to keep a family going, and a government check to assist these families is only a token of help. Like their parents and grandparents, today's Appalachian family is unable to rely on its own resources, and instead, dependency on government is a necessity for survival. Because of their husbands' unemployment situation, Appalachian women are forced toward a new role.

Some women have been asserting individual desire to keep their families from falling into the age-old dependency of welfare assistance, and are seeking jobs to bring home an income supporting their loved ones. Contrary to beliefs of outsiders, there are Appalachian women who feel humiliated having to go on welfare. They not only want to work, but realize the importance of an education for better employment opportunities. As men's jobs disappear, and they cannot gain employment, women have taken entry level positions mostly in hospitals, nursing homes, health clinics, retail, or fast food stores. Unfortunately, those kinds of service jobs generally provide a meager salary. In many instances, income that women have been bringing home since the 1980's cannot fill the void of a husband's paycheck. Some women say their husbands sulk, in turn drink, and become hostile as they have to grow dependent on their wives' salaries, leading to a stressful situation, resulting in abuse, separation or divorce.

The devastation that family breakdown brings leaves mothers moving in one of two directions. Either a woman gives up on life, which in turn could lead to anguish and frustration; however if children are involved, it makes matters worse, because they may wind up having behavioral problems at home and in school. The reverse direction occurs, when a mother sees herself in an entirely different role by seeking and taking action. Any change in a woman's role, however, will have far-reaching implications for her career and family.

A growing number of eastern Kentucky women are opting for educational and professional goals first. Some have gone back to high school to complete their diploma; others pursue a college degree to either go into education or health related occupations. What these women have in common is the desire and ability to change economic and social conditions that for many years plagued their ancestors. They are now identifying needs as well as developing self-determining ways to achieve their goals, and are able to turn things around for themselves and their family.

Sons Of The Family

Sons in past Appalachian generations wanted to be just like their fathers, who worked in coal mines for years. However, today's youth worry that they will inherit their fathers' legacy of constant illness. Many men had to leave the mines in their prime because of the debilitating black lung disease. Their sons feel being a miner does not justify risking one's life. They are pursuing different areas of interests by finishing high school, or planning to enter college. Others are attending vocational technical programs, preparing them for a trade. Those sons that stay home with very few goals for the future face limited opportunities for employment and can only hope to find odd jobs in coal mining, timber industry and farming. Even if work is available, the salary is not enough to maintain a half-way decent standard of living. Though many Appalachians have never gained an economic foothold in society, there are young men who want to escape from an inopportune future. Some are illegally raising marijuana, because for them it is the only way to survive. They don't like what they are doing, but dread existing on by-products of poverty and handouts that they have grown up with.

During World War II, eastern Kentucky was a major source of hemp for the U.S. Government. Farmers were making a good living, since it was needed for ropes on U.S. Navy warships. Grandfathers and fathers of today's youth had legally farmed this difficult growing crop, which required tedious work and nurturing. The government's contract with Appalachian farmers to grow hemp used for twine, rope and coarse fabrics, ended after the war. Through transferring the knowledge of growing this plant, it became a natural avenue for sons of eastern Kentuckians to gain a fast buck by producing marijuana. Even though this is an easy way to make money, many would rather work in the mines or timber industries for an honest and decent day's wage. There is very little use of marijuana locally, and growers take their product to people in other parts of the country. Today, outside forces viewing the opportunity of monetary gain have impinged upon eastern Kentucky growers. With these outsiders coming into the region violence is occurring, which had not been experienced before.

In 1992, the Drug Enforcement Agency along with state and local law organizations destroyed over 900,000 illegally grown plants, valued at more than 1.4 billion dollars. State authorities estimated that this was probably not quite half the crop for that year. The D.E.A.'s budget in 1990 to eradicate the growing of marijuana in eastern Kentucky was 3 million dollars. However, due to increased production, the budget quadrupled by 1993 to approximately 12 million. Growing marijuana and its distribution is so diverse that it compounds the problem for law enforcement to get a strong handle on this situation. Growers generally run a small operation or manage it themselves. Their greatest concern when cultivating the plant is to protect against thieves, poachers and animals, by setting up booby traps that leave an animal or human maimed or dead. As the law catches up with growers, they have moved the planting to public land, such as Daniel Boone National Forest or on inaccessible state land, while others use old warehouses or barns, which makes it difficult for federal and state agencies to ferret them out.

Distribution and transportation of marijuana vary in order to avoid law enforcement agencies. The loosely knit structure of small operations use anything from private cars, house trailers, and planes to carry marijuana to its destination. In addition, the relationship of eastern Kentuckians to illegal growers has led to problems for government, regarding arrests and convictions. Relatives, extended families and clans are loyal, and it is this bond that law enforcement officials find hard to break. It even carries over into the courts, when local people are assigned to serve on a jury regarding a marijuana criminal offense. There is a better possibility of prosecution if a trial is transferred to another jurisdiction, where chances are that members of the jury would not be related to a defendant. Government prosecutors had to move many cases to the federal level, to ensure getting a fair trial.

Rural Appalachia's crime problem differs considerably from urban America. The youths have grown up in an atmosphere of commitment for the well-being of people in the community, where everyone knows each other. By this type of upbringing they fear to offend members of the community. Petty crimes such as mugging, robbing neighbors, or the local store are generally nonexistent, because they sense that everyone is looking over their shoulder. It is a paradox that for years physical barriers of Appalachia have been a hindrance to its people, but on the other hand, the mountains do serve as a benefit by controlling crime from outside and within the highland country. Besides, crime in Appalachia's hollows, hamlets and villages is not as open and obvious because law enforcement handles problems with less bravado than in cities, where the media covers every story.

If killings occur in Appalachia, they often have cultural characteristics, which have been with the hillfolk for generations. One of the greatest social problems is that men have fallen to drinking. Sometimes a family argument results in an unfortunate act of emotion, where one relative kills another. One such double homicide received national attention during the past year, when two brothers were drinking and had an argument, which led to the shooting death of each other. The unfortunate and continuing saga of this type of incident is that this family had experienced several violent deaths since the sixties.

Domestic violence is a major problem and can be traced to degenerating family circumstances which stem from poverty. With alcoholism, suicide, abuse and homicide, a main concern is that often the mental status of some youth relate to deep feelings of insecurity, inferiority, and inability to cope with everyday frustrations. In others, their mental attitude is manifested in a desire to escape the reality of endless deprivation and deterioration of their life, which could lead to an underlying inclination for self-destruction. Some families have experienced poverty for years, and problems are intensified by lack of effective role models or positive experiences, which causes young people to lose perspective.

For generations, poverty has had a devastating effect on individuals, families, and the total community. Frustration of their situation restricts the youth from releasing energy in a positive way, which in turn creates problems that keep mounting beyond any form of solution. Many of those who cannot find work sit idle instead of attending school. A major worry pertaining to youth has been the reoccurring record of becoming parents too early and quitting school before graduation. Some of their mothers and fathers have experienced the same format of life, by getting married and having children at a young age, creating economic and social conditions which they were not able to overcome. However, in many instances young men in Appalachia have not faced up to the obligation of being accountable as a parent. In the past, if a young female was pregnant at an early age, the male generally felt responsible to be the child's father. In recent years, the young generation has become more complicated and adverse in their behavior, which results in greater consequences.

Daughters Of The Family

Early parenthood and leaving school before graduation has been and still is a major problem in Appalachia. The continuing increase in pregnancies of unmarried young daughters has put an added burden on them and their families. Parents still have that strong cultural bond to take care of their children, no matter what the consequences may be, and one can only admire them for this love and dedication. Despite economic and social problems, many maintain very close family ties, and if a daughter is in great despair because of early pregnancy, they respond by caring for her and the child.

When teens become parents and quit school, they are lacking in skills and credentials, often unable to secure employment and raise a child at the same time. Their option for the future leads to a welfare dependent existence, and too many are not mature enough to cope with the demands of adult life. Unless something meaningful is available to prepare them adequately in meeting the challenges as a young adult, welfare will be taken for granted and dependency on government aid could be destructive to the individual's initiative.

There are leaders and groups in Appalachia who are devising ways to serve the needs of young teenage mothers, which include assistance in health, education, other social and spiritual areas. Many programs are not new, but time has shown that they serve a purpose through strategies that are effective. One such educational program, sponsored by the Christian Appalachian Project, helps young teen mothers and other adults prepare for high school equivalency certificates. This approach is unique and has been a benefit to those who want to help themselves. Using a converted "Little Red School Bus" as a classroom which travels throughout counties, an educational foundation is offered for people to achieve their potential, by providing access to learning experiences and services, including job-related opportunities. The role this project plays goes beyond education-al experiences by establishing a sense of belonging and developing friend-ships that support working toward personal goals.

There is another side to the story of today's young Appalachian women, because ambitions of daughters are changing. Some are no longer content to get married and raise a family, however many of these girls will admit they are not planning to stay single very long. Opportunities in higher education are greater today for young women who entertain ideas for professions, and getting married seems less important. Positions for females with an educational background and college degree are expanding. Many have ambitions to return home even though they are creating inde-pendence within themselves, but would like to combine marriage with a career. Strong family and community ties which they sustained and trea-sured all their lives, are the basis of this allegiance. Young women of today have developed a sense of direction for their future, but the urge to come back home is very strong. This is based on family life, where the daugh-ter is cherished by parents that includes a mother, whose self-sacrificing love was always present and a father, whose work ethic had been inde-structible. He was fearless of the dangers in mining, yet gentle and giving, which provided the young Appalachian girl with a sense of security and belonging that lasts a lifetime.

Writings about the culture of these people have always included the family as a basis for survival. Since the time of their forefathers, east-ern Kentuckians were separated from other people, yet have survived as a family through the many generations of isolation. The child-parent rela-tionship of unconditional love is their strength. A warm and telling exam-ple of this kind of "family connection" is characterized in the autobiogra-phy "Coal Miner's Daughter," by world famous Loretta Lynn from Butcher Hollow. The Appalachian family is generally synonymous with caring, concern, and understanding of their loved ones, and from the start, ties are close. As a young girl becomes a woman, she experiences conflicts with the outside world that contradict what was taught by her parents, teachers, and religion. The Appalachian young woman may not appear to be emancipated from traditional ways of life, for she is torn between the pride of her culture, values instilled by her family, and the mixed messages of "outside" society.

The Elderly

Nothing symbolizes hardship more so than past experiences of the elderly in Appalachia. They have had to overcome great obstacles and impoverishment that confronted them by living in the mountains. All their lives they had no other choice but to work long and hard hours for minimum wages in order to survive. Health insurance was non-existant in those days and complicated life even further. Poverty still lingers in Appalachia and most elderly are without any kind of savings. Almost ten percent of them had no telephones in 1990 and in certain backwoods areas approximately 25 percent were without this service. There are quite a few older people who occupy the dwelling they were born and raised in. Even though they would like to share modern facilities and material things to accommodate old age wants and needs, reality collides with their way of existence. In some areas as many as 17 percent of households do not have plumbing, and the use of outdoor privies still exists. Coal or wood burning stoves as a heat source are common, and in certain pockets of the region approximately twenty nine percent of people use coal, which is a major cause for house fires. Other worries are added to already existing problems of the elderly: diminution of strength, agility, visual acuity and physical disability increase the burden of daily existence. Yet, they are people of strong positive attitude and accept life the way it is.

Most of the elderly people do not drive, let alone have a car, and transportation is hard to come by for those that live by themselves and in remote areas. Though there are senior citizen's centers in this region, the need to serve these poor elderly becomes a problem for persons who want to help. Old people are proud and independent, and tend to resist any form of assistance. They feel that their neighbors and friends in the community would think less of them if they accepted a helping hand. There are private nonprofit groups that provide access for transportation to visit doctors, health clinics, hospitals, grocery stores, and delivery of free meals is also available. These individual groups, like the Christian Appalachian Project Elderly Visitation Program, work with the aged who live in isolated areas. CAP volunteers visit homes and help with housework, home repairs, personal care and other services.

The poverty picture of elderly takes on many different scenes. It is not uncommon to see old people walking alongside roads, collecting aluminum cans to help financially get through each week. Existing on fixed social security that is way below the poverty level, the Appalachian elderly could provide lessons to social behaviorists and economists in studying survival of poor people. Living all their life on a meager income and in despair, these people have been able to survive, although some are malnourished and sick. Senior citizens unable to get to a grocery store on a regular basis may not eat for days. For that reason, problems of poor nutrition can lead to bone fractures, osteoporosis, dental disease, physical inactivity, and consequently depression. A significant 1993 study of findings from the University of Kentucky Sanders-Brown Center on aging cited that 28.3 percent of people sixty-five years and older, in forty-nine counties of Kentucky, are poverty stricken. This research further stated that in nineteen of these counties, poor elderly exceeded 34 percent, and eight counties recorded more than 40 percent. In conclusion, the fact remains that as people get older, the poverty rate increases.

Growing numbers of elderly women, having raised children while husbands earned a living, today are widowed and on their own. For many who outlive their husbands, old age retirement is inadequate and financial reserves are non-existing. Destitution and despair increases when social security benefits are meager as life continues in loneliness. Dr. Graham D. Rowles, who conducted the University of Kentucky study, pointed out that employment opportunities for elderly Appalachian women are extremely limited. If a widow is fortunate enough to receive the share of her spouse's pension and social security benefits, she may be able to stay above the poverty level. However, women suffer financially more in old age, because they or their husbands had not worked long enough to gain decent social security benefits, which are based on a person's work history. Some husbands may not have had pension benefits at all. Also, for years Appalachians were paid less than in other regions of the country, affecting their pension or social security. According to Dr. Rowles' study, in fifteen counties forty percent of these elderly women lived at the poverty level, while in two counties, Wayne and Owsley, it was more than fifty percent.

The inherent nature of Appalachian families typifies that adult children will always be available to take care of their aging parents. However, offspring moving to other parts of the country has become a disadvantage for some elderly. These adult children are frustrated with anxiety, fear, guilt, and sadness, because of not being able to take care of their parents from faraway places. In many cases, the old people don't want to move out of their homes, because they have lived all their life in this region, and that's where they want to stay; even if it means being alone.

Although there are elderly persons living by themselves in remote hills and hollows of eastern Kentucky, family responsibility and closeness are the strengths of their culture. Older people need help, and as part of their commitment, love and caring, Appalachian adult children or relatives without question, have been there to provide for their aged parents. They have met practical and emotional demands with mountaineer spirit, exemplifying strength of character. However, family members find themselves in a quandary, when certain physical and mental conditions of their parents deteriorate, being unsure how long they can help. Even when relatives and neighbors are able to assist, many find the job so demanding that answers have to be found. Appalachians are proud people, even though they live in less than ideal situations and have been reluctant to admit their status of poverty. In turn, denial of elderly needing medical and social service support presents a caveat of problems. Many do not give thought to the vital role these services play in keeping them well. It would be advantageous for health care professionals to form a partnership with private and non-profit organizations that educate senior citizens and their families about the importance of alternatives for care offered in each community. While family members and relatives are concerned for the elderly, local health care personnel and services should monitor and identify needs of older people through a comprehensive community approach.

Children Living In Poverty

The history of Appalachian children living in poverty leads us to critically question the nature and speed at which our country has been responding to this escalating crisis. As the 20th century enters its final years, poverty has increased, perpetuating conditions that bring misery to our children. It is known that failure of the federal government to develop a sound national policy toward poverty in the 1980's and early 90's, had its greatest effect on children. In Appalachia, many generations have lived in poverty, but for children to grow up in poor conditions of great proportions is unjust and inexcusable. The contrast of their status from other young people in America has gone unnoticed, or was ignored for too many years.

However, since the early 1980's, attention has been given to all other children in our country who were impoverished. As a result, the social consciousness of many groups has led to extensive research on poor children. One such effort included a 1991 project from the "Children's Defense Fund," based in Washington, D.C., citing that over one-fifth of American children were living in poverty. This is approximately a twenty-five percent increase over the decade of the 70's. Dr. Marion Wright Edelman, President of the Children's Defense Fund, further explains that extraordinary high levels of child poverty have become pervasive in our nation, and more concentrated in rural America. With the greatest percentage of the United States population centered in urban metropolitan areas, one would assume that they have the highest rates of children living in poverty. However, research compiled from published and unpublished resources indicate that in 1989, the forty counties with the highest rates in our nation were all rural.

Even though the past decade has shown a phenomenal national increase, the trend in Appalachia has been consistently high for many generations. An extensive and immeasurable amount of poor in the highlands is a major reason why Kentucky ranks as one of the top four "poverty" states in our country. To go a step further, research by the U.S. Census Bureau in 1990 not only cited that the percentage of eastern Kentucky children living in poverty increased from 1980 to 1990, but it also showed the following counties having an even more shocking rate, which need immediate attention. For example in Owsley County, which tops the list, child poverty increased from 58.2 percent in 1980 to 63.8 by 1990. Knott County showed a rate of 42.4 percent for 1980 and moved up to 46.4 in 1990. For Harlan County the 1980 figure changed from 31.7 percent to 40.3 by 1990.

There are two factors relating to children of impoverishment that have been researched, discussed and must be considered if conditions are to improve for the rural needy. First, problems experienced by poor children today are much more extensive and complex than years ago. The second reflects disparity in distribution of services and funds by government to urban settings as compared to rural areas. Each group, whether rural or urban, warrants equal attention, because poverty in Appalachia and the rest of our country is not insurmountable and can be overcome. However, contradictions of federal inaction toward societal conditions warrant that prevention, intervention, treatment services, and support for the child of poverty have never been in greater need. Failing to take necessary action in overcoming the deprivating conditions of poor children have reached a point of no return, and it is very important that they receive timely care to avoid horrible consequences. We are concerned with the future that affects not only the young, but also the rest of Appalachia's society. Inaction toward providing health care, education, and other social or family strengthening services can be considered passive abuse, and it is demoralizing for parents to see their children's quality of life not improving, let alone realizing that they become a greater burden on society in adulthood.

In the past, when our country experienced recovery, the middle class family was generally affected, and socioeconomic changes were beneficial to them. This has not been the case in Appalachia, where poverty continued to grow, which led to greater problems and frustration for needy families with children, who were ignored. It should be noted that the largest number of eastern Kentucky's poor children live in a two-parent family, which is not the case in most of our nation. Further worsening this situation, the pregnancy rate of Appalachia still ranks among the highest in America. Also, families of this region are larger than the national average, and the younger a mother the more likely her child will grow up poor. A full-time minimum wage job is often not enough to lift a family above the poverty level. Appalachia's poor children receive little health care compared to others, and high quality care is less accessible to children of unemployed or low income parents.

According to the 1993 Census Bureau annual poverty report, 39.3 million Americans lived in poverty, of which 40 percent were children. During that year, seventy-five percent of the working population in some eastern Kentucky areas were earning less than the poverty line, which amounted to 14,763 dollars for a family of four. In communities where the only income was federal assistance, the average totaled half that figure. As a result, hunger has been a constant presence for too many Appalachian children and must be eradicated. A study by the Tufts University Center on Hunger, Poverty and Nutrition Policy cited that in the whole nation from 1985 to 1992 there had been a fifteen percent increase in the hungry, which totaled thirty-million people. In certain eastern Kentucky communities, three out of four families qualified for food stamps, of which more than half went to children. Federal government's statistics showed that a record 26.6 million Americans were on this anti-hunger program. The U.S. Department of Agriculture reported on March 2, 1993, one out of ten Americans received food stamps, which was 38 percent higher than the three previous years.

According to a study by the Food Research and Action Center (FRAC), nationally one child in eight is hungry on a regular basis. These children become vulnerable to missing school more often, being frequently late, and performing worse than those who are poor but not hungry. U.S. government congressional figures also show that more than twenty million Americans, including children, depend on soup kitchens or food banks. Traditionally, individual caregivers of Appalachia have been the one saving grace for many poor who are hungry, and struggle to maintain their sense of dignity. The role of these individuals, groups, churches, and organizations, providing kitchens to feed parents and children with donated food or money, have for many years been the biggest benefactors for the needy, who live in a dehumanizing grip of poverty. Without these contributions, the magnitude of this problem and all its ramifications would increase much more.

One reason why there are still some Appalachians struggling today is illustrated in the following story, about a young family with three children. Paula, (not her real name) a 23 year-old wife who married at fifteen, expected her first child when she just turned sixteen. Her husband Lloyd, age 27, had to leave home and look for employment in other parts of the country. Previously, he worked in the mines part-time, then was let go, and after his unemployment benefits ran out decided to look for a job in the big cities. I met Paula at one of the mission kitchens in eastern Kentucky, and she did not know where her husband was, only that he worked part-time "here and there," unable to get a full-time job. Lloyd like some other young adults, was in a predicament of not qualifying for certain employment situations because of his illiteracy. Paula said, "I do not get mail from him, since he doesn't know how to write very well, and I can't leave Appalachia to join him because we have no money to move. Occasionally, he sends a few dollars home, but does not make enough money to rent a room, so he sleeps in his car that he took with him." Paula's income was a meager monthly welfare check and food stamps that were not enough to feed her and the children.

The saving grace for a person such as Paula is that she and her husband have close family ties, and their parents give whatever they can. Paula and her children could not afford leisure activities. In fact, they had never been to the local hamburger joint or fast food chain to enjoy "that kind of food". Their home was a shanty with an outdoor privy and no running water. A well was the only source of water, and its contents needed to be boiled before use. Whatever food her in-laws and parents contributed helped feed the children. Paula's oldest child missed school more often than not, because "he always has a cold," and her two-year old daughter was constantly bothered by ear and throat problems. The other son had severe coughs that sometimes were uncontrollable, "ending with deep, wheezing sounds." I asked Paula if the children had been to visit a doctor or health clinic recently, and her response was that she didn't remember "because it was so long ago." Paula's concerns were basic, as she talked about her children "having three good meals a day." She felt that this not only boosted their morale and attitude, but hers as well. They definitely were not healthy looking and appeared to be underweight, but the tragedy is that Paula's sons and daughter represent many poor and hungry Appalachian children, who often suffer from malnutrition, leaving them at risk for numerous health problems.

Needed Health Care For Children Of Poverty

Although some improvements in the health care system of Appalachia have been made in past decades, there is still great concern for poor children. This stems from the fact that they are not immunized early enough and will likely suffer complications leading to disease. Children who don't receive the necessary vaccine such as MMR will not be protected against measles, mumps, and rubella, and if their parents fail to take the initiative, or community health programs are not available, children are at great risk. Timing becomes very important, and immunization must take place early; generally the first of two MMR shots is given at fifteen months and the second later in childhood. However, there are poor children who do not get protection until they go to school, when immunization is an entry requirement. This leaves a period of years for susceptibility to serious infection. In addition, when the young are unprotected by MMR vaccine, they place expectant mothers at an increased risk for rubella. In turn, the unborn baby of a pregnant woman can end up having serious health problems if the mother never had the disease or was not immunized.

When children lack the necessary health care, they can also become exposed to whooping cough, called pertussis. On December 17, 1993, the Center for Disease Control and Prevention from Atlanta noted an increase of whooping cough throughout the country. Teenagers and adults were coming down with this highly contagious infection of the respiratory tract, and could have been easily passed on to a susceptible infant in their family. If young children become infected, they are particularly at risk for serious complications, such as pneumonia, seizures, inflammation of the brain, or it could lead to death. One can never tell the potential for a resurgence of childhood diseases like polio if immunization is neglected. Research has shown that poverty is linked to low immunization rates, poor nutrition, and high infant mortality.

When large numbers of children are in poor health, we all pay the price; not only in terms of more diseases in the community and increased health care cost, but also in lost educational opportunities and ultimately decreased productivity. We do know, and research has told us that sick children don't learn well in school, resulting years later in absenteeism and poor performance in the work place. One should also remember that children die sometimes of illness, disease or injuries, without justification of cause. High infant mortality is inexcusable. All families, regardless of income, should have medical care so that their children can live productive and healthy lives. Effective and preventive measures can make life easier and safer. Parents and children have to be educated, and government needs to invest more in health care for all. If we are to adhere working with the poor Appalachian child, then their family must be provided with opportunities and services that can help to lift them out of poverty.

The Coal Miner — A Changing Role

During the 1980's and early 90's, the coal miner's role changed in basic and fundamental ways. For years mining was the major industry in eastern Kentucky, and generations of the male population depended on it. Today, many jobs have yielded to mechanization, which has forced the layoff of coal miners as corporations showed greater profits. In May 1992, the U.S. Bureau of Labor Statistics released a report indicating that the coal mining industry employed 146,800 workers in 1990. This was a drop from the highest total of 650,000 fifty years earlier. At present there are approximately 35 thousand eastern Kentuckians employed in mining. Appalachians, whether working underground or in strip mining, find themselves in three types of job situations: full-time, part-time, or on a contract basis. Miners on contract usually work for small mining operations and in most cases do not have benefits, such as health insurance.

Strip mining during the 1980's and 90's has shown a great increase in coal production. Even though underground workers have changed over to strip mining, fewer jobs are available, because heavy equipment is doing the work of many men. Overall, the ranks of coal miners are disappearing and have not been replaced. Salaries appear to be better where the United Mine Workers Union exists, however, most eastern Kentucky coal miners are non-union. Today, the U.M.W.U. is less relevant to this region and virtually non-existent, except in pockets of some counties, while years ago, it was established for improvement of working conditions and fair wages. For many Appalachian miners the Union has served its purpose and coal companies that employ non-union laborers have circumvented ways to overcome employment costs through layoffs, lower salaries, cutting benefits, employing part-time or contract workers, and eliminating health insurance. The 80's and early 90's saw value of the worker decrease, yet coal mining still remains the main industry and shows growth.

Continued frustration of the obstacles that plagued miners for many years, along with loss of jobs, now forces each man to look at the uncertainty of his future. Except for coal mining and timber harvesting industries, most jobs in Appalachia are low paying. In the past, as difficult as it was to work in mines, and financial rewards were not great, miners at least had an income to support themselves and their family. As a result their economic presence was important to the region. Through the years, there were entire communities that once depended on the coal industry for their economic lifeblood. Today, people look to government subsidy, Medicare, Medicaid, or disability pension in order to exist.

Eastern Kentucky's unemployment rate in the 1980's and early 90's was much higher than that of the State or national average, for eight of the top ten "unemployment" counties are located in Appalachia. In areas such as Mud Creek of Floyd County, up to seventy-five percent of the population able to work are unemployed, because there are no other industries. Overall, a greater percentage of people are living below poverty level in Appalachia than in any other region of our nation. Large coal corporations are still powerful, and mining profits have led to a new class of owners. Increased mining operations that are mainly small family-owned and run, have sprung up throughout the region, and provided few jobs.

The frightening reality of being a miner is that it still ranks as the most dangerous occupation. Even though the U.S. Mine Safety and Health Administration, along with other agencies are policing the safety of mining, many violations, mine explosions, cave-ins and other deadly accidents continue to plague the industry. Death and injury do not play favorites with miners' lives. For example, on January 20, 1982, seven men were killed by an explosion in a Floyd County mine. It was a family-owned mine and most men died. The blast was fatal to the owner's three brothers, his son and three relatives, and was so powerful that the force spewed parts of a coal conveyor belt and other equipment out of a tunnel, sending blackened dust all over the surrounding hills.

Days later in neighboring Pike County, two miners were killed on January 22, 1982, working in another family-run mine, when a fifteen by thirty foot slab collapsed on top of them. This incident was the fifth mining disaster in the Appalachian coal fields in less than two months, and thirty-three miners died during that period. Nationally, over the years, a total of approximately one hundred fifty thousand miners died working in the coal industry, and one million five hundred thousand were injured. Regardless of increased safety measures and devices, explosions still occur. They happen through different circumstances, but emission of methane appears to be a major cause. This odorless, colorless flammable gas is found in coal beds and is normally prevented from reaching explosive levels by regulating forced ventilation. Although mine explosions don't occur that often, the magnitude of their effect can result in numerous deaths and injuries.

Efforts to Overcome Damage

Even though laws have been passed to provide better mining conditions, coal companies found ways to circumvent and manipulate the federal government's good intentions. The Coal Mine Health and Safety Act of 1969, spearheaded by Congressman Carl Dewey Perkins of eastern Kentucky, along with the Surface Mining Control and Reclamation Act of 1977, were developed to cover health, safety, and overall damaging results of the mining industry. Kentucky's State Government, in cooperation with the federal enforcement agencies, has given attention to curb illegal actions of wildcat strip-mining operators. "Wildcatters" flouted the law by removing coal without permits and avoiding restoring the land to its original use. Federal law calls for reclamation of the land after stripping top soil and coal, however this was ignored by wildcatters, who left parts of Appalachia environmentally devastated.

People's hands were tied in fighting the various coal interests that destroyed environment and land. This injustice came about by a 1956 Kentucky Supreme Court ruling, conveying that owners of mineral rights had approval to strip mine, regardless of consequences. Community activists of the 60's and 70's battled against scarring and destruction of their land and experienced individual victories, but the war was never won. However, their pride and fighting spirit did not cease and they have continued to take action against mineral rights companies.

The 1956 court case *Buchanan versus Watson*, served as the basis for a number of subsequent legal actions to overturn this landmark decision by eastern Kentucky activists. People suffered for many years from results of the Buchanan strip mining ruling that has favored coal companies. However, in 1987, through the persistence of well organized activists, landowners won a small battle. The Kentucky Supreme Court ruled that property owners had to be compensated for surface destruction, but the principle of the Buchanan decision stayed, which led to further advocate group activity throughout the state. In 1988, Kentucky voters approved a constitutional amendment that protected land owners against strip mining destruction. People who had owned property in the late 1800's and early 1900's signing away mineral rights, could not foresee that devastation would be the result of strip mining, which was unknown at that time. These people who signed their names on broad-form deeds with an X, would not have done so if they had known that their land would be left useless. The 1988 amendment emphasized: when landowners consented to strip mining, coal should have only been removed by methods that existed at the time of signing the broad-form deed. Landowners finally gained leverage to control usage of their property. However, battles were not over, because coal companies did not stand by to lose all the revenue they would gain.

The damage done over many years left much of the landscape with vast piles of stripped surface materials. Since the beginning of strip mining, surface damage of some areas was never restored, and procedures for careful reclamation were ignored by certain companies. Waste products that were not spread out properly and landscaped, produced sulfur dioxide, which escaped into the atmosphere and created acid rain. The mining companies' excuse was that methods for effective reclamation of stripped land were too expensive and would increase the cost of coal, as well as energy obtained from it. However, they were cognizant that strip mining was more damaging but cheaper. Thus, coal became an advantage to users as a source of heat and industrial manufacturers knew it. It should be noted that this industry's major consumers are electric power companies, and today, more than fifty percent of electricity in the U.S. is produced in coal-burning plants.

Opponents to the 1988 State Constitutional Amendment continued to claim that mineral rights owners were being prevented from doing business. Their argument was that strip mining is the most economically feasible way to mine. Defending the amendment before the Supreme Court was Attorney General Chris Gorman, who debated that the deeds could not convey a right to something unknown at that time. He further pointed out that the land owners had not intended to bargain away the surface. On July 15, 1993, a Kentucky State Supreme Court ruling banned unwanted strip mining, thus reversing a long history of decisions that favored coal companies. An activist group, "Members of Kentuckians for the Commonwealth," led the 1988 campaign for amendment ratification and was elated, but sad that this decision came thirty-seven years too late.

Leading to the State Supreme Court's decision was an outcome of a case in Johnson County, where coal mining mineral rights owners challenged the 1988 amendment. Some opponents see this decision as precursor to having the United State's Supreme Court review this ruling. Results of the statewide work of community activists finally brought positive change to the people of Appalachia. Thirty years ago, no one would have imagined that this was possible, yet the State of Kentucky responded to people's wishes and their advocate leaders. In turn, the power of coal companies had been diluted by cooperative community action and a point was made that if State Government is unable to use its regulatory sword, it should take a page from the advocate's book to approach a battle the best possible legal way.

Such an incident occurred where a coal company's plan to mine under Lilly Cornett Woods, one of eastern Kentucky's last tract of forest, was blocked by action from the Commonwealth. This 550-acre forest, owned by the State and located in Letcher County, is administered through the University of Kentucky. The Commonwealth's intention was that this land should never be used for mining, but the coal company that owns mineral rights is opposing such action. With assistance of environmentalists, the University, which uses this land as a living laboratory, expressed strong concern that underground mining could create potential environmental devastation. Circumstances of certain conditions, such as acidic contamination of water-sheds, refuse fires, and instability of slopes, could give way to a different physical structure not only in regard to the land, but also to those trees that are standing for centuries. The need to

165

preserve state-owned Lilly Cornett Woods and a privately owned 2,000 acre tract of Harlan County land is unquestionable, since this is all that remains of a forest that originally covered over seven million acres of eastern Kentucky.

It cannot be stressed enough that prevailing conditions of this region are the result of an industry which has controlled natural resources carelessly to the detriment of land and people. Inequalities that characterized the past of Appalachia are too obvious to today's populace. Those few responsible for Appalachia's economic affairs were callous and oblivious in their actions. As the past has shown, these people and their corporations controlled economic life along with varied political and social institutions of society. No longer are these conditions acceptable to the people of Appalachia or the State of Kentucky. Today, leadership in eastern Kentucky and the State are in the hands of a new generation of people, who are knowledgeable, concerned and care about what happens to its citizens and their future.

A Family Fights Back

With a ban on unwanted strip mining, the battle of Appalachian mineral rights is not over. Many people are reaching out to solve problems and rebuild their areas. One example is the Wright clan of Letcher County. Dan and Juanita Wright, seven children and their families all live on the same property that was ravaged by strip mining. Mr. Wright is a coal worker, who in his spare time farms a little piece of land that was not utilized for mining. Dan and Juanita, like many landowners, had been battling not only the coal corporations, but also a natural gas company, which owned mineral rights to neighboring land, and simply went ahead crossing over the Wright's property to start drilling. Mr. and Mrs. Wright and their family were concerned that it would create many problems and disruption, along with ruining a dirt gravel road they had built. This steep, winding road was the only access to the Wright families' homes.

The uniqueness of this story is the role that Appalachian women played. Outsiders have a misconception that they have been passive, but nothing can be further from the truth. Through determination and drive, fifteen Wright family women defended the property by blocking their private road, preventing a huge twenty-wheel truck that carried a bulldozer from reaching drilling sites on the other piece of land. Spirit and desire of the Wright clan not to be "bamboozled" by a natural gas company, forced legal action against Dan and Juanita. However, people throughout Appalachia heard of the Wright family's plight, and a strong citizens' group joined in a legal battle to force the company to pull back.

The Battles Continue

Kentucky's ban on strip mining had given impetus to arguments for restrictions on oil and gas drilling, and the advocate group "Members of Kentuckians for the Commonwealth" led the fight against such mineral rights interests. Their major emphasis was for the state legislature to pass a law, which required input from land owners before oil or gas drilling began. Surface owners were concerned, if drilling occurred on their land, contamination could take place and protection of ground water would be necessary. The people also wanted to have a say where drillings should take place on their property. Arguing to the contrary, mineral rights owners claimed that oil and gas drilling would not create the same devastating results as coal mining. They felt that mining disrupted the land more than oil and gas drilling, and therefore should not be judged in the same light.

There are many questions confronting Appalachia about mineral rights and implications relating to the land and people. In retrospect, it is easy to analyze the cause of continued problems that people face today, and the broad-form deed is a constant reminder. With this inequitable piece of paper, the greatest moral disservice to people of Appalachia was created. The deed, developed before the turn of the century, has been a basis for frustration, disappointment and anger. Many important issues have been skewed relating to what it represents — a justification to take advantage of mineral rights. Therefore, it is the distortion of this fundamental issue of justice that most radically affects Appalachian people.

With positive leadership and group efforts in eastern Kentucky, results are beginning to show a balanced sense of justice in every part of the community. This declaration however, does not guarantee that the forces representing Appalachians against mineral rights owners have been successful. For this is just an early stage and does not show the total picture of how coal, oil, gas and other natural resources play a part in the future of Appalachia, whether economically or environmentally. One must also question what effect the decisions will have on the people. Who will sacrifice or benefit, how and why?

In regard to the coal industry's future, which has been the main source of eastern Kentucky's economy for decades, questions about longevity and direction seem to emerge. Opinions and research have presented two viewpoints. Some say reserves of coal have scarcely been touched and estimate that perhaps as much as seventy billion tons still remain in the ground. On the other end of this spectrum, critics are projecting "easy money mining" will be exhausted in the not too distant future. The question is, will the coal industry continue its way of desecrating land, leaving people desperately poor and exploited, or cooperate through reclamation?

167

Appalachia is a region of Kentucky with many excellent natural resources. People should look at oil, natural gas and other geological treasures with greater conviction and a stronger direction, so that ways of the past will "desist." The State of Kentucky and its people have to come to grips with these problems and must face them. Hardly any corporation has resisted the temptation to gain financially from mining, without putting back necessary reformation by bringing the land and consequently people "back to life." Even now, mineral rights owners and their corporations are moving to expedite legal action in overthrowing the 1988 State Constitutional Amendment which benefits Appalachian people, as well as all Kentuckians.

Justice has been rearing its head in forcing the State to effectively assist land owners and other citizens of Appalachia in many ways. The feeling is that there has to be a bringing together of all forces from this region and state, to get involved with problems at hand. Furthermore, it is important to combine all natural resource interests in working cooperatively with the people and State government. Decisions will have to be made that inevitably make the best and most efficient use of natural resources. To arrive at solutions is of great importance and must come about with intelligence, understanding, respect, and environmentally sound results. If successful, the land will yield to wishes of the people. This is a formidable task of providing Appalachians of tomorrow with a more comfortable life than their forefathers. They were unable to achieve this, due to their lack of knowledge in foreseeing the destruction and havoc that generations thereafter had to live with. Positive action must prevail if Appalachia wants to change in order to secure a better future.

Farming — Continuing Decline

Through the years, government policy toward small farmers has kept them economically in the red. Measures were introduced that have slowly led to elimination of family farms in the region. Many of those who remain are daily raising the question of how to survive, and there is realization that agriculture in Appalachia has lost its clout over the years. On top of this, members of congress have criticized an overstaffed bureaucracy of the U.S. Department of Agriculture. If a major trimming of this government agency occurs, the need to guide Appalachian farmers should not be lost in the shuffle. In the early 90's, the Department of Agriculture was criticized by Washington politicians and media, regarding size and numbers of subsidies. Its role was questioned concerning responsibility and accountability within the organization. Appalachia's farmers worry, because the impact of losing assistance from the government would lead to extinction of most family farms.

The U.S.D.A. Agricultural Stabilization and Conservation service office for Bell and Harlan County has expressed great concern. They felt, if farms and service offices go by the wayside, this region will have many land conservation problems. There is also a need to avoid erosion, otherwise lack of soil-saving measures will lead to outcomes that reminds one of the destruction left by strip mining. The implication of eagerness by some Washington politicians to trim the Department of Agriculture goes beyond the cutting of certain services and subsistence. In counties such as Bell, there are flood plains that have to be preserved, for if they dissipate and wash away, farming land of Appalachia will be useless. Consequences would be alarming if soil is allowed to run off into creeks, tributaries, the Mississippi River and finally washing into the Gulf of Mexico.

Even though the U.S. Department of Agriculture performs important functions for this region, there are signs that indicate lack of communication and understanding relating to Appalachian farming needs. For example, Washington's record keeping of farmers who operate in Bell County was four times higher than the local ASC service count, which resulted in the Senate Agriculture Committee placing the Bell-Harlan Counties' unit on the "hit list" to reduce field offices. Government merits praise for cutting budgets and needless expenses, but all too often regions such as Appalachia are overlooked by decisions that would be important to the people and their land. The urgency to preserve and improve their existence has constantly been ignored.

Federal government has to understand that techniques for good farming, continual planting, and advice about insects and pesticides are necessary for a farm to function daily and effectively. Even large farms such as the Henderson Settlement, 1,300 acres of cultivated land run by the United Methodist Church, which provides low-cost food to people of Pineville, would flounder if government ignores the necessary process to avoid wasteful deterioration of vegetation. Through the years, floods often left deposits of soil elsewhere with significant deterioration to farming land. Today farming requires concerned management and government assistance to be productive.

Forcing unwanted conditions on Appalachian agriculture placed the farmers in an untenable position of practicing subsistence farming for years. They raised crops and tended to animals just enough to satisfy their own needs, and if successful, provided food for other people throughout Kentucky. When their forefathers came to the hills of this region, small family farms were the accepted norm. Over the decades, farms disappeared through various circumstances and those that remained did not grow or diversify. Today, farmers fear that lack of government concern and land buyouts by large corporations might lead to closing the door on small eastern Kentucky farms. Of all people living on farmsteads in Appalachia, the majority earns money by doing something other than farming. According to the U.S.D.A. Agricultural Stabilization and Conservation Services office in Pineville, there are approximately 538 full-time farmers in Bell County, which has a population of 35,000 people. Although this is a relatively low figure, most Appalachian counties have a much smaller ratio of farmers per population.

Demands on a diminishing agriculture workforce to produce more food has been a bane of existence for the Appalachian farmer, and many remaining small operations are finding this to be a difficult task. Helping to fuel this demise is the government's agriculture policy, which appears to be out of date. For years, mid-sized farm families had to abandon their land because of certain federal action that benefited the larger owners. Osha Gray Davidson, nationally recognized author of "Broken Heartland: The Rise of American Rural Ghetto" explains that federal policy, in spite of trying to help save the family farmer, funneled seventy-three cents of every program dollar into 15 percent of the nation's super farms. While writing this book, I have alluded to the plight of small farmers and how federal government has ignored their existence as an institution of our country. There are many reasons given by others before me, as to the direction of our government regarding agriculture since the Great Depression. My concern is, why has there been a pattern of indifferent attitude and action by so many administrations, which led to a disservice of an occupation that our country cannot afford to do without? Perhaps, the answers may be found in positions of authority.

Farming is an extraordinary pursuit not only in Appalachia, but all over the world, and makes it possible for people to exist. The soil upon which farmers toil is a remarkable gift that grows food to nourish our bodies, therefore top priority should be given to farming, since it is the foundation for our existence. As caretakers of this precious earth, farmers produce what today's and tomorrow's society needs, and their role should not be ignored. Instead, bureaucracy of our federal government has closed the door on small farms. From the beginning, mountaineers tilled the soil regardless of how meager their income, however they were economically independent. Today, as a farmer works his land, he feels like being in solitary confinement, facing each day with an unknown future, because of the many constraints that are placed on agriculture.

Health and Health Care

One of the most talked about social problems since the 1980's, which has gained public attention and support, is the need for a strong and healthy America. Providing a health care program for all people is without a doubt one of the most important issues of our time. Polls taken over the past ten years overwhelmingly favor reform, and national health care has become the top priority of today's federal government. This is understandable, because close to forty million Americans are without health insurance, and approximately fifty million have piecemeal coverage. "Families USA Today" reported on September 16, 1993, that 2.2 million Americans are losing their health insurance each month. This is a contradiction, for our nation is considered the leader in medicine, which includes: care, facilities, research, technology, procedures and training. Yet, there is great disparity between those people in our country who can afford high quality care and those that are poor and need health care benefits.

Over the years, health status of most Americans has shown a steady improvement, however the poor of Appalachia have not benefited, and many critics consider this situation unacceptable. One of the basic weaknesses is that health care has been rationed irrationally, or withheld from the needy. Debate over health care has become more heated, and even Congress has not provided the necessary leadership for solving this issue. Doctors, hospitals, insurers, and employers usually don't agree on many issues, however, there is a strong consensus that piecemeal health coverage is absurd, costs are out of control, and the current system is unworkable and inequitable. As workers lose their jobs to the present economic situation, they are also confronted with the reality of not having health insurance. For many unemployed people, this is the first time they are hostage to medical bills. Change in premiums of health insurance is shifting from employer to employee, as they feel the dent in their pockets through larger deductions. Many look at this as a pay cut, and rightfully so, because it shows in their take-home paycheck.

Appalachians without insurance coverage, the working poor who cannot afford health care, and others prejudiced against by insurance requirements because of pre-existing health conditions, are left out in the cold. With more part-time work in the mines, timber industry, farms, and lower paying service jobs, there are now greater numbers of Appalachians who encounter poverty at one time or another, with the result that they cannot afford health insurance. People may climb out of poverty, but are also confronted by the risk of returning to it, and face uncertainties in maintaining an income level or have to go back on some form of government assistance.

Public welfare has been constant in Appalachia and for many, poverty is a vicious cycle. Unfortunately, not everyone in America understands the problems of poor people. There are financially secure individuals who view impoverished human beings that receive welfare as "pariahs," burdening society. How can people look at it in this way and feel that welfare benefits are often too generous, when there are families with meager monthly incomes who cannot afford health care, let alone qualify for any type of program? It should be every citizen's right to have at least basic health services. If access to basic health care is not available, problems will be much greater in the future, not only for unfortunate individuals, but our society as a whole. However, by waiting much longer to rectify this problem, it will be too late for some of our citizens, because they need help now. Unfortunately, this includes the elderly, who are paying proportionately as much money for health expenses as they were prior to being eligible for Medicare.

In the final analysis, our health care system is in critical condition and will continue to deteriorate uncontrollably, unless government takes positive action. The 1980 average health care cost for a family of four was 2,600 dollars, and surpassed 8,000 in 1993. Analysts project that by the year 2000 the cost for this size family will be at least 14,000 dollars. The change in health insurance premiums, with larger deductions from employee wages, is making it harder for many Americans to survive. In rural Appalachia, people are in poorer health than their urban neighbors, and have a difficult time finding health care and paying for it.

Appalachia's Continuing Health Problems

It has been said that there are too many people in the U.S. who cannot get appropriate health care, even though we are living in the most modernized country in this world. If that is the case, then immediate attention must be given to the continued weakened health status of Appalachia's inhabitants, for they are the hardest hit in America and generally do not have options for health care, which exacerbates their problems. The rural poverty rate of eastern Kentucky has been higher than the national level ever since our government started gathering data many years ago. According to the U.S. Department of Health, thousands of Americans die daily of maladies that could have been prevented through up-to-date or effective treatment. Getting immediate medical attention is crucial, but even if a person in Appalachia can get some form of care, services generally are limited.

A 1991 report from the Center on Budget and Policy Priorities, a Washington, D.C. based research organization, cited that fewer health care services are available in rural regions of America, compounding the problem of finding affordable medical care in thinly populated areas. The report further pointed out that nationally at least 111 rural areas had no doctor. The unequal distribution of physicians in our nation is evident, because there are only 97 practicing doctors per 100,000 people in rural America, while 225 are available for the same number in urban settings.

This report further indicates that the difference between rural and urban health conditions in our society is more visible than ever. Rural insurance coverage for people under 65 years of age is more costly than in urban areas. Compounding this problem is that a greater percentage of rural businesses do not provide health insurance to employees. In Appalachia, many of these businesses are small operations, and with rising costs associated in providing health insurance to their employees, expenses have increased around 20 percent annually since the late 80's. This has hit small businesses hard, as they face higher costs and lower profit margins than larger corporations. The result is that the working poor find themselves unable to pay for health care services. Among the younger or middle-aged poor in the U.S., there is a greater portion of rural population that lack health coverage.

Another report, released in 1993 by the U.S. Department of Health and Human Services, shows that the cost of running welfare programs such as Medicaid, is rising twice as fast as there are people enrolled, and the federal government's share of benefit payments have increased immensely. An interesting fact is that high administrative costs and bureaucracy have created a need to streamline not only Medicaid, but the total welfare system. Another concern is that rural poor were not getting as much Medicaid compared to the urban population. Since a greater amount of poverty-stricken people lived in rural settings, it is a paradox that the urban poor were benefiting more from Medicaid. I realize that this is no utopia, but the way some people in our nation had to exist is uncalled for. When states do not function equally under a democratic structure, one begins to question the motives of politicians. Another example of inequality is that rural states tend to have more restrictive Medicaid eligibility, and their programs offer fewer health care services.

Health care has bypassed too many people, and the need should no longer be ignored. Our government must look at areas such as Appalachia, before establishing a national health program, otherwise people will be trapped in the same continuing cycle. If government fails to distribute health care opportunities for its citizens to live a healthier life, then certain people of Appalachia and other parts of our country will continue to live in poverty's grip. Although medicine in the United States is the most advanced, for poor Appalachians progress of medical breakthrough has little meaning. Their major concern in life is basic medical care, which other Americans may take for granted.

Need For Doctors

The supply of physicians in Appalachia has grown at such a slow pace, even the national average of only 97 rural doctors per 100,000 people is higher than in eastern Kentucky. In Knott County, which epitomizes this crisis, there are four physicians for a population of approximately 18,000, and it does not take a mathematical genius to figure out that there is a critical shortage of doctors in this region. Many are not only working in their own counties, but also provide services in nearby communities. For the poor people who live in remote areas of Appalachia, getting to a doctor is a monumental task. On top of this, health clinics, doctors and staff are so overloaded with work that a patient may have to wait three to four hours before being treated. Access to care is a problem, but some critics say that quality of care is even a bigger issue. However, community health centers have a positive record by providing the best possible level of quality care for those who are medically indigent, insurance poor, or have no money to pay customary fees that are required by the private sector. There are some doctors in Appalachia who only work with those patients that can afford to pay or have insurance. However, most physicians are committed to providing decent medical care for the poor, regardless of having a private practice or working with a non-profit health clinic or hospital.

At present, it is difficult to entice physicians and other medical personnel to this region, where the shortage is much greater than the national rural rate. Physicians in eastern Kentucky work longer hours than the national average and their salaries are considered amongst the lowest in our country. Commitment and dedication of working with the poor have less financial rewards. Doctors provide more charity work in Appalachia than in other areas of our country. Although these practitioners provide care for the poor at reduced fees or no charge, volunteer efforts, as admirable as they are, have not been able to reach all needy, who are isolated by poverty and the mountains. For many doctors, basic care for all Appalachians is the major concern, and if a person receives immediate attention, it alleviates more serious problems down the road.

Health Clinics

A plethora of studies justified a decision by our government in the 1960's to authorize funding of community health clinics throughout the nation. Today, these non-profit centers provide comprehensive preventive care, as well as basic services in family practice, pediatrics, internal medicine, obstetrics, gynecology, and family dentistry, along with giving help to other health needs of the poor. In Appalachia, these are the only facilities in many communities that have complete physician continuity of care. Health clinics also provide transportation to a hospital for the indigent, as well as other patients who need this level of medical attention. Their specialty in bringing medicine to the needy of Appalachia exemplifies one of many good deeds, which emanated from the "War on Poverty Program."

Health clinics in Appalachia did not travel a smooth road. They encountered obstacles, mainly by the Administration and bureaucratic federal government structure of the 1980's and early 90's. Even though these clinics reduced infant mortality, low birthweight, rheumatic fever and middle ear infections, improved prenatal care and increased immunization of children, government funding was cut back. The lack of foresight and caring for the poor, including vocal opposition by certain lawmakers, made it a difficult task to provide the desperately needed non-medical services for those "hard-to-reach" families. Education, counseling, outreach and support programs are also necessary to combat health problems, which are prevalent throughout Appalachia's rural areas.

Some people fail to realize that a good system of primary care, which provides a preventive program, has a better chance of decreasing the many ills of poor people. However, long range implications of not offering preventive medicine lead to greater expenses as illness strikes. There is a need to restructure the thinking of decision makers to realize that costly health care, as it is today, rewards a payment system which promotes high-technology care rather than a strong preventive approach. Health clinics are an ideal segment of the medical community that can improve access to cost-effective care. Since introduction of these clinics in Appalachia, their achievements have more than fulfilled the purpose to upgrade the health of communities. Doctors, dentists, along with other professionals and helpers, have worked extremely hard to improve the health status of poor fellow citizens. Individuals and groups that started and directed these organizations, whether medical professionals or lay people, have made a tremendous impact which cannot be ignored. Their influence is mainly due to drive in getting things done, and passionate faith for the causes they serve. To be succinct: health conditions of Appalachians would be devastating if it were not for these people.

Eula Hall
The Miracle Of Mud Creek

One such determined person is Mrs. Eula Hall, who overcame

many obstacles herself and sacrificed to help the poor people of Appalachia. Eula Hall founded the Mud Creek Health Clinic, which is named after a winding stream that snakes through the Grethel area. She is an example of what an individual with perpetual drive, love, and concern can do to help the less fortunate. For over twenty-years, Eula Hall, with the assistance of only a few doctors, nurses, staff and volunteers provided medical, emotional and social help, going beyond the realm that one might expect from a health clinic in more influential parts of our country.

The clinic has worked miracles for people in this area of constant poverty. Nearly seventy-five percent of the 17,000 people of the Mud Creek area are living below the poverty level. Eula Hall is responsible for the success of bringing help to this area's needy through her compassion, and is the reason why many of these poor people are alive. Mrs. Hall is not an M.D., nor does she have a nursing degree or high school diploma, but what this wondrous woman has, is unbelievable honesty and a kind heart to lead people out of the doldrums of poverty and despair. Like other Appalachian leaders, Eula Hall found what she was looking for in life not far from where she grew up. In retrospect, her background leaves one with amazement and admiration for this woman.

Born into poverty at Joe Boner Holler, Pike County, near Greasy Creek, where physical, economic and social barriers of Appalachian life were evident, she experienced hard times. Eula grew up poor, and was many times embarrassed to go to school, because she did not have paper and pencil to write with. Children of poverty were treated differently in schools, creating feelings of inadequacy. Eula Hall told how she smashed a rock, trying to use pieces of it as a substitute for pencils. Poverty to her meant growing up with no books, magazines or newspapers, and very few toys. Her home may have lacked electricity, indoor plumbing and many other necessities, but she never stopped dreaming of wanting to help the needy. Growing up, Eula experienced all the unfair ills of poverty, including malnutrition, sickness, and lack of health care. Children quit school for many reasons, and Eula left with an eighth grade diploma, but is very proud to note that she accomplished this in five years.

At age fourteen, she traveled to New York State and was employed in a government canning factory. Recruiters had been sent to eastern Kentucky to find people eighteen and over to work in this industry. Their selection process was not very efficient, for Eula Hall was able to convince the recruiters that she was eighteen years of age. Eula arrived in New York with a busload full of Appalachians, who were all promised a weekly check, but worked almost a month without compensation. Originally, they also were to receive free transportation to New York. Instead, their salary was withheld to pay for transportation, room and board, which left nothing for the workers. Being cheated of their salary along with their rights, Eula and the others organized a strike against unfair labor practices. However, company management called the local police and state troopers, who then charged these young Appalachians with inciting a riot. Some of the workers over eighteen years of age ended up in jail for six months, and Eula, along with the remaining younger boys and girls, were sent back by bus to Pike County, Kentucky.

Eula Hall married at the age of seventeen, had five children at home without assistance of a doctor, and never received any prenatal care. Unfortunately, Mrs. Hall experienced personal sorrow, when one infant daughter died and a son was born deaf. Even though her own family was of most importance in her life, she never stopped being concerned about poverty, and found ways to help the hopeless and disadvantaged, realizing that someone had to look after them, or they would not survive. She always felt it was important to build confidence and self esteem and show that people care.

I first met Eula Hall in the early 1960's during the development of Volunteers In Service To America (VISTA). She was always ready to help people in need, and when some poor parents of children in a new Floyd County school were complaining that discrimination took place in the lunchroom, she got involved. The only children that had been able to buy a 25¢ lunch in the school cafeteria were those whose parents could financially afford it. Poor children did not have money for lunch and sat on the cafeteria stage, watching their classmates eat. Eula Hall and over a hundred other parents started the Eastern Kentucky Welfare Rights Organization and marched to Prestonsburg. In an all out battle with the county superintendent they won, and children from poor families got free or reduced lunches. Thus, a string of activities started to help the poor, leading Eula and EKWRO to seek justice in overcoming inequities that were occurring in public assistance and the food stamp program. Eula did not stop there, energy and drive carried her and other activists to battle the coal company operators. She encouraged people of Bull Creek to fight strip mining from coming into the area and devastate their land. The people organized and succeeded to stop operators from further damaging their properties.

Welfare groups that Eula became further involved with were concerned about a health care program in Floyd County. They did not feel that the program was dutifully serving the poor. Local politicians, along with certain medical doctors benefited financially, while the people were getting poor medical service. However, the Welfare Rights Group was successful in having this program canceled and a reorganization came about. Mrs. Hall also was very active in leading the black lung movement, creating an effective instrument for the miners. Even through her own struggles in the sixties and seventies, she actively participated with a group of activists who unselfishly strived to end poverty and powerlessness. Amid the darkest areas of Appalachia, Eula has been a continuing guiding light for her people in overcoming health and social problems.

In 1973, Eula Hall found a way in responding to the needs of other people, by starting a community clinic on Tinker Fork. As their "Social Director," she brought public attention to the necessities for health care of people in this area. Volunteers came to her beck and call, and the United Mine Workers Union contributed operating funds. As Eula's vision became reality, a trailer was used to provide health services, and she found herself in the midst of poverty-stricken people who were suffering from all kinds of illnesses. Mothers were holding listless and malnourished babies, showing love and sorrow on their faces, and Eula knew that she was confronted with a monumental task. Mrs. Hall did not stop with a health clinic, she also started to distribute food and clothing that were donated. Emergency transportation for patients to places like Lexington was also provided, so that people could have operations to ease suffering or save their lives. If a patient was unable to get transportation, Eula would drive this person in her secondhand van, which was donated by a local funeral director.

Mrs. Hall never shied away from public issues. After initiating and directing a health survey study with help from University of Kentucky students at Prestonsburg, research showed that almost all local drinking wells were contaminated and she immediately organized the Mud Creek Water District. Her worry was that polluted drinking water could lead to epidemic conditions of hepatitis, typhoid and diarrhea. As a result of Mrs. Hall's leadership and voice as Water Commissioner, her concern was heard throughout Kentucky. She is a legend in the State and has used her public recognition as health advocate leader, by drawing attention to the plight of unsanitary water and its consequences for Appalachia. The State of Kentucky responded by providing the Mud Creek Water District with a grant. Under Eula Hall's direction, over 800 families today are receiving clean water in their homes.

In 1982, the original facility in Mud Creek which served as a health clinic, burned to the ground overnight. It was completely destroyed, including over 14,000 patient records, medical equipment, and supplies. Eula was devastated, but despite finding herself in a quandary, she immediately gave a powerful illustration of personal responsibility and determination. The following morning, Mrs. Hall went into action by surveying the damage, dragged out a picnic table, placing it under a willow tree, and persuaded the telephone company after extensive arm twisting to install an outdoor phone. A retired doctor volunteered to help out, and with a makeshift pharmacy, they continued to do business. By noontime, with a picnic table, telephone, a doctor and small pharmacy supplies, the Mud Creek Clinic was functioning again. I have seen courage before, but Eula Hall is incredible; she was not going to give up and continuation of the health clinic became her most important concern. She persevered by looking for ways to rebuild, and donations from Appalachia and other areas of Kentucky were slowly trickling in.

Mrs. Hall found that in order to gain public attention, she had to go on television or radio, and let newspapers write articles about the plight of her clinic; but she did not stop there. The Appalachian Regional Commission, a federal agency working with depressed eastern Kentucky communities, promised Eula if she raised 80,000 dollars, they would supply the difference to build a new health facility. Through her commitment and creativeness, Eula received over one hundred-thousand dollars. People sent coins and dollar bills from every state of the nation, and Eula was so proud and grateful, regardless of the amount.

The new Mud Creek Clinic opened in November 1984, when the United Mine Workers Union was no longer functioning as financial backer of the clinic. The nonprofit Big Sandy Health Corporation, a federally funded provider, is now operating this facility. Everyone knows that the clinic turns no one away, and if a patient cannot afford to pay for medication, Eula will pick up the tab. With so many people living below the poverty level in this area, word has spread to Virginia and West Virginia about the Mud Creek Health Clinic, and people have traveled hundreds of miles knowing they would get help.

Mrs. Hall has fed the hungry, nursed sick people, and guided illiterate needy by serving as their speaker on many occasions, regarding legal matters, disability benefits, and oppression. She became a Water Commissioner in order to get clean water for her people, she campaigned against corrupt politicians, fought injustice and battled for miners, who were dying of the dreaded black lung disease. Eula Hall has appeared before the Office of Hearings and Appeals, arguing cases for people in need. The justice system was awed and amazed by her explicit descriptions about the ills of disabled, poor, illiterates, and explained why they should have the right to claim benefits from social security, aid for dependent children, food stamps, workman's compensation insurance, or other forms of aid. Mrs. Eula Hall, who has helped the many needy, is one of the most loved and famous people of eastern Kentucky.

Recently, Trinity University in Connecticut gave Mrs. Hall an Honorary Doctorate of Humanities. Visitors from all over America have come to see her work at Mud Creek. Writers from national magazines and the *New York Times* expound on this woman, who has lived among the poor, heard their cries, and helped them with compassion. Eula Hall's office walls at the clinic are crowded with honors, citations, testimonial acknowledgments and her honorary doctorate, which are true measures of appreciation and recognition. Unfortunately, there is no more space on the walls for any more of her accomplishments. Summing up her great deeds, one acknowledgment came from the internationally prestigious Common Cause Annual Award in Washington, D.C. Mrs. Hall and former Supreme Court Justice Thurgood Marshall were the 1992 honorees. The citation to Eula so aptly reads: "To Eula Hall, whose grit and love of people brought health care to a needy town in Appalachia."

Today, in spite of illness and advanced age, Eula Hall's childhood dream to help the poor has come to fruition with the development of her community health center. She never lost her love for giving to the people, whether poor, sick, maimed, or despaired. With the help of two dedicated doctors, a physician's assistant, four nurses, two pharmacists, a lab technician, one x-ray technician, two mental health workers, along with records and admissions personnel, Eula Hall's Mud Creek Clinic responds to the needs of over 5,000 patients a year. On the desk in her office she has a little name plate that displays the title "Social Director." This humble woman is more than the clinic's social director, even though she insists that she is a "registered nothing."

Eula still travels all over the area, continuing to give her all in a selfless manner. Her dedication to help the people goes beyond the clinic, by distributing free food, clothing, medicine and counsel to the homebound. Her four-wheel drive Chevrolet Suburban, a gift from the Kentucky Department of Human Resources, has traveled roughshod over remote mountain terrain, valleys and bottom land, and if necessary serves as the emergency unit, carrying people to either a clinic or a hospital, regardless of distance.

People who had the opportunity to work with Mrs. Hall call her a heroic figure. As one very dear friend, Dr. Ellen Joyce, stated, "To work with Eula, is like working with a saint." Eula's children and husband Oliver Hall, who is a retired miner with heart and lung ailments, are proud of her work and accomplishments. Mrs. Hall who has heart disease and arthritis, keeps on going, because she wants to live out the dream of "helping her people." Appalachians know this woman for her compassion, dedication and meaningful work in helping the needy, despite her own hardships. Their love, appreciation and admiration run deep for this exceptional person of human kindness.

Appalachian Hospitals

During the 1980's up to the present, certain economic and demographic trends had a significant effect on rural hospitals, even to the extent of some having to close down. Medical facilities, particularly those in

Appalachia, struggled to keep their heads above water. This difficulty was further fueled by dramatic changes that took place in the health care system and the lack of population growth in some eastern Kentucky areas. As with the rest of America, workers have been losing their health insurance at an alarming rate. Consequently, demand for services among the needy of Appalachia is at unprecedented levels. Since the early 1980's, financial contributions from the government were shrinking, and hospitals, along with other health services had been operating on a tighter budget. In certain situations, some medical facilities have been watching "red ink" spread throughout their ledgers. Many hospitals have concern that low reimbursement from Medicare, which pays approximately eighty percent of the cost for treating elderly patients, is one problem.

Hospitals' troubles took off in 1984, when policies from the government were revised regarding payments. Before, Medicare payments were based on a charge for each case, but since 1984, the change led to a set fee for each type of illness. In large city-urban hospitals for example, where caseloads are big enough, profits and losses on individual patients generally even out. However, in small rural medical facilities, a couple of high cost cases can lead to financial disaster. In the poor communities that eastern Kentucky hospitals serve, there are few patients with health plans to absorb those costs. Making matters more difficult, rural Appalachian hospitals received as much as forty percent less than those in a city-urban setting giving the same treatment.

There are other health system trends that occurred during this period, which affected hospitals of the highlands. Some were hurting because of shifting care from inpatient to outpatient services. Restructuring of the health care industry, with increased competition for patients and rapid advances in medical technology, left rural hospitals in further despair. Financially, many cannot afford the new equipment to run a small facility on a competitive basis, and restricted reimbursement by public and private payers has resulted in conflict, regarding cost-containment and access goals.

Despite the view of many people that hospitals have developed accepted standards and services, not all provide a uniformity of care for the patient. Rural medical facilities are diverse, and each has its own range of problems. Nevertheless, they do have some common concerns such as employment problems, trying to keep experienced personnel from migrating to city-urban areas, where salaries are much higher. Problems of wages are further compounded by the fact that Medicare pays rural less than city-urban hospitals for labor costs, and the reasoning for this is that cost of living is lower in the highlands. However, this has proliferated the problem for rural hospitals to recruit and maintain good nurses and other health professionals. Competitive salaries cannot be met by these medical facilities and income increases have been lagging considerably since the 1980's. Most hospitals depend on a base of loyal employees, who are from the region and do not want to move away from eastern Kentucky. Thus, employees find themselves in the middle of a financial and social struggle. They are torn between looking for better working situations elsewhere, or responding to pressures and problems of the general decline that plague rural hospitals.

In the 1980's, these facilities were making strenuous efforts for survival by paying large fixed costs to continue functioning, so that patients would not go elsewhere. Nevertheless, rural hospitals lost inpatient admissions during this period. Trying to maintain services, the fixed costs still existed, but reimbursement declined. These are only a few of the problems confronting Appalachian hospitals. Private insurance programs have become another concern in containing the cost of hospital care for individuals. The insurers bargain with hospitals to reduce charges in return for increased patient loads.

Without the infusion of a solid national plan and action, rural hospitals continued their downward spiral, which did not seem to concern some congressional leaders. Their argument was that increasingly more patients had been abandoning small rural hospitals for better equipped urban facilities. However, it is difficult for many who live in the backwoods of Appalachia and have transportation problems, to travel 200 miles to Lexington or Louisville for medical service. In the late 1980's, rural hospitals in America were still seeking financial aid from congress. There were critics who felt that even the help given to these facilities or doubling medical payments would not halt their decline. Since that was the case, rural area hospitals had to experiment with innovative and alternative ways to keep their doors open for the people.

During the latter 1980's, an urgent need arose that called for government to make decisions, significantly affecting the speed and direction in solving problems of Appalachia and rural America. In response to congressional request, a national conference took place in December 1987, co-sponsored by the Rural Health Association and Foundation for Health Services Research, which provided government with important information, relating to rural health policy issues and services research. It was clear that there was a need to identify, evaluate and disseminate data on successful innovative rural health care models, along with issues and problems to understand or guide intervention efforts. This period was characteristic for dramatic increases in health care delivery initiatives, which were launched at state and community levels. There was a widespread concern that government knew very little about the relative effectiveness of federal programs in rural areas, such as Appalachia. The need for physicians and other health care personnel in rural communities was also emphasized.

Recommendations resulting from that conference included analysis of differences in practice patterns between rural and urban physicians, and the effects on quality of care. Development of ongoing physician education projects to identify recommended practice patterns was also helpful to the government.

Finally, research of Medicare reimbursement that had been a point of disagreement, revealed the disparity of compensation between rural and urban medical facilities. Congressional attention was attained, and as a result, changes in permitted Medicare compensation between rural and urban hospitals are experiencing today a narrowing of the gap. There are signs that reimbursement between rural and urban services will be equal eventually. Many considerations are particularly important for Appalachian hospitals in improving their situation, and the decision of facilities that are too small an operation to sustain an adequate range of services is still a nagging problem. Lacking financial resources, it is almost impossible for these hospitals to maintain any standard of service, unless through innovative practices or alternative approaches.

From the 1980's to the present, health care priorities in Appalachia dealt with illnesses that have plagued its people for decades. There are not enough doctors, health professionals, staff and prevention programs. Research has shown that health needs are on the increase for mental as well as physical care. Above all, too many people in eastern Kentucky cannot find a way to pay for medical services. A major shift in their needs and conditions are leading them to depend more on health clinics for treatment. Many issues of health care in Appalachia have not been discussed, however they are also important. One such issue is the need for leadership in health care communities giving a sense of direction, desire to search and experiment, innovate, and build for the coming years. Advances have been evident in this region over recent years and the results are showing promise. One might say without exaggeration that leadership is the basis of health care improvement for Appalachia's future.

Grady Stumbo, M.D.
A Leader For The People

Through the years, small villages and towns in eastern Kentucky have bred a surprising number of people with leadership qualities. Among those stands tall a gentleman, whose deeds and leadership are known throughout the mountain country and beyond. Since the early 1970's, Dr. Grady Stumbo has provided a strong voice in the ongoing demands for better health care of Appalachia and Kentucky. It has been his desire to make the roles and needs of his profession known, as health care reform takes place not only in Kentucky, but throughout the country. A decision made by Grady Stumbo in the 1960's had a profound effect on people of Appalachia and the State. Growing up in McDowell, Kentucky, Grady Stumbo's ambition in life was to graduate from college, acquire his necessary professional credentials, and come back to Appalachia as a physician and leader. Dr. Stumbo has faced a number of challenges in over twenty years of service, and has never lost sight of the goal to help and serve his fellow people.

I remember in 1964, standing outside the Alice Lloyd College administration building with President Will Hayes, Ralph Lewis, Director of Publicity, and a college student, named Grady Stumbo. This young man exemplified the kind of person who would be very successful one day. In our conversation, Grady was asked what he would like to do in life, and his answer was definite and concise, with an aura of self-confidence. He wanted to get his medical degree at the University of Kentucky and come back to help the less fortunate in Appalachia. Talking with him, I had the feeling that he would make meaningful contributions, whether it be in Appalachia or elsewhere. Before attending Alice Lloyd College, Grady grew up in an area of Kentucky that had experienced a great amount of adversity, lacking economically and socially. Depressed conditions existed for generations, and young people generally had very little positive experiences from adults, who were always hardworking and goodhearted, but impoverished.

Many youth, including Grady, had strikes against them in wanting to achieve an education, and deprivation of the surroundings never left their minds. Deterioration of the Appalachian spirit and ambition made it quite difficult for young people from areas of poverty to attend college, and deal with the transition of societal differences. The hope of Alice Lloyd College, as espoused by its founder, is that each student should receive a solid foundation for their respective mission in life as leaders. Today, in an excellent promotional publication entitled "A Light Unto the Mountains — Alice Lloyd College," Dr. Grady Stumbo's words to that effect appear in writing. He wrote: "I can honestly say, my years at Alice Lloyd helped me to focus on my goals and provided me with an important springboard to achieve a career in medicine. It's a warm memory for which I'm thankful." Alice Lloyd's legacy lives on in Grady Stumbo, whose humanitarian leadership is evident in his contributions to mankind.

When Dr. Stumbo finished his medical work at the University of Kentucky, he was determined to achieve the goal of opening a non-profit health clinic in Appalachia. In 1972, not far from McDowell, Kentucky, where he was born, Grady and his longtime college friend Benny Ray Bailey, opened the Eastern Kentucky Health Clinic in Hindman. He hoped to provide health care for people in the area, so they did not have to drive long distances receiving medical services. Grady knew from the beginning that he would be caring for "the poorest of the poor". With Benny Ray Bailey as administrator of the health clinic, they started serving the needy.

When a doctor works with the poor in Appalachia, his salary is not commensurate with that of urban doctors, where the middle and upper class can afford to pay the medical profession that serves them. To be more specific, the salary of an Appalachian physician is about two-thirds of what an urban doctor earns. In Dr. Stumbo's situation, if a patient cannot pay the 5.00 dollar visit fee, care is never refused. Approximately twenty percent of his patients are unable to pay, and a doctor has to be a humanitarian in order to function in this type of environment.

Dr. Stumbo's endless work schedule and responsibilities are carried out under grueling conditions, and he is totally committed from morning until evening and sometimes beyond, which is true dedication. Since Grady knows his patients and their financial situation, his devotion to them extends beyond a general family practitioner's medical work. I remember Dr. Stumbo telling about a gentleman who had a very critical back condition that warranted a specialist to perform an operation. The patient was indigent, so Grady called the Lexington-Louisville area to ask various surgeons if they would do him a favor and operate on this gentleman free of charge. He finally found one specialist who consented to perform the life saving surgery. About six weeks after the operation, this patient came into Grady's office with tears in his eyes, kneeling before Dr. Stumbo and giving thanks for his help. He asked Grady for the name and address of the doctor who had operated on him, so that he could write and thank him for "curing his illness." Grady Stumbo told me that "This is the kind of satisfaction and appreciation that makes it worthwhile to keep on helping the less fortunate."

Dr. Stumbo is concerned about his people in many ways. Because there is such a lack of doctors in Appalachia, he and Benny Ray Bailey would like to open another non-profit clinic in a backwoods area. "The doctor shortage in eastern Kentucky is not new," states Stumbo. "I remember back in the sixties, when Dr. Denzil Barker, the only physician in these parts, had to look at a patient with limited diagnostic equipment. Since there was no specialist in the area, he would send the person on to Lexington or Louisville for further extensive examination." Today, Dr. Stumbo is worried about the need for primary care doctors in Appalachia, because nationally there are only 15 percent of medical school graduates wanting to become family doctors, pediatricians, or internal medicine physicians.

It is a fact that doctors in America accumulate large debts before graduating from medical school and starting their respective practices. Their training is the most extensive and expensive of any profession, which requires years of hard work and responsibility, but compensation is poor. Grady stated: "As an intern making seventeen thousand dollars a year, and in many instances working around the clock, monetary rewards do not start until after a doctor puts up his sign outside the office door." When physicians open their practice, they are older and in greater financial debt than other professionals. On top of this, most cannot afford to work in a rural setting like Appalachia, where income is so much less compared to urban America.

Dr. Stumbo's concerns are based on his comprehensive knowledge of the health and health care situation in Appalachia as well as the whole State. In the early 1980's, he served as Secretary of Human Resources for the State of Kentucky. He believes there should be greater emphasis on recruiting the young Appalachians for a future in medicine. "Home grown" doctors understand people of this region better, for they can identify with the culture and social problems. Dr. Stumbo points out, a physician has to understand that people in Eastern Kentucky are poor and proud. Many of them are reluctant to receive charity and instead use home remedies, which is a long-standing custom of their culture. However, if a doctor grew up among them, people accept and trust him immediately. Grady is a strong believer that a local physician can have a great impact on the poor. He should know, because he is a product of Appalachia and has experienced how grateful these people are for his help.

Dr. Grady Stumbo is a devoted physician as well as medical director at the Eastern Kentucky Health Clinic in Hindman, and Wayland. He also visits elderly patients at a nearby nursing home and afterwards goes on to work at Hazard Regional Hospital. Since the new route 80 was built, it takes Grady only about twenty minutes from Hindman to Hazard, but I remember the old winding hairpin curve road that used to take a good forty-five minutes to drive from one town to the other. Dr. Stumbo is a medical man who travels extensively throughout the area, and results of his work are showing. He is a strong advocate for preventive medicine and has worked with other health professionals in developing programs for the needy and poor of Appalachia. His aim is to set up a system that will give people of poverty early access to health care, so they don't have to wait until it is too late or expensive to get treatment. Grady was exposed to preventive medicine when he was a student at Alice Lloyd College. Like all students, Grady participated in the Outreach Program and worked with the poor and their children in Knott County, helping each to uplift themselves through good basic health habits, so that they could maintain a positive image and live healthier lives. Even today, this county is still one of the poorest in the United States, but through Grady Stumbo's continued efforts and the assistance of two other physicians, a dentist, and health professionals, the infant mortality rate is only one-third the State's average.

Dr. Stumbo also believes that a person's mental health plays an important part in improving physical well-being. Continued poverty and unemployment has a tendency to affect the mental state of a patient, and more complex conditions and ills have increased through the years. Grady, along with Benny Ray Bailey, realized that clinics are unable to handle many mental illnesses. Consequently, they became instrumental in bringing the first rural psychiatric facility of the State to the Hazard Regional Health Complex. This recently opened Psychiatric Hospital is unique. It belongs to a large rural medical park, consisting of a Regional General Hospital and facility that trains Rural Medical Interns from the University of Kentucky's Center of Excellence in Rural Health.

Grady Stumbo is on a mission to improve the health status, as well as economic and social standards for his people in Appalachia. He is a firm believer that the Kentucky Education Reform Act, if completely implemented, will have an important impact on the future of children in Kentucky, and has dedicated his life in order to make changes not only in the field of medicine, but also in education. Grady is very passionate in his conviction that change has to come about for Appalachia by a new breed of local leaders who understand the plight of poor people. He further believes what benefits Appalachia will also be positive for the whole State of Kentucky.

Intangible factors of knowledge, educational and professional background, as well as energetic spirit are part of Grady Stumbo's leadership qualities that have lifted him into the political arena. His first hand experience of growing up in one of the "backwoods areas" of Appalachia, and being educated in a deficient public school system before going on to college and medical school, provide sufficient evidence of a vigorous and dynamic person who overcame many odds to succeed. This, combined with the talent to mobilize people and resources, have helped bring attention to Grady Stumbo as a leader. Today, along with being a medical practitioner, Dr. Stumbo is chairman of the Kentucky State Democratic Party and was twice considered for governor on the primary ticket.

Dr. Grady Stumbo, wanting to help fellow citizens through constant encouragement and rectifying the inadequate conditions that deter growth as well as improvement for Appalachia, has not ceased to amaze people. Grady, along with State Senator Benny Ray Bailey and Attorney Bill Weinberg of Hindman and other community activists throughout the State, who are called the "new breed of leadership," has been responsible for change, which was previously unimaginable. They were able to win a victory in 1988 over the broad-form deed that had favored coal corporations since the turn of the 20th century. Battles that started by commu-

187

nity activists in the 1960's were continued by a younger and more astute group of politicians, professionals, business people and homemakers statewide, being led by Grady. They fought a statute which was giving coal companies the right to play havoc with people's lives, their homes and land, because the broad-form deed had been devised in such a way that mineral rights were signed over to the speculators and corporations, leading to exploitation. Also, extracting coal from mountains through strip mining that started in the 1950's, led community activists in the 1960's to bring about the environmental movement, which was carried over in subsequent years by the present leadership group.

For decades companies had been strip mining with disregard for the people and their land, providing little or no compensation. They had their own powerful means by setting up a financially exorbitant statewide sponsored media campaign to win votes of the people in Kentucky. However, grass-roots community groups were too strong in their belief, voice and organization, as 80 percent of the State's voters elected to vote for the passing of a constitutional amendment, expanding landowners' rights to protect their property. Grady Stumbo today takes pride in this victory and is happy with the outcome of issues that will benefit his people.

Changing an area that for years has been ensconced in poverty is an enormous and politically formidable task. The complexity and tenacity of economic and social ills of Appalachia are so daunting that many individuals with good intentions of reform all too often became discouraged in their efforts to help the people. Our government's responses to Appalachia's problems have usually been from two political directions. One wanted to help and the other showed lack of concern. However, when a man like Grady Stumbo comes along, changes are assured, it is obvious that his work for the people is not yet finished. Dr. Stumbo is a craftsman of unlimited enthusiasm, not only wanting to provide the best for Appalachians in health care, but also confronting economic and social problems directly. He and other new leaders have been responsible for development of the rural model regional medical park at Hazard. Though success may not be of an instant nature, since these facilities are relatively new, there is a strong indication that the magnitude of this endeavor will have a significant impact on Appalachia's communities.

There have been critics who question the role of physicians in politics. However, it is my opinion that we should have more people like Dr. Grady Stumbo, who not only play important leadership roles in their profession, but also get involved in improving the economic and social conditions of their community and country. It seems that one profession is allowed to run the nation, and maybe this is what's wrong with society today. From the beginning of our nation, people of all professions and occupations were involved in building its solid foundation. They had intelligence, understanding, wisdom, and leadership to make the kinds of decisions that benefited the people. In recent years, our government "micro managed" the economy and social issues by depending on too many people who had lost touch with reality, instead of looking to individuals like Dr. Grady Stumbo, whose contributions mean so much to society.

Dr. Stumbo has a message to all potential leaders that if Appalachia is to survive and overcome the ills of poverty, people with leadership qualities must come forward. Grady Stumbo further believes that sharing responsibility by the total community for immediate and long-range plans is necessary to make change in eastern Kentucky. Ultimately, progress must come from the grass-roots approach of each local community. He is convinced that what happens on this level can either make or break the future of Appalachia. Dr. Stumbo has been a recipient of many honors, including the outstanding Rockefeller Award that he and longtime friend and working colleague Benny Ray Bailey accepted for their health care contributions and humanitarian efforts.

Benny Ray Bailey

While health care delivery at the county level stands out as a primary source to combat the ills of people, there is a strong need in receiving support from the State and federal government to provide remedies for improving Appalachia's health status. As a state legislator and chairman of the senate's Health and Welfare Committee, Benny Ray Bailey has become one of the state's driving forces for change in rural health, especially in Appalachia. Mr. Bailey, who runs the Eastern Kentucky Health Clinic in Hindman and Wayland since 1972 with his friend Dr. Grady Stumbo, has been instrumental in many health projects that have benefited the people of Appalachia. Bailey, an eastern Kentucky native and Alice Lloyd College graduate, was born in the tiny hamlet of Orkney. In his childhood he saw first hand how poverty reared its "ugly head" at people. He realized that health care was unequally distributed and withheld from the poor of Appalachia.

Today, as Administrator of the Eastern Kentucky Health Clinic, he has helped bring health care to those people whose medical needs were ignored. His efforts have not stopped at the local level, and he has moved to a leadership role in the State Senate that acknowledged the rise and recognition of this learned politician. With state legislators from the region like Mr. Bailey, the impression of past politicians is today replaced by forward thinking leadership. The "good old boy" reputation that had plagued eastern Kentucky politics for years, is now being replaced by astute leaders with vision, who understand that working for the people is a responsibility, not a means of using a public office for one's own benefit. For years, eastern Kentucky politicians, geared toward the elite of communities, were able to wheel and deal for the benefit of self-indulging cheers. There is no doubt about Benny Ray Bailey's conviction to fight for the poor people, which has been evident through his genuine concern and action to improve health care in medically underserved areas. He and Dr. Grady Stumbo are trying to revolutionize medical care residencies, so that training can take place in rural health care facilities, such as local hospitals, health clinics, and even in private practices. This practical approach of "on the spot" training for interns, will help them understand the realities of people's needs.

Benny Ray Bailey sees preventive medicine also as a key to improving the health status of eastern Kentucky, and what better way for a young medical resident to gain firsthand experience than to live and work among the people of Appalachia. He is also aware that recruiting doctors, nurses and technicians into rural areas is truly a challenge to Kentucky's health reform plans. Mr. Bailey's front-line work at the state level has led to the Health Care Reform Act of 1990, and he was given credit for the drafting of this bill. The Health Reform Act, introduced by Bailey and fellow senators, included the need for a new State rural psychiatric hospital to be part of the medical complex in Hazard. The significance of this unique facility is that it serves patients who are referred by respective local mental health facilities from twenty-one eastern Kentucky counties, including Bell, Breathitt, Clay, Floyd, Harlan, Jackson, Johnson, Knott, Knox, Laurel, Lee, Leslie, Letcher, Magoffin, Martin, Owsley, Perry, Pike, Rockcastle, Whitley, and Wolfe.

In the past, eastern Kentuckians had to travel hundreds of miles in order to get service at a psychiatric hospital. This led to frustration of patients and their families and caused further neglect to provide needed help for the mentally ill. Lack of proper mental health services in Appalachia brought about brutal indifference for these unfortunate human beings. The majority of them lived with their parents and were without professional mental health care. Benny Ray Bailey and his colleagues realized the need to do something about this inadequate situation. With tenacious drive, he demonstrated sustained competence and a strong sense of ethical responsibility to the less fortunate. Through Senator Bailey's leadership, extension of the 1990 reform bill was passed on April 15, 1994, and is considered a major step by the Kentucky General Assembly in improving availability and accessibility of health care in the Commonwealth. His work and leadership were acknowledged, when he and Dr. Grady Stumbo received national recognition for their humanitarian work with the poor — The Rockefeller Award.

When Benny Ray Bailey met Grady Stumbo and other classmates at Alice Lloyd College thirty years ago, they had talked of wanting to make definite changes for Appalachia. Their common bond of compassion, caring, and concern for poor people was understandable, for they also came from poverty, and the vision of giving service and leadership to these unfortunate individuals was utmost on their minds. Benny Ray Bailey and Grady Stumbo have turned that dream into reality, despite all the difficulties they have encountered. Benny Ray is working hard as a Senator to represent his people, and if he along with other new leaders succeed, the future for hillfolk will look brighter, and poverty can be overcome. He has been largely responsible for the history-making success of the new Regional Medical Park complex in Hazard that should have a great impact and help change the health situation of Appalachia. Mr. Bailey is a person of strong character, fairness and sincerity in helping other citizens. He personifies the true spirit of a public figure through good example, hard work and devotion to duty.

A Model Rural Regional Medical Park

A significant step in the evolution of health care delivery in Appalachia is the Eastern Kentucky Comprehensive Health Care Complex at Hazard. The cooperation of surrounding counties and their physicians has provided a modern regional Medical Park, consisting of centralized health care resources that serve, enhance and articulate with other facilities, rural clinics, and practitioners. This was fueled by the need to provide a unified system of community-based health care, so patients did not have to travel to distant urban medical centers. Uniqueness of this medical complex is that it contains a fusion of specialist physicians in a centralized rural health care community, providing a combination of medical facilities with a broad range of comprehensive services. The Regional and Psychiatric hospitals will be tied in with a teaching center to ensure the most technologically advanced diagnosis and treatment.

In developing the regional hospital, emphasis was placed on providing optimal quality of care that calls for highly skilled physicians, nurses and other medical practitioners, and the latest in diagnostic and therapeutic equipment. The opportunity for a regional hospital to perform more surgical procedures is an advantage of importance. It is documented in research studies that the rate of survival is much greater in hospitals that perform higher volumes of surgery. A second facility that opened in July 1993, the one-hundred bed psychiatric hospital, is the first of its kind in Kentucky that involves state government and private non-profit health

191

care cooperation. The Appalachian Regional Health Care Organization built and equipped this new mental health center through tax exempt revenue bonds. Kentucky's Cabinet for Human Resources has contracted with ARHCO to provide professional personnel and staff for evaluation, supervision, and treatment of patients who require psychiatric services. For those whose needs go beyond basic treatment, this facility is a godsend, and the kind of care provided by the Regional Psychiatric Hospital is a necessity. This quality of care, which was lacking for too long, is part of the ongoing change of maximizing access to every available up-to-date resource of health care delivery.

The third phase of this medical complex came about through the efforts of people like Dr. Grady Stumbo and Benny Ray Bailey. Both men had been campaigning for years to achieve greater medical care in Appalachia. One area of concern and a major dilemma was the lack of physicians, namely general family practitioners. Dr. Stumbo espoused two ways of solving this problem. The first dealt with setting up a cooperative working relationship with the University of Kentucky Rural Medicine Program, by establishing an Eastern Kentucky Rural Based Residency Center in Hazard. Interns will be trained in family practices, with hopes of being placed in underprivileged areas of Appalachia. Another way Dr. Stumbo, State Senator Bailey and other concerned professionals would like to improve primary care service is through recruitment of young men and women who are natives of eastern Kentucky towns and villages. Hopefully, this modern rural teaching hospital will also provide the kind of exposure that entices young people of Appalachia, and it appears that this undertaking looks promising.

At this time, it is difficult to ascertain the long range implications of professional staff regarding the rural model health park. There are people who may express concern that specialists, leaving smaller hospitals to join the Regional Medical Center, may have a negative effect on those rural areas. These and other matters need to be dealt with by all concerned parties. However, as decisions are made for the future, it is hoped that professionals providing health care to the people of Appalachia look forthright and fairly at all possible avenues for better quality of care.

Small rural hospitals provide important services, even though they are often less sophisticated. They fulfill a significant role by offering emergency medical services, routine care and diagnosis in areas that are many miles away from the Regional Hospital, or the more distant hospitals of Lexington and Louisville. These small medical facilities have been the foundation for rural health care and should be recognized for the role they can play through improvement. However, with development of the Regional Medical Center, greater access to quality care is available, which should not be a duplication of what has been provided for people in the past, but an extension of services and care that will lead to higher survival rates and longer life. Research should show over long term that this operation will prove to be beneficial for upgrading the health status of Appalachia. At this early date, signs point to a successful health care approach that can serve as a model not only in Appalachia and the State of Kentucky, but for all of rural America.

Education

During the 1980's and early 90's, there have been many calls for improving education of all children in our society. In the wake of these "exhortations," increasing attention was given to the challenge of educating children, who are most at risk of school failure. Unfortunately, such youngsters come mainly from families that live in poverty. In 1983, the National Commission on Education wrote a 36 page study entitled "A Nation at Risk" that stirred our country by stating: "The education foundations of our society are presently being eroded by a rising tide of mediocrity that threatens our very future as a nation." Reports coming from the U.S. Department of Education very seldom create excitement for the population. However, even national newspapers warned that "A Nation at Risk" frightened the country, by shaking people's faith in the most basic institution — schools. In many educational circles, the Commission evoked emotions that propelled a host of educational reforms throughout the United States. Research studies showed negative results of education, and how it was declining. With all the hoopla and reaction of concerned citizens, this report talked of "fundamental change," but proposed already known recommendations, and only marginal improvements were experienced by educational reform programs during the 1980's.

Education in Kentucky suffered continuously, and above all, the schools in rural Appalachia struggled even more due to many obstacles that were placed in their path. Inefficient school systems, built on a weak financial base, lacked amenities which should have been available for children. Further compounding the situation were deteriorating facilities, low teacher salaries, poor criteria for selection of teachers, outrageously politicized school boards, nepotism and patronage that trapped eastern Kentucky's children in schools of mediocrity.

Financially, eastern Kentucky counties have been in very poor condition for years. Their tax base was too low, and hillfolk had difficult times paying taxes. Some people were so desperate to make payments that in certain instances they had to sell the only mode of transportation, their automobile. Poverty and unemployment have constantly been a major reason for this region's inability to provide quality education for all its children.

Schools in wealthy counties of Kentucky enjoyed strong financial support, and during the late 80's, more than 3,000 dollars were spent per pupil each year, with extra money for "state of the art" computers, band equipment, music programs, field trips, and other activities. In rural Appalachian counties the scene was quite different. Schools could not afford to spend more than 1,900 dollars for a pupil per year. Students attended classes in buildings that were badly in need of repair, and teachers dipped into their own pockets to pay for paper, workbooks and other supplies. The income from local taxes in eastern Kentucky counties was insufficient to run schools, and in Floyd County things were so bad that the State took over the school system. A 1988 audit revealed that students raised more money for their schools by selling candy and magazines than the county school district received in local taxes.

Kentucky Education Reform Act of 1990

The gap between wealthy counties of Kentucky and poor rural Appalachian schools had a negative impact on providing quality education for all its children. This prompted action that was unprecedented and unheard of not only in the commonwealth, but throughout our nation. Education forged a coalition of districts that wanted to sue the state for equitable funding of all schools. In November 1985, as a result of deteriorating conditions in poor school districts, a complaint was filed in Franklin Circuit Court, challenging the equity and adequacy of funds provided for education of all Kentucky children. Plaintiffs were the Council for Better Education, consisting of sixty-six school districts, seven Boards of Education, and twenty-two public school students. The lead counsel in this case, former Governor Bert Combs, presented the suit on behalf of plaintiffs from counties throughout Kentucky. Judge Ray Corns issued a decision in October 1988, stating that the State's General Assembly had failed to provide an efficient system of common schools. He further declared that the system of school financing was inefficient and discriminatory. Defendants included the Governor, State Superintendent of Public Instruction, Treasurer, President Pro Tem of the Senate, Speaker of the House of Representatives, and the State Board of Education and its members, who then appealed to Kentucky's State Supreme Court.

The plaintiffs under Bert Comb's leadership argued that use of local property taxes to finance schools were depriving students in poorer counties of their right to equal education. This was upheld by the State Supreme Court. However, the highest court in Kentucky did not stop there, but clearly stated that it was holding the entire state system of elementary and secondary education unconstitutional. The court said:

> "This decision applies to the entire sweep of the system
> — all its parts and parcels. This decision applies to all
> the statutes creating, implementing, and financing the
> system, and to all regulations, etc., pertaining hereto. . .
> This decision covers the creation of local school districts,
> school boards, and the Kentucky Department of
> Education to the minimum foundation program and
> power equalization program. It covers school construc-
> tion and maintenance, teacher certification — the whole
> gamut of the common school system in Kentucky...Since
> we have, by this decision, declared the system of com-
> mon schools in Kentucky to be unconstitutional.
> Section 183 places an absolute duty on the General
> Assembly to recreate, re-establish a new system of com-
> mon schools in the commonwealth..."

The General Assembly viewed this decision as a stroke of good fortune to launch a new era of educational opportunity, which would ensure a strong economic, social, cultural, and political future. Boundless energy and enthusiasm by political leaders finally succeeded in proposing a clear cut strategy and time table to achieve what some people think may be an impossible task. Others feel, this could be one of the most dynamic and ambitious challenges of statewide educational reform in the nation. In 1989, many people hoped that reform would lead to a complete reversal of the direction taken in previous years. Politicians in Kentucky generally do agree that schools are a reflection of today's society, and through the years, inequality in education has been a major concern. Responding to the opportunity for change, a legislative task force on education reform appointed three committees: curriculum, government, and finance; and through study and discussion they gained a broad perspective of possibilities for restructuring schools in Kentucky. The State then moved toward development of the Kentucky Education Reform Act of 1990. This act became law on July 13, 1990, and the schools were given new life. Thus, the State Supreme Court's mandate that the "System of Common Schools" receive adequate funds to achieve its goals, was a beginning toward equity throughout the state.

Access to quality education is supposed to be available, regardless of where a child lives. This massive reform, which established a new funding system, was designed to close the gap between the state's richest and poorest districts. The sweeping changes of K.E.R.A. have brought Kentucky to the forefront in education innovation. No other state has enacted such a change and provided support with a significantly higher level of educational funding. One outcome of this reform included a sharp tax increase for individuals and businesses. It should be noted that this was welcomed, because parents wanted better schools for their children rather than lower tax bills. Business groups had also expressed the need of better qualified school graduates for their workforce.

New gubernatorial appointee, Education Commissioner Thomas Boysen, had set forth a reform of the Department of Education. The legal mandate was to create an educational structure that would serve as helpmate to individual schools rather than dictate to school districts. Commissioner Boysen initiated a new department, the Council on School Performance Standards, which was responsible for drawing up a long term plan, specifying broad educational goals. School boards and local councils had to decide how to meet these expectations. Every district in the State of Kentucky in "Step One" was supposed to have at least one school based council elected and in place by June 30, 1991. Over the next four years every school is required to establish a council, which would consist of two parents, three teachers, and a principal. They are responsible for drawing up the curriculum, overseeing school budgets, hiring or firing of teachers and other crucial decisions that were formerly made by district administration. Along with restructuring the State Department of Education, Kentucky developed strong rules against nepotism. It also created a new election process for local board members, which called for them hiring only the school district superintendent and board attorney. The superintendent was allowed to employ all other employees, such as staff and supporting services personnel.

These changes take time and require patience from all participating persons. Modifying attitudes and ideas of teachers, administrators, and the public is a difficult task. However, much needed improvement in controlling schools was implemented for the Kentucky Education Reform Act to succeed. Accurate knowledge about benefits, to upgrade school districts, can at the present only be surmised. As of today, no school district has included the entire reform into their system, and it may take until July 1996, before such data would be derived from the K.E.R.A. This is how long it will take to complete the development phase, testing of various models, and analyzing project results that are called for by the time line schedule.

At this stage, the Kentucky Education Reform Act has made important strides for positive change. It is aimed toward improvement of education for all children, and as one briefly glances at the features, Kentucky has passed a most significant reform act. Features of K.E.R.A. include:

State-funded preschool education for all at risk four year olds and handicapped three and four year olds.

Family Resource Centers and Youth Services Centers to provide services in or near schools, in which at least twenty percent of the students match federal poverty guidelines.

Technology in Education has been emphasized and available for learning experiences. Upgraded technology, including a telephone in every classroom connected to the state education television network to benefit children and staff, is a top priority.

An ungraded Primary School Program will replace entry level to fourth grade of the elementary school course of study. Successful completion of this program must be met before a student enters fourth grade.

Guaranteed minimum per pupil spending level. Starting the 1990-1991 school year, overall state financing was supposed to increase each subsequent year.

An autonomous, teacher-majority Education Professional Standards Board is established as the certification authority.

Schools are to provide extended services for students who need additional time for instruction to meet the learning outcomes. Local school districts will receive state grants for the extended school services.

The Kentucky Education Reform Act did not move along without a hitch. In 1991, local teacher associations in Boyd and Floyd counties encountered opposition by school boards and administration. Through the Kentucky Education Association, local officials were taken to task when superintendents and school boards had resisted many changes, including mandated salary increases, which led to a teacher walkout. This was the first strike in Kentucky since 1976, and in both counties, the community gave its staunch support to teachers, as local officials gave in. Educators throughout the state felt that action of teachers, thus reinforcing the K.E.R.A. accountability structure, would ensure change. Probably most significant is that each community took the ultimate step in supporting teachers and mandates of the Act to oppose efforts by administration and boards that were deterring educational change.

By starting anew, the Kentucky Education Reform Act has emphasized accountability and directed its attention from "input" of education (buildings, classrooms, teaching degrees, books, etc.) to "outcome" of the educational process. There is now a new sense of urgency in Kentucky, focusing on productivity of its schools in the 1990's. Academic achievement and behavior of students are society's most concerned investments for the future. Although this treatise has long been an awesome responsibility of educators, it has now become a specific directive from the legislature, governor, and courts.

Previously, educators have used traditional procedures of evaluating their school systems. The national accrediting agencies have provided antiquated guidelines for excellence in education. In general, they analyzed facilities, equipment, and staff, with little attention to classroom procedures, students' abilities, knowledge, or skills that resulted from the teaching and learning process. However, through education reform, a new door has now opened, with Kentucky recognizing and demanding that schools be administered more systematically. Explicitly defined measurable goals and proof of accomplishment are major necessities. In responding to this need, accountability was initiated into the total state educational system in 1990. Now, four years later, schools are inundated with written documents on the subject of education reform.

Any educator will testify that accountability is no easy task. On one hand, there is a concern for tightening the legislative purse strings at the state level and an auditing system, demanding that schools provide proof of wise and prudent spending; on the other hand, in order for Kentucky to implement this program, there will be rising costs. Monetary help is needed for improved teaching procedures, qualified teachers, expansion of student services, developing new offerings such as pre-school, ungraded primary programs, along with maintaining various other activities and services.

The number of children and families being served by this educational endeavor is colossal, because of their individual demands for improved programs and expanded curriculum. In addition, educators are dealing with many variables that imply a heterogeneous complex group of factors, which are not easily ponderable. School systems must deal with the human factor of attitudes and values, culturally and socially, as well as the economics of financing education. Although accountability in Kentucky schools is the major topic, there is very little research information on how to justify the role of education in maintaining this program. Another major concern is that we were told for too long that education was immeasurable and untouchable. Research has also been controversial, because of the difficulty in measuring abilities of students.

Nationally, educators have considered and rejected merit pay, because there were too many intangibles involved. However, Kentucky is moving toward a new approach, which should have the opportunity to be evaluated. It has incorporated the total school as to success or failure of its educational program. In the past, any student who did poorly, failed, or dropped out of school was considered uneducable or not receptive to learning, and teachers were not held responsible. Some educators feel Kentucky may have come up with a strong answer to this situation. The K.E.R.A. system of school-wide bonus for all staff members is based on total school performance, not individual teacher merit. This team approach brings about a sense of cohesiveness, which has never been attempted in such a way that it affects an entire state system.

Tied in with this merit performance approach is the persistent failure to meet institutional objectives, in turn, these schools will be declared "in crisis." When this happens, outside managers are sent to evaluate each school situation, and if necessary recommend elimination of the professional staff. Parents would have the option to take their children elsewhere, and ultimately the school could be closed. There are people raising questions about this aspect of K.E.R.A.; but patience is necessary, because nothing like this has been tried before. Local schools that are experimenting with site-based management also have many concerns. There has been reluctance to force certain action or penalties on various weak performing schools. However, if an isolated rural school fails to perform, where are students supposed to go? Another question is, do the children transfer to another school that may have similar problems? Will education deteriorate for youngsters that are left in those poor performing schools? There are many more questions that need to be answered. Developers of the reform plan have thought about them and realize that there are going to be weak schools. However, some educators believe that working in a team environment may be the answer. If the structure is set up appropriately and in a non-threatening way, the weak link in a chain can always be repaired.

When a system of accountability is established, subjectivity becomes less of a problem in determining effectiveness of the educational program. Teachers and staff evaluate in an objective manner the problem at hand and prescribe alternative approaches to overcome the known deficiency. However, if teachers and administrators are confronted with an unknown reason for failure, the problem cannot be solved. The purpose of developing and implementing K.E.R.A. has a simple answer. A school, its staff and faculty must work as a team with community involvement, so that the process of planning, implementing and evaluating the program objectively will bring results. If change is required, the professional staff will know how to make improvements.

As one reviews the Kentucky reform program, it is difficult to argue the general principles involved. In fact, there are many benefits a school district would realize by implementing K.E.R.A. The reform act does not require acceptance of any specific set of values in education. Emphasis is entirely on making explicit, rational aims and objectives for various programs and courses of study offered. Most of the newly proposed segments of K.E.R.A. provide support to assist teachers in implementing goals and plans for students. It means however that schools must better identify their educational objectives and then measure outcomes of student learning.

One major motivation for the development of objectives is that it will give school district leaders, teachers, and people in the community an understanding of their present situation and "where they are heading." It will also provide effectively coordinated activities, leading to identification and elimination of functions which are unnecessary in the educational process. School district leaders, teachers and staff will be able to concentrate more on establishing priorities. Given the limited resources of these districts and their myriad of functions, individual schools and education officials may put more energy on the most pressing needs, and eliminate those that are of marginal importance. Data that is available to decision makers at critical points would lead to a generation of better informed educators. Concentrating on the quality of information should also help to pinpoint research needs, expose pertinent data, and identify the total cost of activities. This is in contrast to prior budgeting and accounting practices that used to hide complete costs. The serious effort to develop "output" measures for school district programs should lead to a better understanding of their purpose, which is a task that will consume time and energy.

Minimizing Risks of K.E.R.A.

Predictions about the long term success of K.E.R.A. appears to look complicated because of uncertain attitudes in financing. It becomes increasingly apparent that Kentucky's inability in meeting its commitment to fund education could threaten the basic foundation of the reform act. Implementation of K.E.R.A. will be slow under the best circumstances; however, since ten of the last twelve state educational budgets were cut, this presents a disturbing picture of financial commitment to schools. It seems questionable that the State government was realistic in its financial projections to support education reform. Adding to this problem, the governor and legislature still have to contend with anti-tax sentiment, engendered by passage of the spending portion. Some legislators who supported K.E.R.A. lost their jobs during the 1990 and 1991 elections. People also have to realize that implementation of the Kentucky Education Reform Act calls for added expenditures and cannot be looked at as a financial shortcut.

There is danger of future conflict that the governor and legislature must confront. They have to find a way to prioritize education at the head of their funding list. The question at hand is whether the state will stick with K.E.R.A. Nationally, all too often worthwhile educational programs were not allowed to continue, either through political or bureaucratic meddling. The result is that Kentucky education has also been quick on shortening vital programs, and up to the present time, it has taken a back seat in regard to the national scene. The reform act is potentially the most solid and practical proposal that exists anywhere. If the Kentucky Education Reform Act does not have an opportunity to evaluate and study its successes and defeats, then the potential to improve quality of education may not be accomplished. As an added bonus, if the state would continue this program long enough and fine-tune it, there is a greater probability that Kentucky schools will achieve their goals.

Apparently the "fathers" of K.E.R.A. have considered an appropriate approach to these concerns and questions by establishing the Office of Education Accountability, a branch of the Legislative Research Commission. The State was aware that a carefully designed system for gathering necessary data on continued progress of the total K.E.R.A. program called for monitoring the education system. Constant up-to-date information through various processes and evaluation is needed if legislature wants to be on top of the reform act. Currently, there are different types of information being used by the Office of Education Accountability to fortify K.E.R.A. These include (a) reviewing the state's system of school finance (b) verifying accuracy of school district and state performance (c) investigating unresolved allegations of wrongdoing at the state, regional or district level and (d) reporting to the Legislative Research Commission.

The possible advantage coming about with this legislative branch is that the State Education Department and school districts will be committing themselves to rigorous self evaluation in order to get program funds approved by the State government. In essence, the Office of Education Accountability is a needed third party independent audit for not only economic factors, but a whole range of anticipated useful by-products for K.E.R.A.'s continuation. This approach should work toward securing knowledge of optimum relationship between "input and output" in any given educational program. If the goal for the O.E.A. is to serve as an objective independent body, then this approach will provide new credibility in the educational process by forming a basis for discovery and improvement of good practices in education. In turn, those who are working with the legislature will feel that their schools are becoming more responsive to needs of students and community. What better way for the State to justify its allocated resources and funds for K.E.R.A.?

There are many other issues that should be considered with caution as the reform act goes through various stages. Future conflict is possible between people working together at the local community council level of administrators, teachers and lay people. Schools have the responsibility to open a communication network that is free of personal biases and subjective actions. People who are involved will need to be trained in order to effectively implement this program. During their training, an analysis should be required at all levels for the purpose to sharpen educators' judgment, supplement their wisdom, and provide more information as important decisions are made. After all, there is no substitute for an experienced, sensitive, and discerned educator, whether it be a teacher or administrator. Education is a complex process that must provide professional action and activity.

There are some concerns relating to parental involvement in implementing K.E.R.A. Although there appears to be a willingness of school administrators and teachers to involve parents in this new educational process, a lack of participation from them has been evident. A recent survey authorized by the State Department of Education cited that very few parents attended local school council meetings. Even in the election of community members for school councils, voter turnout was very weak. One of the greatest difficulties in school-community relations is that for too many years parents did not get involved, and it has become difficult to change this pattern. The need to alter this calls for a communication network of information that is based on a sound philosophy of integrating parents into school affairs.

One approach to communication is the development of procedures that are based on local characteristics and trends, which should be creative enough in stimulating response from the community. Apparently, too many individuals seem to forget or don't realize that their community is the "rightful owner" of schools, and maintaining them means serving the people. Because of this, educators have a responsibility to provide as much knowledge as possible about the total picture of a school to the community. The negative attitude and lack of parent participation which exists today is probably an indication that for many years a weak school-community relationship prevailed. Schools had removed themselves from the people, and until recently, old traditions of the educational structure led to negative feelings by the community. In essence, many do not know how to respond to this change of a new educational direction. It is true that there will be parents with negative, apathetic, or lax attitudes toward what schools are wanting to accomplish, but this should not be an excuse for educators to have anti-feelings toward the community. Creative endeavors are necessary in order to work with parents, regardless of their present posture. The direction each school takes to improve parent involvement and participation will only strengthen and bring to fruition implementation of the total K.E.R.A. program.

Another area of concern is the emphasis on being able to measure results, which is a major characteristic of the reform act. The responsibility of making decisions by participants should be supported in such a way that they are not tempted to abandon purposes which cannot easily be quantified. Conflicts will arise, but sound educational practices have to take precedence over the requirements of a specific objective, should the two ever conflict. The Reform Act is not a substitute for common sense in administering a program. If this is lacking, the Act by itself will not lead to the development of an improved educational program. When reform was implemented in 1990, there were not many educators knowledgeable or trained in this accountability system. Caution was exercised by school districts since inception of K.E.R.A., and four years later, it is still the byword. Teachers and staff have to be carefully trained and merits of reform demonstrated, before anyone can say with certainty that schools are moving ahead in achieving their respective goals.

In an education reform which is oriented toward productivity of objectives, it is important that accountability be shared by all people involved in this program. Assessment should occur at intervals suitable to appraisal and replanning, but the establishment of objective standards will require the maintenance and analysis of longitudinal records. Quality measurement can be done by following the individual child over years through their entire process of educational experiences. Although most schools have some form of information concerning students, they usually do not receive much on probable weaknesses of the educational program. Each experience for a child tends to be placed in separate compartments, and the result is lacking recognition of basic problems or fluctuation in quality of the educational program. Studies must aim at accountability, either through verification of student learnings, curricular or operational changes.

Kentucky is moving toward a new age in education, and whether schools are in Appalachia or other parts of the commonwealth, they will be held accountable by state agencies working at a new level of sophistication. Bureaucrats and committees will want to know more than educators have yet been able to tell them, and in this eagerness, they will be proper agents for the public. I suspect, educators have no choice but to seek a drastic increase of public support for the schools in Kentucky. The consequence for all educators is a new requirement of candor, and schools must now become open to themselves, each other, public authorities, and indeed to all.

The call for accountability in education is a summons to review and reform the educational system. For too many years, educators nationally have confused measurement of results in education with limited and restrictive assessment, such as standardized achievement testing of the normal curve based variety. Also, to be fair in our judgment, we must admit that educational research has provided very few valid methods of measuring the actual results of education. Currently, various contemporary approaches that are being used throughout the country for accountability in education are not as strong as we would like them to be. However, the State of Kentucky has taken an organized step toward finding more valid and appropriate means of measuring outcome. It is identifying programs rather than objects of expenditure, and attempts to get the greatest return on investment of resources. Above all, it involves identifying objectives, and finding alternatives for allocations of resources, which should provide for a solid base of outcomes.

The ultimate success for carrying out educational reform is the school. Basic sources are the community, teachers, administrators, and students. This should never be forgotten by school leaders who are implementing those elements that deal with the larger issue of accountability. Hopefully students may become "proactors" rather than "reactors" to the various forces that are common energies in educational work. The result should be improvement of education for children and a much more enhanced opportunity for a fulfilling and happy life as they grow into adulthood. Their chances of succeeding as adults should be more promising, with expectations that some become Appalachia's future leaders.

Individuals and Groups — Leadership

Looking back at history and researching its impact on Appalachians, one realizes that certain individual and group actions have played an important leadership role in saving many people, who lived in poverty. Given the circumstances, persons of conviction and dedication have stepped forward time and again, sacrificing for the less fortunate. No matter how little an impact they had on fellow Appalachians, it seems to hold true that their work and efforts show in the salvation of the needy. The importance of self-help through guided commitment, caring and concern has been the standard for successful humanitarian leaders since the time of Alice Lloyd, Mary Breckinridge, and Katherine Pettit.

In recent years, Appalachia has seen the formation of voluntary groups pursuing goals with greater community involvement than ever before. This trend, which started many years ago when groups were organized to provide for justice and social services, has mushroomed and includes almost every possible socioeconomic concern of today's society. The scope and scale has magnified the role of community involvement to the point where individuals, such as politicians, professionals, business people, clergy and religious helpers, along with concerned non self-serving citizens, are leading and working cooperatively to help the region improve its status. This grass-roots community approach involves non-profit self-governing groups that are showing success in easing the burden of poverty. They are altering a trend that had been reserved in the past for government. However, action taken by these groups makes it necessary to extol their leadership role, which reflects the phenomenon of will and determination to accomplish goals. Regardless of their different directions, they have a common bond of responding to needs of the poor. The following groups are presented as a sample of the varied forces that are representative of what is happening in eastern Kentucky today.

Kentucky Educational Television Network
Virginia Fox, Executive Director

Even though certain groups nationally have been fighting the use of media in education for years, one must face the real world of experimentation and innovation today. In the field of educational television there is one notable example that was tried and proves to be successful. Innovative action by Kentucky's Educational Television Network has given children of remote rural areas the opportunity to take courses, which their respective community schools were not able to offer. In the mountain region, where students attended high schools, there was a lack of certified teachers for advanced courses in math, science and foreign language. However, the K.E.T. Network provided access to excellent learning programs.

The success of offering these courses came to fruition through the vision and drive of Virginia Fox, herself once a rural student. Under her leadership, along with former Executive Director Leonard Press, Kentucky Educational Television, the largest land-based public television network in the nation, broadcasts directly to over 1,800 schools and public institutions throughout the state. Actually, 88 percent of Kentucky's students use some kind of K.E.T. programming in the classroom, and public television is also available to every household throughout the commonwealth. K.E.T.'s unique and innovative approach in providing services has led to national recognition. In 1991 the Ford Foundation and John F. Kennedy

205

School of Government at Harvard University honored K.E.T., by giving it the prestigious Innovations in State and Local Government Award. This national acclaim was further recognized by Vice-President Al Gore who stated that students in rural locations are fortunate to have access to superior teachers through educational television programming.

Virginia Fox is K.E.T.'s Executive Director today and strongly believes that "Students in every area of the state, no matter how remote, should have an opportunity to take advanced courses." Through her initiative the State's educational television network was given a grant in the 1980's for a closed circuit satellite system that included a link to every one of the 1,300 elementary and secondary schools. Students receive instruction on television and interact with teachers, using their keyboard and telephone to deliver responses or questions to the studio in Lexington. Student input by voice and data helps teachers modify instructions according to needs. This state of the art system was developed not only for enrichment programs, but also offers many types of learning experiences, enhancing the overall educational offerings.

When Kentucky Education Television began to deliver high school courses via satellite in 1989, math was lacking throughout the state as well as science and foreign language. Kentucky Education Department research showed that 78 high schools did not provide physics, 50 offered no math courses beyond Algebra II, and 40 percent of foreign language teachers held only a minor degree in the language they were teaching. Major reasons for these shortages were continuous lack of funds and the small size of many schools. With little revenue coming in, these schools could not afford to hire new teachers, and the number of students interested in particular advanced courses was not sufficient to justify the expense. Lack of articulation between secondary schools and college concerned Kentucky's higher education institutions, because many students were spending their first two years of college taking courses they should have received in high school. Higher education was hindered to help the students reach their full potential and had to offer college preparatory courses.

Since starting the first advanced math course in 1989, in which one teacher and 126 students participated, K.E.T. programming has increased immeasurably, and all types of courses are now serving over one million people. It means that K.E.T. is providing for students in classrooms or at home, and gives people who live in remote areas access to expert, up-to-date information. The system has expanded its services to include professional development seminars for specified groups or organizations throughout the commonwealth. Another major contribution is making educators across the state aware of latest changes in all phases of the 1990 K.E.R.A. In the 1992/93 school year, K.E.T. was very active in producing over 100 hours of training sessions and teleconferences for Kentucky educators. Using this educational network has made it possible for organizations to conduct successful conferences via the satellite system, which include: Partnership for Kentucky School Reform, Kentucky Cabinet for Human Resources, Kentucky Workforce Development Cabinet, and the Kentucky Science and Technology Council, Inc.

Another shining achievement of this non-profit organization is the series "GED on TV." This program is geared toward adult students who never finished secondary education and are intending to prepare for the high school diploma equivalency examination. Since 1975, more than 15,000 students in Kentucky have earned their GED's after completing this television course. In 1982 K.E.T. expanded "GED on TV" to other states and was very successful. Over 1.2 million students nationwide have passed their GED exam after viewing the series. High school courses offered on K.E.T. are also in demand. For example, during 1989 and 1990 a high level probability and statistic's course enrolled 561 students from 129 schools outside of Kentucky.

One of the most fruitful decisions was made by the State legislature, when it called upon K.E.T. for assistance in helping Kentucky's Educational Reform Act find solutions to problems of equal access to quality education. K.E.T.'s response has been one of enthusiasm with the highest level of quality in innovation and experimentation supporting education reform at large. The focal point of creating favorable climate and setting for new ideas and practices in educational television required a cogent direction, aimed toward developing a national model, addressing educational equity.

With development of a strong educational telecommunication infrastructure and limitless possibilities, it is important to carry forth a "total commitment" to innovation and experimentation. The need to help foster community development and create programs related to teaching people new job skills is an admirable undertaking that this public service organization plans to add in the near future. Clearly, K.E.T. is proving its importance to the children and adults of Kentucky. It has gone beyond nominal involvement in education and other service program offerings. In fact, its impact on Appalachia should make us look forward to the coming years with optimism and hope. This volunteer tradition of assisting community and service organizations has been strong, and there is every reason to believe that K.E.T. will continue contributing as an important agent for change.

Community Health Care Clinics —
A Positive Impact

The characterization of community health care clinics as a positive force came about in the 1960's, and had a great impact on the health status of Appalachians. In general, these clinics have been a benefit to the needy and community. The extent of their contributions in Appalachia can only be understood when one looks at the common concern for providing quality health care services, positive attitudes and humanitarian endeavors by health professionals and personnel.

When community health clinics were started, they offered needed services to a large portion of the population that had been without any form of care. Since its inception, community health clinics have provided for the needy, regardless of their financial status. Today, questions are being raised about the health care clinic's role and its effectiveness for the future, if or when this nation comes up with a national health care plan. Some of these inquirers are blunt and critical, perhaps even unjust, and view that with a national health plan, people will forsake the local community health care clinic and seek out better medical care, assuming it is superior. Critics feel it would modify purposes and roles of medical and health professionals, as well as other areas of health care. Unfortunately, they are also citing lack of comprehensive services, which community health clinics are aware of and have been trying to improve.

There was some validity to this, because government funding in meeting expectations had not been sufficient, but these medical facilities tried their best to be effective despite financial limitations. This is why critics had a reason to claim that health clinics were not doing the job expected of them. It must be understood that some of these individuals were against development of community health centers from the start. However, even staunch supporters, along with the Administration, medical and health professional personnel admit that comprehensive services are not as they would like them to be. A major reason is the lack of physicians, dentists, other qualified professional personnel, equipment, supplies or appropriate facilities.

In spite of the problems community health clinics face, it is clear that they are a very important and effective provider for those people who are in dire need. It must be recognized that some of these clinics offer outstanding service, and in certain instances are known to engage in innovative and benefiting health care practices, such as preventive medicine. One should also remember that over all health care has come a long way in Appalachia over the last 25 years. This was not expected or hoped for, considering the tremendous needs of the past. Credit must be given to individuals and groups who had the desire and fortitude in organizing and developing this important addition of service to fight the ills of poverty.

A person who represents this leadership group is Lois Baker, administrator of one of the largest rural health community organizations in America. She is a strong advocate for preventive as well as curative care. Like all the other health clinics in Appalachia that are providing service for patients with low or no income, the Mountain Comprehensive Health Corporation is involved with family-oriented preventive services. Mrs. Baker is also very enthusiastic about the role of medical and health clinic leaders, and her own energy and commitment to help people of this area is certainly evident. Comprehensive services which she envisions for Whitesburg's citizens will soon become reality with the construction of a multi-million dollar state of the art community health clinic.

In essence, it appears that the mission of community health care centers is heading in the right direction by providing comprehensive services for the total family, which range from preventive to curative care. Where the need for referral to specialized services is required, community clinics become the first basic and probably most important step in helping the patient. After examining and taking into account the community health clinic movement, these non-profit self-governing organizations have accomplished much more than they have been given credit for. Effort, drive and wanting to help fellow Appalachians cannot and must not be equated with accomplishment, because those who are willing to provide the best health care to people sometimes are denied resources and support. For these clinics to achieve continued quality service and success, resources and moral support are essential. In turn, community health care clinics can play a bigger part in changing the future of Appalachia.

A Small Community Fights for Survival

In Appalachia's ongoing battle to overcome poverty, one small community has taken a unique direction toward developing solutions to many problems, and its story should be told. The basic premise is, when people reach the lowest level of existence but are given an opportunity for self-survival, they become motivated to effectively work for change. The town of David is not exactly a thriving community, but proudly holds its own by virtue of the people's enormous persistence and determination. By actions of its residents and outside humanitarians, the legend of this revitalized community was born.

Explorer Daniel Boone used the area around David as his winter camping ground and would roam this beautiful land, called Lick Fork of Middle Creek. The valley, well nestled in the isolated backcountry of

Floyd County, and a "whistle's reach" over the hill to Magoffin, has been called by some "pristine land." Boone first visited here in 1767, and considered it one of his favorite hunting grounds. The isolation of this area did not offer opportunities to mineral rights speculators and coal companies during the big boom of the 20th century. Inaccessibility of Lick Fork was a major reason why this part of Floyd County was not exposed to the coal industry until 1940, when core drilling occurred to determine the feasibility for serious mining. By that time, Appalachia's production of "black gold" was at its highest level.

The starting point for the chronicle of David as a coal town began more than two decades after other communities had experienced this mining phenomenon and were on a downtrend. In 1941, with the onset of constructing a few dwellings at the mouth of Rough and Tough Hollow, the Princess Coal Company began its operation. By the end of 1941, just prior to World War II, approximately 100 residences had been constructed and this coal town officially was named after the company's president, David Francis. In those days, David was not a typical coal town, in fact it became known as a model community for the mountain region. Through cooperation by the company and miners, certain developments brought recognition to this small mountain settlement. For example, effective action of its people working toward a common cause occurred in 1950, when a swimming pool was built by the miners for families of the area. While mining practices were considered up-to-date, the operation was financially profitable, and families lived in adequate dwellings that had not fallen apart by the forces of mother nature. As a result, the community developed a deep sense of pride and desire to grow economically, socially, and culturally.

Good working conditions along with community life were being recognized by newspapers from Louisville and Huntington, as well as in mining magazines; even a government film had espoused the effectiveness of cooperation in David. The whole town participated in activities and organizations that ranged from scouting on their own campgrounds to women's clubs. Even a singing group, the "Patsy Teenagers," was started by the wife of a company engineer, Betty Fiedler. Under her direction, and later headed by Katherine Frazier of Prestonsburg, the singers traveled throughout the country and appeared on national television. What David had going was community spirit, which emanated from a corporation that shared a positive relationship with employees and their families. It was a generation of workers who showed loyalty to family and work, as well as pride in sharing camaraderie with fellow workers and neighbors.

I saw the town of David for the first time in 1964, which was after its peak years, when the Princess Elkhorn Coal Company used to employ 600 miners at the Lick Fork site. In the 60's, Appalachia had been experiencing a great recession, unemployment was high and the coal industry had diminished its workforce, replacing men with machines. For the people of David good times came to an end in 1968, when the coal company's president closed the operation. From that time on this industry did not evoke a sense of pride in its workers, even though another coal company bought the mining operation, but functioned on a limited basis until 1972. What did occur thereafter were sporadic efforts of strip mining by different small independent companies.

The town was sold by David Francis in 1968 to another company, which then turned around and disposed of properties at different intervals. With Princess Elkhorn Coal Company no longer in charge of the community, any legacy that had remained was now locked within the people. They were hurting, and part of their efforts and actions to make this a good place to live were hampered, thus all the progress and achievements made over a generation were lost "overnight." Within a short time, dwellings that they were renting quickly turned into shambles. The number of workers and families had been reduced to a "precious few." David became a shadow of what it once was, held together by people who were committed to help the community survive. At this time the Brothers of Charity from Philadelphia, along with concerned citizens led by Ashland "Hawk" Howard and the David Community Development Corporation, brought about the revitalization of this small coal town. Since the early 70's, people have been able to purchase the homes that they formerly rented. With a church and federal loan, the DCDC bought the town of David in 1974, and also financed a new water system. Property was purchased by a non-profit alternative institution known as David Independent School, which is nationally recognized for its service to youth and people of the region. After the Brothers of Charity left this community, the Sisters of Mercy from Martin continued their work by establishing human development programs and business ventures that proved to be effective in providing employment for people in the community.

Today, many human development programs are headed by Sister Ida Marie Deville, who had been a school principal in Texas before coming to help this area. Under Sister Ida Marie's leadership and guidance, education is the basis for various endeavors that the community attempts. Through a training program certain residents are helping to build new structures, which include housing. Sister Ida Marie is a strong believer that the results of this approach will be evident in future work that these people could be involved with. David Appalachian Craftsmanship, through its cottage industry, employs over 100 persons who are able to supplement their income. The many crafts that are produced in David are sold throughout the country. In a discussion with Lucille Johnson of this non-profit organization, she noted that "the residents have developed self-esteem, which is important in order to gain a sense of direction."

It would have been easier for humanitarians, such as Sister Ida Marie Deville, to work in urban areas of America. Instead, she has resolved to stay in the heart of poverty — Appalachia, where the community of David stands as an oasis of hope, giving people a chance for survival. What I have noticed is that these people are anxious to change their lives and do not want to depend on welfare, for they are proud to work, even if the income is meager. With the support of such givers as Sister Ida Marie, the town of David will survive.

Indeed, the Appalachian Crafts projects, training people for work opportunities, and the David Independent School, are shining examples of how to revive hope in adults and rescue children with educational problems. What this highlights is the overall importance of simple good deeds in remedying the economic and social ills. It is true that these are only small solutions to massive Appalachian problems, but they are stepping stones for a new start. When Sister Ida Marie decided to come to David and help the people, she did more than commit to serve them. Sister Deville also provided the leadership that would help them reshape their future. An example of the people's great appreciation for Sister Ida Marie is the annual education scholarship, awarded in her name, to a deserving youth.

The David School
Dan Greene, Founder

It wasn't too long ago that a great number of youth were dropping out of the public schools in Floyd County. This became a subject of concern, but very little was done to overcome the crisis. However, in the early 1970's that began to change. Concern for these young people led Dan Greene to pioneer a school that dealt with difficult problems — educational and social. Dan Greene is a leader on a mission to broaden education opportunities for children who were not given a chance to succeed in regular public school programs. In 1972, the unique independent David School opened and provided an alternative in dealing with students who left local public schools early. This was precipitated by the fact that the dropout rate in Floyd County had reached 40 percent.

Dan Greene, who came from New York State to Floyd County in 1968 as a church volunteer, found that many children lacked wholesome educational experiences, and looked for ways to help them. He envisioned a non-sectarian school aimed at guiding these youngsters of poverty, whose families' incomes were very limited. The type of student selected to attend this alternative school had a background of deficiencies that included apathy, despair, parental indifference, and a general lack of concern.

With the aid of two helpers, Dan Greene raised funds to build a school that would eventually become a nationally recognized model, creating opportunities for effective learning and meeting the needs of those dropouts who were unable to function in regular classroom settings. Other reasons for these students coming to David School included seeking better self-understanding, developing and improving skills of learning, and exploring new talents. The education offered provides guidance on an individual basis through varied approaches that encourages the student to overcome his or her deficiencies. This may be acquired collectively, through study groups, seminars, or individualized tutoring, which is the major source for learning.

These and other factors provide the kind of environment that makes learning a challenge, encourages self-responsibility, and fosters success in a young person. The dream Dan Greene, his faculty and staff have, is to turn around the attitude of young people who lost interest in education. They have succeeded by offering solid learning experiences and encourage work responsibility. Specific extensions of this effective philosophical approach have led to the establishment of student-run services, where they gain valuable work experience, as well as improve mathematical, reading and social skills.

One of the chief obstacles to the School's success has become one of its greatest strengths: all students are from low income families. They have learned to cope with their limited resources, but are required to participate in a community service program, where they give back to the people. Realism of giving to others leaves no doubt that this school is preparing its young students in becoming responsible to themselves and their community. Experiences that were gained at David School had a positive impact on each individual's future. The more secure a person feels, the healthier his or her family environment becomes.

Another major factor of success with this program is parent involvement. From the start, it emphasizes the importance that parents be involved along with their children. One key element is that faculty and staff are visiting with parents at home to gain support from them in sharing responsibility and helping the children. With this type of family attention, parents can encourage offspring to achieve educational goals, which are made possible by the school's overall positive attitude and special efforts. Results have been outstanding for the David School Program, and even the most disadvantaged adults want to do a better job of parenting. This approach is just one type of guidance and support that has led to enthusiasm of all involved persons.

Unfortunately, young people in Floyd and other counties are dropping out of public school at an increased rate. There is a need for students to succeed, and David School has been showing the way. For those students who have come to this non-profit school for help, more than 95 percent complete high school and are prepared for life in the real world. Within a few years, David School has transformed young people in gaining a solid base for learning. Results are evident in the high academic achievement records of its students, and the school has been recognized as a vanguard for dropout prevention initiatives. This acknowledgment is noteworthy, because one of the most valuable contributions is that it has given new opportunities to those youth who previously were excluded from most public school educational programs. Recognition of David School has come from the Appalachian Regional Commission, Kentucky State Dropout Prevention Commission, and by many local school boards. The school was also honored by former President George Bush for its humanitarian community service program. *Readers Digest* called Dan Greene an "American Hero in Education." Finally, credit must be given to this fine educator, his loyal faculty and staff, for ensuring that their students overcome many obstacles. This sets the stage for encouraging more youth to succeed in school, so they can be ready for life as productive and effective adults.

Workers Of Rural Kentucky (W.O.R.K.)
Stella Marshall, Director

Since the 1980's, too many people in Owsley County seemed directionless, and life to them had no purpose or meaning. According to official government reports, this county is Kentucky's poorest, and census figures cite that 47 percent of all families live in poverty, of which more than half are children. The unemployment picture shows that 50 percent of the physically able population cannot find work. In 1985, a nun from the Sisters of Saint Francis, Noel Le Claire, was sent by her order to work with people of Owsley County. Two years later, Sister Le Claire and a group of concerned citizens, who were mainly women, formed Workers Of Rural Kentucky, Inc., a non-profit organization.

When Sister Le Claire asked members of W.O.R.K. what they wanted for their community, the answer was unequivocally a need for jobs, so that people could get off the welfare support system. Appalachians are proud and do not like to be called poor, for they take exception to this label. What these people want is to work and make a decent living to improve their situation. Motivation is extremely high and understandable, since they have learned to survive in one of the most impoverished places of our nation. Working together, Sister Le Claire and the group organized to create opportunities for members and other interested citizens.

In spite of many obstacles such as financing, their aim is to help low-income people become entrepreneurs, start businesses and provide jobs. Since public grants were not available, whether local, state or federal, W.O.R.K. approached church groups, individuals and organizations to help contribute for the start up of this worthwhile community project. Money was raised through bake or yard sales and other grass-roots fundraising efforts. The Christian Appalachian Project (CAP) also contributed through organizational and development training programs, helping W.O.R.K. effectively get off the ground. Some members even traveled to Hazard Community College to take entrepreneurial classes. Learning experiences that these novice organizers gained from CAP and HCC services proved beneficial for developing strategies and upgrading community economic and social conditions.

The organization, located in Booneville, encountered tough times at first, but has helped women start small business ventures which required very little capital. Even though nobody is getting rich, businesses are still functioning, and the effectiveness of opportunities has transformed lives by improving self-esteem and confidence. Membership is open to all persons of the community, especially the low-income, who want to obtain employment through W.O.R.K. Private non-profit organizations are the main source of funding in order to increase the efforts of fighting poverty. Even though this program focuses on self-employment as a way out of welfare, it collaborates with other groups in promoting justice and improving the quality of life in rural southeastern Kentucky. W.O.R.K.'s objective of self-employment addressed a long-standing oversight in the region. Their concern is that most of the federal money has gone toward Appalachian infrastructure development, while very little is spent on the people.

The uniqueness of starting a business in backwoods Booneville, Owsley county, and succeeding or surviving, is a tribute to the ingenuity of this organization. According to 1990 U.S. Government Census Reports, per capita-income in Owsley ran at 5,791 dollars, compared with the national average of 14,410. Data about this area shows that living conditions are inadequate for too many residents. Twenty percent of the homes are without plumbing, and one in three do not have a telephone.

Housing is a challenge for W.O.R.K. and they want to make it their major objective. Three years ago, when Stella Marshall took over as director of the organization, its mission was to build low income housing. Ms. Marshall, a native of Booneville, is one of many people who did not want to stay on welfare. She is an amazing woman despite a limited educational background and enduring an abusive relationship with her former husband. Generally, the physical and mental results of such a situation would render a person incapacitated. Instead Ms. Marshall is a mother with great strength and persistent leadership qualities, guiding underprivileged people to astounding challenges. Today, W.O.R.K. is looked at as a "big economic development success in this area" says Ms. Marshall, and a great deal of credit should go to this woman of determination.

People who criticize businesses managed by women of low income may question the focusing on self-employment projects as a way out of welfare. They do not see long range stability for small businesses and criticize the lack of overall effectiveness on the economy, due to limited backgrounds of these people. However, there are philanthropic foundations very favorable to the approximately 200 programs in 41 states that aim at helping poor people to finance small businesses. Organizations such as the Mott Foundation, have recently given attention to businesses conducted by low income women. Mott saw potential in these ventures by lending over 5 million dollars nationally, with results showing an 80 percent success rate. The bottom line is that people are working and feel proud of their accomplishments.

Pride and self-esteem were generated through success of businesses and availability of jobs, which has led Ms. Marshall and her organization to pursue new horizons, as additional projects are just getting underway. A dream came true when W.O.R.K. joined Habitat For Humanity and another group from Breathitt County. They started to repair homes and helped with other small projects which are very much needed. Their goal for the immediate future is to build new homes and repair as many older ones as possible. Two years ago, attention was given to poor mothers who were faced with lack of opportunities. Realizing that it could serve a dual purpose, W.O.R.K. initiated grants for mothers who have young children, so they could start their own child care operations. On the other hand the organization knew that day care in Owsley and Lee Counties was needed for children, so parents could go to work or further their education. From all indications, it appears that this effort has been successful.

The expansion of this organization's services has led to the development of a Tutor and Literacy Program for children and adults at risk. Also, members of W.O.R.K. have moved toward education as a source of self-improvement; some completing their GED, others enter college study for the first time. The knowledge these helpers have gained from their actual work experiences is immeasurable and fulfilling. Group members like Ms. Marshall have attended the University of Kentucky Commonwealth Leadership Program, and others participated in Berea College's New Opportunity School for Women. This program is open to poor women between 35 and 55 years of age and offers a 3-week program of varied learning experiences. W.O.R.K.'s many projects have just started, and there are some obstacles to overcome, however determination and enthusiasm of its members serve as a solid foundation for success.

Christian Appalachian Project (CAP)
Father Ralph W. Beiting, Founder

Ralph W. Beiting, while studying for priesthood at a seminary in the 1940's, had a vision that someday he would help poor people of Appalachia. Today, Father Beiting is a legend who exemplifies what can be done through selflessness and dedication by nurturing people, with persistent drive in challenging the ills of poverty. He has provided the leadership and guidance for a most dynamic organization of giving individuals, whose common bond is to help the impoverished. Since he started the interdenominational non-profit Christian Appalachian Project in the 1950's, thousands of volunteers have joined this organization to share Father Beiting's "vision" in alleviating poverty. As CAP continues to grow, it may seem difficult to believe that so many volunteers have helped the less fortunate of Appalachia in different ways. Having lived in eastern Kentucky myself, I know how grateful poor people are toward those who give of themselves. Persons who have never seen the reality of poverty cannot imagine that help and goodness from humanitarians represent a priceless treasure to the needy.

From the time Father Beiting started his first mission parish, which included Garrard, Rockcastle, Jackson, and southern Madison counties in eastern Kentucky, he has always been concerned about reaching as many less fortunate people as possible. Fortunately, with the Roman Catholic Church sending him to establish missions throughout Appalachia, he was able to expand CAP. During the beginning of this organization, Father Beiting set goals that were aimed at providing food, clothing and household goods for the poor. In the meantime he was developing a support system of volunteers which was critical for the growth of CAP. Around the mid-fifties, Father Beiting started a much needed camp for youth of the area, who were underprivileged. Immediately after opening the youth camp, other long lasting ventures were added to build a solid foundation for those poor who wanted to help themselves. They included used clothing stores that were called "The Attic," Bible schools, emergency assistance, and a dairy farm. Their success led to further undertakings, such as a woodworking shop, greenhouse and a factory making Christmas items.

Although these businesses were not aimed at creating an extensive amount of jobs, they had a significant impact on the local economy. The dairy farm, which began with six donated Holsteins, operated by native Garrard County volunteer George Purcell, has been very successful. Today it provides economic benefits for extremely poverty-stricken and financially poor Jackson County. By using imaginative solutions to problem situations, one of the most successful enterprises began back in the 1960's and

217

is still going strong today — the Christmas Wreath Factory. It employs ten people throughout the year and nearly 150 during manufacturing season.

Since the beginning, Father Beiting's Christian Appalachian Project has placed emphasis on bringing to the people social and economic opportunities that would help lead them out of poverty's grip. Operating on a sound philosophy of "helping people help themselves" during the early 1970's, workers of CAP realized that several important elements were necessary for healthy economic growth to occur. Emphasis was given to human development, addressing short and long term needs. Planning and programming CAP services for long lasting projects included child development centers, counseling services, college scholarships for high school seniors, tutoring of teenagers and adults working toward high school equivalency certification, and adult literacy instruction. The organization has also been successful in developing teen and youth centers, a health advocacy program, life skills training, and supported employment opportunities for people with disabilities. CAP did not stop there, and wherever another need appeared, it proceeded in developing necessary approaches to overcome problems. One such area of concern pertained to elderly people and other adults, who were making transitions in their lives. Through construction of residences, CAP was helping them adapt from insecure situations to full independence. Also, social services and counseling have been provided so that these people could effectively make adjustments to alleviate traumatic experiences of change.

Stories detailing many efforts of CAP are well documented in the national media. Magazines and newspapers have reported the success of short term projects such as emergency financial assistance, home repair service, visitation of elderly people, spouse abuse shelters, food and gift baskets on holidays, a respite facility for families who have members with disabilities, and a family recreation complex. This is only a segment of growing human development programs that CAP has initiated. One in particular had been brought to my attention during a visit to eastern Kentucky. I met parents of a disabled child, who were given instruction by CAP services on how to teach their pre-schooler. In caring for their dependent child, they had a difficult time trying to find professional help, until a friend told them about CAP. They could not express their gratitude enough for the commitment and caring given by this organization, and were elated with the progress of their young child.

Due to the success of services, expansion of the organization has coincided with the transfer of Father Beiting to new parishes. In the 1970's, he was designated to serve five more counties: Pulaski, Owsley, Casey, McCreary and Estill. This move brought an increase of CAP volunteers to help the poor in these counties. During 1981, Father Beiting was also assigned a mission parish that covered Floyd and Magoffin counties, and as a result, the needs of these people also had to be taken into consideration. As the years progressed, contributions of this organization have become more evident. Driving through Floyd County during the 1980's, I noticed a red school bus parked next to the side of a road, where people worked inside, while others waited to enter the vehicle. The bus was used by CAP as a service program facility for tutoring teenagers and adults, who were working on high school equivalency certifications and also offered adult literacy instruction. This created an unforgettable picture, seeing concerned volunteers helping those who were making an effort to change their future.

In 1991, Father Beiting's next assignment was the mission in Lawrence County. This established an opportunity for CAP to develop programs in Lawrence as well as Martin county. Whenever Father Beiting was assigned to a new parish, CAP programs sprang up to help the poor of that area. The remarkable work of this missionary and his organization through many years of service captures true devotion of Christian giving. Their actions are so well known throughout the country that I even heard a national radio newscaster in Florida talk about 350 students from thirty-two colleges, who wanted to forsake their 1994 spring vacation in order to volunteer in Appalachia and repair homes or work on other short-term projects.

This organization has an extraordinarily unique way of operating, and whenever there is need, it will initiate action. When CAP received a large donation of books in 1986, it launched a program known as "Operation Sharing." Along with other goods, including food, garden seeds and home repair supplies that were donated from a number of sources, a distribution network was started. Today, these as well as other items are shipped to grass-roots organizations of all Kentucky counties and to an additional twelve Appalachian states. If emergency needs occur elsewhere, Sharing will expand services to states outside the Appalachian mountain range. The impact of "Operation Sharing" has been overwhelming for thousands of people who have benefited from its contributions.

As influence of this organization increased in a number of counties, economic development became a central force in helping to change the very nature of poverty. During the 1980's, CAP initiated another program that helped communities get attention for economic development potential. Working with groups by providing technical advice to already existing organizations, it further supplied small grants for local development. By 1991, CAP had formed the Appalachian Development Corporation (ADC), a for-profit, wholly-owned subsidary. The need for people to be employed had been apparent and the demand for existing businesses to provide jobs was not met. Entrepreneurs who were seeking financial resources to get started in a new venture had encountered frustration. ADC took the most direct and cost-effective way, brightening the outlook for individuals and communities. Their mission is to buy existing businesses or begin new ones that will employ 30-35 people, and locate them in underdeveloped areas of eastern Kentucky. As with everything this organization got involved in, it could not afford to ignore the need for economic growth and acknowledged the problem of unemployment. Therefore, ADC was ready and willing to develop initiatives for business growth and employment in Appalachia.

As CAP continues to expand offerings of helping the people, success could not have been possible without the many volunteers and workers that have contributed. Its goal to include volunteers is a benefit that cannot be extolled enough, for today over hundreds of men and women are daily playing an important role in its many programs. On top of this, more than 600 employees, of which 300 are on full-time basis and the remaining on part-time or seasonal programs, are positioned at all levels of the organization, and support the multitude of ongoing activities.

Through the years, the Christian Appalachian Project has symbolized resourcefulness, energy and drive by ordinary people, providing extraordinary action with efforts to improve lives of the less fortunate. There are many individuals who deserve gratitude; whether employee, volunteer, or financial contributor to CAP, they all have helped by sending forth a positive message that is being heard loud and clear. It relates to the vision of a young seminarian almost fifty years ago, who is a priest today, and wants to fulfill that dream by continuing to help the less fortunate with the assistance of dedicated people who are sacrificing their personal life in order to serve others in need. The inter-denominational Christian Appalachian Project, which requires financial and other resources to keep it going, is the largest non-profit private service organization in eastern Kentucky. As the 20th century winds down and the 21st is approaching, this dynamic operation will continue its mission "to help the people help themselves," by providing opportunities for overcoming the hopelessness of poverty.

Hazard, A Model for Community Change

Appalachia's communities have been criticized for living in the past, lacking many services for appropriate human existence and development. Some critics even said that living conditions were too dirty, unsafe and depressing. Outsiders considered these communities "backward," yet the people were forced to exist this way and survived despite their problems. However, one community is demonstrating its desire to change. Hazard has turned toward progress over the past years through dynamic leadership and a concerned group of individuals, who are working for a better future.

Contrary to most communities of eastern Kentucky that have been struggling to redirect their economy after coal industry employment began to decline decades ago, Hazard has taken aggressive action for development over the past 16 years. Industries and businesses are now looking at Hazard, and consider relocation because of its excellent geographical setting. It lies on the banks of the Kentucky River's North Fork, bordered by junction route 80, (Daniel Boone Parkway) and route 15. This city is an example of what happens to communities located on or a little way off a modern highway, which are built to help improve the region. With the construction of route 80, access from other communities to Hazard has made travel much easier and faster. For example, a ride from Hindman in nearby Knott County used to take 45 minutes thirty years ago, driving on a treacherous road that wound and twisted around the base of mountains. Now it takes a comfortable 20 minutes on the new scenic route 80. Hindman may not have grown in past years, nor has industry shown any significant improvement, but with the highway bringing these two communities closer together, a tremendous change is occurring in the area, affecting both places.

When Mayor William Gorman and the city commission, consisting of Elizabeth Duncan, Dr. John Gilbert, Herman Maggard and Ben Roll, were elected into office in 1976, Hazard and its surrounding area was in the throes of continued high unemployment. Streets and roads leading into the city were deteriorating, as well as gravel and hard-surfaced roads that came from the hollows. Entering the outskirts of Hazard at routes 80 and 15 interchange today, posts such as "construction ahead" greet the visitor. One can see bulldozers, excavators, bucket loaders, rock crushers and giant trucks moving like an army of ants, busily cutting off tops and sides of mountains, restructuring these giant towers of stone into tiered levels to make room for a medical building, modern shopping center, new national chain motels, restaurants, other facilities and beautiful homes, which makes one realize that this is a forward looking community, planning for the future.

Hazard is only a small city, wanting to show growth in many ways. It is incomplete in what its leaders have planned, yet there has been progress. Consequently, it should be of interest to all who care about Appalachia's future, because the success of Hazard may represent a key element in the region's ongoing quest for economic development, which positively affects social conditions of the city, county, area, and region. One might ask, why should people care about a community that is not the

221

biggest in the region, and does not even have the largest area of land to build on? The answer presents itself by looking at the fact that because of growth, there are one-third more jobs available than Hazard's total population of 6,000. People from villages and towns in Knott, Letcher, Leslie, Breathitt, as well as Perry County, are using the new major highways, commuting to work in this city. It astounds outsiders that over 180,000 persons live within one-half hour from Hazard, which is serving as the focal point by bringing them together, providing a sense of civic identity and presence. The outlying areas, with ideal country living conditions of "peace and quiet" and clean air, cannot offer its residents the types of service and economic muscle like a community such as Hazard.

Contrary to what people believe, immediate surroundings and the total region also profit through job opportunities because of the economic boost by this city. The spin-off leads to the working people buying not only in Hazard, but in their own local stores, restaurants and gas stations. Even the banks and other services will benefit, for growth of Hazard has definite positive implications beyond city and county borders. Mayor Bill Gorman and the city commissioners, who are a respectable, vibrant and progressive administration, have concern about the need to grow economically and socially. Because of solid achievements, Hazard's government ranks today among the most forward thinking and effective in Appalachia.

Traditionally, many communities known as "progressive and vibrant," tend to base their growth on a solid foundation of services that effectively and efficiently enrich the community and area. Hazard is a good example, for it has cohesion and upward mobility, and one of the most modern "model rural health and training centers" in the United States is located here. Some boosters consider this city the "focal point and business center for eastern Kentucky." The expansion of Hazard brought much needed small businesses and industries to this community over the past years. Construction, both commercial and non-commercial, has been on the increase. Extending recreational benefits of the immediate surrounding area, from beautiful lakes, state and national parks, will provide additional opportunities for comprehensive activities that enrich the quality of life in these communities.

The city is proud of its safe drinking water supply, and has expanded water service to nearby areas of other counties. Planning and construction of water lines are ongoing, as the area's needs are being met. Hazard and Perry County have been key allies for a unified plan to develop many services, such as government facilities and other projects that are providing credibility and show results of their cooperative efforts. They include new fire stations, elementary and secondary schools, vocational-technical and community college facilities. Even surrounding counties worked together in a myriad of endeavors to improve the Appalachian way of life. Today, counties throughout the area and region that are in dire need of many services and help are bolstered by astute leaders, who even cross political party lines in order to accomplish change in Appalachia.

Other key forces, like certain coal companies, are pitching in and contributing to the betterment of communities. Cypress Mountain Minerals Corporation, which is considered a leader in using reclaimed land with its "Starfire Project" on the Perry-Knott County line, has been very influential. It stimulated other companies in reclaiming land for recreational and other purposes to enrich community life in Appalachia. Another development, an event center at Avawam on the outskirts of Hazard, and located next to the Daniel Boone National Forest, was initiated by the Sun Company. Land which is being donated to the city by this company, called the Honey Branch Development, will be available and contain a multipurpose facility that includes a 1.2 acre indoor arena, an outdoor arena, a recreational area and a trail that leads to the Daniel Boone National Forest.

Among other noteworthy projects of coal corporations is one by the Kem Company, which received national recognition for its work at an abandoned mine, when reclaiming 600 acres that were needed to make room for the regional airport at Hazard. Leeco Corporation also was honored with a national award for its innovative design and operation of a preparation plant, refuse and disposal area. Another unique contribution occurred in Knott County, between Pippa Passes and Hindman. Land was donated by coal owner John Preece to build a much needed shopping center to service both communities. Benefits go beyond shopping need advantages, by providing a closer relationship between these places.

A most ambitious endeavor for Hazard and Perry County is probably the development of a 100 million dollar woodchip plant, which is moving toward completion by spring, 1995. The economic impact of such a facility would mean hundreds of new jobs, millions in wages, additional tax revenues, and will encourage many people to move into the area. Workers and their families would generate additional money. The industry should have offshoots of necessary services. Most importantly, the positive impact a new industry has on people, community and surrounding area, is immeasurable.

The growth of Hazard has brought questions to the minds of leaders from villages and towns in nearby counties. These places have deteriorated for years and survival is tied to Hazard's success, a growing and vibrant rural center. They are now more important than ever, for not only is work needed because their existence is threatened, but if growth continues in Hazard, employment increases, creating job opportunities. Left on their own, many of these villages and towns would further decline. However, looking at the future role of these communities as a work supply force for growth of the Hazard-Perry County area, they could be imbued with new directions, new uses, and ultimately new vitality.

Looking at the strategic position that Hazard embodies for the area, which includes Perry, Knott, Breathitt, Letcher, Owsley and Leslie counties, it is obviously the physical center. The two major highways converge here: Route 80 from the east, continuing as Daniel Boone Parkway to the west, and Route 15 from the north and south. Even the primary railroad of this area runs through Hazard. Natural features and amenities of the ideal location make it a prime factor for current and future development. Advantages of restoring not only Hazard but also the immediate counties, could serve as impetus for other areas of Appalachia to consider their future. Historically, as any urban or rural setting develops, surrounding communities grow symbiotically. Therefore, industry in a central area of Appalachia would work effectively as a link to nearby towns and villages. It is easier for people to travel toward a central destination rather than heading in different directions, especially when a modern highway, such as Route 80, provides transportation advantages.

Hazard is not only important because of industry, it is also the center for one of the most advanced models of comprehensive rural health care in the country, and provides services that go beyond its city limits, such as safe drinking water. New development of housing, which was never overwhelming in Hazard, is now providing a unique complement to the city's overall growth. This community has a long way to go, but progress must continue to further improve economic and social vitality of the area as the 21st century approaches, otherwise surrounding communities may become "a thing of the past." The link between Hazard and neighboring counties is still tenuous, though as growth continues, this city will play a major role in strengthening the future of Appalachia, and could serve as an inspiration for other areas.

Summation

Since 1980 to the present, eastern Kentucky has experienced an increase of cooperative action due to a broader based and astute leadership. However, Appalachia still continues to demonstrate the need for strengthening its regional goals, even though certain approaches and innovations, public and private, have taken viable steps toward overcoming some of the ills of poverty. The achievement of individuals and groups have led to new found hope in the fields of education, health care and social work.

One of the most significant changes in the 1990's, is the Kentucky Education Reform Act which has provided new opportunities. Through great initiative and humanitarian leadership by a former governor, the case for equal education of all children in Kentucky was brilliantly presented to the State Supreme Court. It took wisdom and vision of the high court to make this important decision. With a charge for action, the State General Assembly, all 138 members, assumed their responsibility overwhelmingly by providing one of the most dynamic state education reform acts in America. Unfortunately, in certain circumstances some legislators whose constituents back home did not agree that inequity of education had to be overcome, were voted out of office. These legislators had believed it was time to take a stand for the underprivileged against obstacles that have helped fuel conditions of poverty for decades.

During this period, the medical field was working diligently to address some long standing issues for an improved health status of the region. Developing strategies and action to combat these matters of concern has required great concentrated efforts because of understaffed medical and health personnel. However, the health status for poor people is showing signs of improvement in certain areas of the region, regarding preventive care, services for children, comprehensive clinic care, and a cooperative system of providing for mentally ill persons.

Even local governments in some communities are taking a lead role toward positive economic growth. Their plan is based on community needs and if proven successful, they can be used as a blueprint. Inherent in the success of these communities is that there are individuals and groups with the desire to work for human development progress. Not all towns and villages have this type of situation, in fact most do not have any diversity of opportunities to enrich the citizens and should confront their problems with candor. Political leadership must make every effort to deal with problems, otherwise the community's future will be at risk. A major concern is the lack of long range goals, because there are greater possibilities for continued decline. However if growth in development is to occur, they must operate on the principal of "shaping the times" through effective leadership. Towns and villages cannot afford to be handicapped by inaction, for the harsh reality is that "progress will pass them by." Through vision, dedication and hard work, communities in Appalachia must look at their assets and make the most of them. The desire for change has to come from leaders as well as the people.

Independent groups and organizations have made their presence more visible in recent years, by providing economic and social programs while helping the poor to be beneficiaries and active participants. This period also brought forth activists, who were concerned about the destruction and further deterioration of the land. Constant battles between mineral rights owners, land owners and environmentalists, led to significant decisions by Kentucky's populace and the State Supreme Court. These important steps were evident of Appalachia's grass-roots-action and commitment for a revitalized region.

All these efforts are heading toward the vision of a common goal. The aim is to achieve a better life and overcome impoverishment, by focusing on talents and resources of individuals and groups that are based on carefully determined priorities. All have an agenda not only aimed at providing for the poor, but also enabling "them to help themselves," which is a much needed ingredient in fighting poverty. A major concern confronting these humanitarians is the limited financial resources they have to work with. The fact remains, innovative initiatives are necessary for their non-profit organizations to gain additional resources of money in maintaining and expanding operations. If ways could be found, these groups and others would be able to meet the needs for a greater number of people, which will have a profound effect on the total region.

Chapter VII

The Future

A Time for Change

Despite many years of poverty in Appalachia, there is a glimmer of hope for its people, who are now given a new opportunity for change. The combination of rising expectation by individual, group and political involvement is beginning to show encouraging signs. Even self-motivating actions by some poor to improve their life symbolizes a positive attitude of hope, and is a turnaround from feelings of frustration for decades. What is now being seen are the results of positive leadership initiatives from concerned citizens. Their plan of action includes: reforming education, upgrading health care delivery, helping needy children, adults and elderly, improving living conditions, responding against devastation of land, as well as working for economic growth through expansion of business and industry, which will lead to employment opportunities. The mountain folk recognize that efforts of our government through the years did not suffice in eradicating poverty, and realize that they need to take the leadership role in solving their own problems. There is movement to achieve success by combating the ravages of poverty, and with each day that resolve is showing results.

With changes taking place in Appalachia today, we see a different trend of fighting poverty. For example, economic and social movement in eastern Kentucky has been initiated by non-profit self-governing groups of people who are sacrificing their personal lives, even though they have no

227

material reason to do so. They are sincere, and strongly believe that the poor should be treated fairly and must be given an opportunity in learning how to help themselves. Since the 1960's War on Poverty, a grass-roots movement in this region has come about, because government was slow or reluctant to totally commit its resources for the needy. Poverty, which escalated for too many years, has become a more complex problem. To some people it appears that government has allowed the gap between the have and have-nots to widen so much, whereby the future of our less fortunate looks dismal.

With this scenario facing Appalachia, the grass-roots movement has taken an effective leadership role by responding to varied needs of the poor. However, there is much more that has to be done, as these individuals and organizations need assistance in building a unified consensus for future growth and prosperity. The result is that people must work together to overcome the economic, political, physical, cultural, and social conditions that are synonymous with poverty. We are knowledgeable about impoverishment and its long term ills, which have provided us with many learning experiences, and understand that no single program or action can solve all the problems of needy persons. The fact is that focusing on each single issue must be viewed as a part of the all-embracing nature of poverty. Although the task of undertaking a comprehensive and integrated plan of action may appear insurmountable, strategies for overcoming these ills have already been established or are being developed.

What I have presented in this book is a view of selected individuals and groups who have demonstrated energy and enthusiasm in finding ways to translate initiatives into action, which exemplifies true humanitarianism. The dynamic force that seems to be the main source of constructive efforts manifested in these individuals and groups, is their absolute commitment to this region and its people. We must recognize the great inspiration that this regionalistic devotion is capable of generating, but it is not sufficient and needs government involvement to help eastern Kentuckians accomplish their cause and achieve progress. A comprehensive partnership among all levels of government, working in support of those individual leaders and groups who have been on the front line battling poverty, is necessary to better understand success for change. In turn, if the administration is sincere in helping, it must come to grips with the reality of working with these grass-roots leaders. Government should serve as an acknowledged backer, and perhaps effective strategies and actions could be developed to serve as model for a broader and greater scope of people not only in eastern Kentucky, but elsewhere in our country. In retrospect, there is not a more appropriate time than the present for Appalachia to strengthen the individualism of its people, which consequently will help bring about change. Agony and cries of the poor must be answered, so their children can live without the deprivation that has been experienced all these years.

The spearhead of this new leadership movement for change and growth is coming from people whose vision for strategies to combat poverty's conditions are on the threshold of developing a better future for Appalachia. In seeking insights and approaches to understand eastern Kentucky's direction, reliable trends must be examined and assessed. Through analysis of the past and present, a positive "blueprint" is necessary for development of the region's emergence into the 21st Century. The hillfolk are at a crossroads, and should not accept the continued problem of poverty as inevitable, because conviction to act now could mean change for the future.

Appalachia's Economic Future

In studying eastern Kentucky's economic situation, it is important to examine the processes by which change can be brought about. Decisions made to effect a positive turnaround call for solutions that will benefit the region. Discouraging realities of Appalachia's past must not deter forward thinking about economic progress. One way this can be achieved is through strategies that encourage combined efforts of grass-roots organizations and governmental agencies. In turn, this will demand great visionary planning for solutions of a better economic future.

As we look at Appalachia today, a crystal ball is not needed to determine that a crisis exists. If a one-dimensional industry is to continue as the main source for this region's survival, the economy will look like an old car in need of repair, sputtering down a road to oblivion. It can not depend on coal mining alone, for with the addition of automation, many men have lost their jobs. After years of exploitation, coal miners are no longer needed, facing life without hope of being called back to work, which is catastrophic for them and their families. Financial devastation reigns, as their future in Appalachia becomes a prolonged cycle of poverty. Therefore people continue to migrate with sadness in their hearts, as the remaining population's attitude and spirit will end up in despairing defeat if their problems do not diminish soon. One must recognize, that poverty has been with eastern Kentucky people for many decades, and any immediate economic solution generally ends up in superficial quick fixes. In fact, conditions in the region call for redirection that includes diversification of industries, which has been a missing ingredient in the past. In order to move toward economic expansion, bold and innovative planning for long term growth should be a major goal in meeting Appalachian needs.

Need For Strong Economic Development

The future for economic development in eastern Kentucky is the most important and critical issue. Reduced growth throughout our country has given rise to competition from other regions and states that are applying aggressive and energetic methods of enticing corporations to relocate. For Appalachia, the discouraging fact that our total nation is in a crisis, warrants greater emphasis on attracting outside companies in moving their operations and jobs to the highlands. This calls for well organized efforts, otherwise unforeseen obstacles will require greater energy to expand economic development. During the past years, many areas throughout the United States have made efforts to persuade American as well as international corporations to relocate. There is even a more dramatic impact when a community lands a major corporation, which affects improvement of employment and personal incomes throughout the surrounding area. One example is Toyota, which opened a plant in Georgetown, north central Kentucky. The many changes that have occurred in this community with the coming of an industrial giant includes growth of existing and new small businesses. Also, higher priority is given to infrastructure projects, and opportunities for operation centers in that part of the state are much better now, since major highways have been built.

As part of progressive action by the State of Kentucky for improving economic opportunities to entice out-of-state industry, Lieutenant Governor Paul Patton initiated in 1992 three incentive packages that offered businesses a decade's worth of income tax credits, covering up to 100 percent of construction and start-up costs. Certain states, following Kentucky's determined effort to improve economic conditions, are developing similar approaches to lure industry into their communities. In response to this aggressive action, states that are losing corporations have reacted with their own incentives, trying to prevent existing industries from moving operations elsewhere. To further complicate the issue of corporate relocation, certain considerations are no longer exclusive to large cities or metropolitan settings. Companies are now looking for areas of uniqueness and financial advantages that help decide where to relocate their operation.

Aggressiveness by eastern Kentucky communities to gain a share of economic projects should be their top priority. Local government policies must be examined to ensure competitiveness with other areas of America and foreign countries, in order to attract quality industry through a strong development program. Besides providing good paying jobs for residents, corporations also donate to schools, children's programs, fund raising projects, sporting events, recreational activities, the arts, as well as other happenings that would benefit the cross section of a community. This is the kind of impact a new company has, and looking at places such as Georgetown, one can also see great pride among the people, for they are working, and long-term incentives look encouraging. What it means is that this place has gained prominence as a thriving community, which is changing people's lives.

With a new company operating in a community, offshoot businesses will be available as extended service of or to that respective industry and become important tools for improving economic growth. The result is that employment in the area should increase. Community growth, ranging from public services, health care and improvement of roads, could multiply. Eastern Kentucky must also realize, by planning roads and adding highways conducive to back country areas, more people will be given a chance to benefit from progress. Conditions of inefficient roads must be eliminated since Appalachia can no longer afford to be impervious to change. Ways and means have to be found by the State and federal government to establish a better road system that is going to make it attractive for industry to relocate or develop in this region.

An advantage of progressive community action is to recognize opportunities that a tuned-in educational system can supply by meeting employment needs of new industry. Research is showing that creative use of education and industrial cooperation, especially through instructional delivery services, constitutes many benefits to a community. As the economy continues to require more skilled workers, immediate and long term, it coincides with the goals of Kentucky's Education Reform Act, which calls for job-oriented training. The simple truth is that eastern Kentucky cannot compete for high-tech jobs by offering unskilled people. Retraining of unemployed persons for the right jobs should be a major objective when establishing such programs in Appalachia.

Government-funded retraining programs also allows the unemployed to study for specific high demand occupations. Some jobs, like computer-related positions in business, medical, allied health, and electronic fields, appear to have long term employment implications. However, when training workers, there has to be a consistency of organized planning and evaluation of the market situation, in order to be prepared for an occupation that has job openings. The need for unskilled workers to acquire education for new opportunities is also a priority, which warrants that these individuals become productively employable. Chances are that illiterate and unskilled persons will be without work and fall further behind, as the employable population sees their income rise.

Corporations intending to relocate, always look for amenities and uniqueness relating to a potential move. Emphasis is also placed on sta-

231

bility of a community and the existence of family values. These are reasons why Appalachia should be able to attract corporations, because their sense of community and strong family foundations have remained relatively unchanged. Another added plus that should also be considered, is the work ethic of eastern Kentucky people. For generations mountain folk have gained respect for "putting in a hard day's work," and are proud of this moral value that they have toward employment.

Cultivating The Small Business

Incentives for relocation are not the only initiative for economic growth, and ways must be found to provide entrepreneurs of small ventures with opportunities. One important ingredient for success of the American economy in the future are small businesses. Projection of U.S. economic growth for the remainder of this century is expected to stay at the same level as the past two decades. During that same period, America's large corporations have been going downhill, losing approximately five million jobs, while small operations gained about thirty-five million.

Small business opportunities need to be explored extensively in each community. With help of regional action, the entrepreneur should take advantage of current economic trends. Above all, they have to be more innovative and willing to face risks. Regardless, whether a potential enterprise is commercial or industrial, it must be closely scrutinized as to local and regional demographic trends, lifestyle changes, and other factors, to successfully survive over a long term. Businesses should be flexible enough to look for possibilities in which the operation can expand in various directions, including government related contracts.

During the past year, national leaders have expressed concern over the future of our bureaucratic federal structure that is too cumbersome. At the present time, initiatives have been of a rhetorical nature, waiting for action; however, if they become reality, opportunities will be made available for local community ventures by government encouragement of private contracting in various industries. Federal government's long range plans call for turning over a greater amount of its operations to the private sector. As it trims bureaucratic services, critics say that efficiency and benefits of private contracting will outdo the present structure. This is one way that the region and local communities can encourage growth of business opportunities, and their perceptual receptivity along with guidance for entrepreneurs will go a long way in motivating them to survive during tough economical times.

Financial Support

When dealing with economic development, it is fairly clear that there are certain basic elements which have to be present whenever progress is expected. One of these is capital, and Appalachia must have access to financial resources, which are the foundation for growth. In order for eastern Kentucky to have any form of success, financial backing is necessary. Pursuing venture capital can come from within or outside the region through various methods. A major goal that community leaders should be concerned with is to lay the foundation for long-term financial resource development. To do this, assistance is necessary through a pool of private and public capital to help start up new enterprises. Beyond promises, leadership has to offer action, the kind that makes private money available to get businesses or industry started. The plan for economic growth also calls for financial commitment from all possible public sources, whether local, state, or federal. To assure continuity of effort and results, private sector leadership in each community should work cooperatively with bankers, professionals, business community and individual citizens in the overall development plan, emphasizing monetary resources. Private and public ventures must be created so that a mixed climate for growth will assure improvement of business opportunities and help lure industries to the region. If it is impossible to start certain business ventures without financial subsidy from state/federal government or other outside sources, community groups should develop a plan through private pledges to get potentially worthwhile businesses underway.

Good Paying Jobs Are Necessary

One of the major areas of concern in Appalachia is that not many hard working people are making a decent living. Even though economic growth may reduce unemployment, it is important for low income workers to have good paying jobs, which will generate a greater impact on the local situation. Earlier in this book it was stated that implementation of a comprehensive development plan should include expansion of training programs for the working poor and unemployed, which is a basis for upgrading job opportunities. Too many unconcerned individuals think since people are working and making money, they enjoy a decent way of life. Unfortunately, this assumption is erroneous and misleading. Presently, many working people in Appalachia and elsewhere find themselves still living below the poverty level because being employed does not mean that their earnings are enough to lift them out of poverty.

The Future

In dealing with economic development, community leaders must give considerable attention to pursuing a direction aimed at industries that supply better paying jobs in order to improve overall income for workers in the region. It may appear to some that just expanding the job market will suffice in alleviating unemployment; however, the difficulty with this approach is that the economic base may not grow. If a person is not making a decent income, community structure stagnates, and the lack of buying power from the working poor will continue to deter growth. Because of this, communities throughout this country have become more innovative. They had to concentrate on development strategies, which call for industries that provide higher paying jobs, rather than generating low income employment. There is a need to aim for growth, so that an upsurge of better jobs can take place, resulting in higher salaries that will dominate the employment scene. An aggressive, innovative, and comprehensive economic development program is necessary if an improved employment picture is to unfold; otherwise plans that appear to be effective could turn into self-defeating deterrents for upgrading the standard of living.

Tourism and Related Opportunities

Over the past 30 years, tourism in the nation has increased tenfold, as more people are using the highways and byways because of recreational and business purposes. There are many factors why it has become one of our country's major industries. Increased leisure time today in comparison to the past provides greater incentives for individuals to take long weekends, short trips, or holiday breaks. Also, advantages of early retirement gives people an opportunity to travel more often, and the industry itself is constantly updating offerings to entice more visitors each year. Increase in demand by the population for expanded tourist areas and places has meant millions of job opportunities at many different levels. This industry is so diverse that the combined elements present an awesome picture of employment opportunities. Included are a full range of jobs relating to food, services, accommodations, entertainment, recreation, and manufacturing items for souvenirs. In certain parts of our country, tourism has become the number one industry of a community's existence. Economic indicators show that it is the second largest retail industry in the United States, earning over 200 billion dollars a year, with future projections calling for even greater growth.

Today it is affordable for many more people to enjoy the simple luxury of leisure opportunities, which could be offered by eastern Kentucky. Accrued earnings can help the economy of towns and villages

234

that are located near tourist areas. Levels of benefits can be achieved for nearby or related communities, however, those individuals responsible for planning and implementing this industry must make long-term commitments in order to be successful. Certain regional leaders have discussed with enthusiasm that the natural physical characteristics of eastern Kentucky's highlands can be a financial advantage. The beauty of Appalachia's mountains is dramatic and has many charming, resourceful amenities like lakes, state and national parks. Yet, little has been done to take advantage of these assets, which could have an enormous impact on this region.

Development of tourism is an essential element for revitalizing the economic and physical core of eastern Kentucky. In order for growth to occur, a proper comprehensive plan is necessary. When one looks at other tourist areas of our country that do not have physical beauty like Appalachia, it is amazing to see how much success was achieved with little effort. A major obstacle of growth is the lack of vision in regard to multiple opportunities and services. One must also have desire to make the most of those assets a region has to offer. The concept of attracting people is no longer simple. Providing a piece of natural park land along with lodging, food and a lake does not mean that visitors will come. There are many other parks, lakes and recreation areas throughout the United States, making competition difficult and complex. People are demanding a variety of activities, entertainment and recreation, all in one location. Traveling from one area to another has become a secondary concern. Innovation for new ventures of tourism can serve as an offshoot, benefiting eastern Kentucky's economy.

The region's parks and lakes are a jewel for tourism, and upscaling these areas should include appealing activities, creating opportunities for outdoor enthusiasts, like water sports, golfing, tennis, baseball, football, soccer, volleyball, basketball, etc. Surrounding these parks, communities could plan for diversification of entertainment centers and activities, build shops, restaurants, convenience stores and motels that are inviting to visitors. Certain innovative concepts, such as a heritage museum, theatre complex, or entertainment park located near a recreation area, would serve as added incentive in attracting visitors.

Hard decisions have to be made, if leaders and politicians want to keep the vision of expansion on track. Growth calls for diversifying present situations, and successful development will require planning and adjustment to take advantage of the shifting economic conditions. The pitfalls of viewing a park and lake in itself as a panacea for growth is inappropriate. It takes time to evaluate the economic situation as to the future character of tourism that communities and the region want to be recognized for. However, activities, recreation, and entertainment are added incentives that business and industry look for when locating to an area. Desire for growth has to emanate from the total community, and if concerted efforts of a comprehensive plan come to fruition, tourism will have a positive impact on Appalachia's economy and provide many job opportunities.

Economic Transformation Through Environmental Action

Visitors who drive on the modern roads of Routes 80 and 23 from Ashland, Kentucky, south through Prestonsburg toward Pikeville and Hazard, view lush mountainsides and grassy hollows. Interspersed throughout the hilly terrain are well-kept small and large homes, house trailers, and old shanties. If a person has not been back to this part of Kentucky for a few years, things appear to have changed for the better. However, go beyond the superhighway into the back country and you will find yourself in an entirely different world. There are many environmental concerns that the visitor perceives. Most notable is the severe damage to large areas of Appalachia's rural landscape caused by the cutting of trees and strip mining. Once these projects were completed, mineral rights corporations moved, leaving unusable barren properties without salvaging the damage by reclamation. Useless earth was left to the people who own the land. They are trying to eliminate the ugly scars left by strip mining, but financially cannot afford to do so. Appalachia's concern is that the ground has laid waste for too long and is a threat to the entire ecosystem of eastern Kentucky. The conditions that now call for drastic measures were not anticipated by Washington's leadership and bureaucrats in the past, because very little direction had been given in regard to environmental regulation. Restoration is needed for the barren land contaminated with residue called tailings, which also carried into streams, rivers and lakes, polluting them.

Appalachians have to take a new approach that will provide for better protection. Environmental problem areas need to be cleaned up, so that life can be brought back to the devastated land. This calls for leadership at all levels to work in consortium with help from the federal government, by providing a planned program that can serve a dual purpose, meeting environmental needs along with boosting the economy. A benefit would be the development of immediate jobs for unemployed people. This idea is not new, and one only has to look back at those Depression years, when the Civilian Conservation Corps was established to assure work and enrich the natural beauty of our country. Restoration of Appalachia and creating jobs should not be a constant form of public assistance, however, it is imperative to help these citizens gain pride by providing them with opportunities to renurture their land. The need to make jobs available and achieve environmental goals for the region are a natural solution that should be placed in the hands of eastern Kentuckians, who are most affected by this action. As leadership of the region looks for long term economic development, education should also be offered for those who are involved in this type of program, so that an eventual move to future employment situations can take place.

Transforming Appalachia's economy through environmental action will surely be looked upon favorably by the present administration, since the "Presidential Council on Sustainable Development" has recently organized. Government is acknowledging community action as a top priority for suggested environmental solutions that go hand in hand with providing work. Local community leaders, activists, and politicians should convene with regional, state and federal agencies to initiate this type of action. It appears to be a hopeful direction for environmental goals and community-devised plans geared toward employment. This could open other areas of industry that are dependent on natural resources, such as timber, agriculture, and even domestic fishing farms. Tourism and the natural surroundings need to be included in this opportunity of development. Each of these natural resource industries should be extolled because of the importance to sustain their existence for the future. It appears to me that the present administration wants to have leadership come from local levels, where environmental conditions are in need of positive action. Solutions that are imposed locally have a greater chance for success. A comprehensive plan for all the above possibilities must come from cooperative action by Appalachian communities and their people.

The Future — Better Health Care

In attempting to forecast health care's future, it is evident that changes taking place today will help make predictions less difficult, if commitment is implemented to improve the health status of Appalachians. Ability to make changes will depend largely on this region's capacity to overcome the many problems of poverty that confront the medical profession. Access to health care for all citizens, along with availability of resources and its use is eastern Kentucky's goal. If this is not enacted, consequences will lead to a greater complexity of problems, which will further fuel the ills of poverty. However, by viewing health care in Appalachia today, one cannot help feeling encouraged about changes that medical leaders are striving for. They have perception and understanding of the implications their actions will bring to people, especially the poor.

Through strong leadership, Appalachia's health situation can be improved and obstacles are no longer insurmountable. Today there is greater hope for health care being able to meet people's needs than at any other time in Appalachia's history. Nevertheless, it will require an effective federal government health reform program with the help of local and state forces to battle the perpetuity of poverty.

Regional Innovation

A current experience of cooperative regional action is the unique development of a model rural medical health care park and family-practice residency program in Hazard, Kentucky. It consists of the Appalachian Regional Healthcare Medical Hospital, Regional Psychiatric Hospital, along with the University of Kentucky's Center of Excellence in Rural Health, located in a modern day campus setting. This accomplishment has clearly cast the region in a role of rural health care innovation. The consequences of this visionary undertaking have also created an economic boost for the Hazard area through increased employment of health care professionals and other personnel. Expansion of these medical services definitely implies an irreversible trend of improved health care delivery for the region and individual communities. A sharper definition and expansion of rural medical training should also have a positive impact. Greater practical working opportunities are offered to the young physician who is confronted with actual rural health situations, and unique on-the-spot experiences should lead to a higher degree of understanding and better quality care services.

Health facilities at the local community level, combined with a comprehensive medical care center such as the Hazard regional complex with its spoke-like network, would also imply a more vigorous direction toward quality of care for eastern Kentucky. This innovative approach should have an impact on the region's ability in responding to certain important trends, created by the pressures of a continuously changing and complex health care system. They include:

1. a shift of focusing from inpatient to outpatient care,
2. use of more advanced and sophisticated medical technology,
3. developing a much needed health referral system for the patient's benefit,
4. adequate supply of rural health personnel and services,
5. and improving access to health care services.

These actions, combined with medical and political visionary leadership, will make health care delivery stronger and more consistent with the region's mission of overcoming the ills of poverty. In addition, Appalachia has the opportunity to place itself in the forefront of rural health care in this country, by demonstrating that the outcomes show improvement in quality of care.

Need For Physicians, Personnel, and Programs

As we look toward the turn of the century, many uncertainties in health care still exist and implications for medical personnel have unanswered questions. The addition of more doctors and other health care professionals in Appalachia is necessary in order to improve the present situation. Recruitment of young physicians by the University of Kentucky Rural Training Program needs to be innovative to show success. Also, addressing the lack of medical personnel, there should be a plan that entices students to remain in underprivileged rural areas. Those who are concerned with the practice of medicine suggest that one way to sustain the stay beyond a training period would be by providing incentives, such as waiving school loans. Nurses and other health care personnel should not be excluded from having similar opportunities. Certain types of advantages, like educational benefits, are no more than a fair exchange for commitment of helping the poor.

The severe shortage of doctors, nurses and other health personnel is part of health care's biggest problem. Presently, this need is much greater in Appalachia than in other rural and urban scenes of America. To entice health professionals, the region must provide stimulating motives, such as good education for family members, housing and other amenities that make it conducive for people wanting to work in eastern Kentucky. Federal government incentives, which virtually dried up during the 1980's to the present, have been a deterrent to recruiting young doctors. In 1970, the National Health Service Corps program was created for improvement of access to primary care in underserved areas. Unfortunately this scholarship undertaking, aimed at health professionals willing to work in rural regions, has lost federal support. Nearly eighty million dollars were spent on this federal project in 1980, yet by 1985 it was reduced to approximately two million. At present, this program appears to have completely lost the support of Washington, D.C. The State of Kentucky, in its Health Reform Act of 1994, is addressing some concerns with initiatives that will assure greater opportunities for persons wishing to pursue medical education. Inherent in the Reform Act are incentives for those attending University of Kentucky and Louisville medical schools. Another alterna-

239

tive that was explored considered the recruitment of prospective young doctors who are from the region. It is a fact that physicians are more apt to practice in rural Appalachia if they come from its communities. Also, it is hoped that the rural physician's training program located at Hazard will give greater impetus to young people of eastern Kentucky who are interested in a medical career.

Challenges for medical personnel have changed considerably in relation to expectations and demand of working in Appalachia. The roles of primary care physicians in rural areas have proliferated, and they are struggling to respond to many pressures created by the evolving health care system. Doctors of eastern Kentucky see too many patients with health problems that are related to unfortunate circumstances of poverty, compounded by the lack of preventive care. Their tight schedule has placed overworked doctors in an untenable position of mainly dealing with curative care situations. With the exception of a few visionary practitioners, health clinics, and other health professionals, Appalachia has been light years behind other parts of America in providing preventive care for the underprivileged. Not knowing the importance of medical care before illness sets in, the pattern of rural families waiting too long to see a physician has been a constant barrier to better health in the region.

Interwoven in modern day life is the need for Appalachia to find a workable balance between the individual, community and doctor. In no area of personal care is this more evident than in preventive medicine. As medical science expanded to meet problems of disease and illness, the situation between physician and patient has changed, and greater attention must be given to preventive care. However this type of care is truly a luxury that the poor cannot afford, and very few understand its implications. Too many people in poverty do not comprehend that if they ignore good health practices day after day, it can lead to regrettable consequences in personal well-being. In spite of being poor, their pride and nature makes them reluctant to receive charity, even if it is thrust upon them by well-meaning health care professionals.

Their cultural beliefs are also a hindrance, since Appalachians are steeped in generations of health patterns and still resort to old ways of dealing with ills and sickness. In today's complex health situations, some of their home solutions are conflicting and outdated. The need for preventive care at routine periods and during early onset of illness or disease is not only life saving, but could also minimize cost. Reluctance to seek health care when the problem is minor can eventually lead to a chronic or life threatening condition. The result is that Appalachian doctors are providing more charity and expensive care for a condition that could have been treated at an earlier stage.

By not getting health care on a regular basis, the poor may

encounter conditions like hypertension, which in turn has led to a higher than predicted rate of cardiovascular disease and stroke among relatively younger adults. Studies have provided important information and understanding of the risk factors that lead to coronary heart disease. People of Appalachia, who have lived all their lives in a traditional way and ate only certain types of foods, do not realize that their lifestyle influences their health. Therefore, education in promoting good health to prevent illnesses should be a major goal. Recent research by the National Cancer Institute indicates the same dietary guidelines that proved to reduce heart attacks and strokes are recommended for cancer prevention. Other studies show that Appalachian women's high mortality rate of cervical cancer is attributed to poverty conditions. Research by Gilbert Friedell, et al. from the University of Kentucky in cooperation with the Center for Disease Control in Atlanta, Georgia, found that incidents of cervical dysplasia, carcinoma in situ, and invasive cervical cancer among Appalachian women were much higher than in the general female population.

One of the most important challenges for rural medicine over the coming years is to increase its competence and ability in improving the quality of life for poor Appalachians. Educating people serves as a major goal in preventive care. They need to be taught that it is important to visit a physician before becoming ill. This is a strong contradiction of mountain folks' attitude, who think that doctors are only for the sick, not for persons who feel well. It appears more advantageous that medical care improve the health of people through preventive measures, rather than provide treatment after the damage is done.

The importance of community acceptance regarding preventive medicine in Appalachia, depends upon informing and educating these individuals of benefits and their impact. This can be accomplished in many ways through cooperative methods. One example is the utilization of "full service" schools in combination with community health organizations, and leadership by physicians as well as other professional personnel. Not involving any of these groups in a comprehensive educational program promoting good health can result in lack of health status improvement. Through cooperative region-wide leadership, appropriate strategies should be devised at first in targeted communities. A logical link with this preventive medicine approach is the Kentucky Education Reform Act that calls for full use of schools in each community to utilize "Family Resource and Youth Services Centers." These facilities, located in or near elementary and secondary schools, could cover a wide range of services and programs, which include training new and expectant mothers, as well as parent-and-child education on health care. Youth centers would provide referrals to health and social organizations, drug and alcohol abuse, family crisis and mental health counseling.

Combining health services and other community forces will increase people's acceptance of preventive medicine. National studies of health care systems indicate that these types of efforts can stimulate positive attitudes of the poor toward their own personal health. Problems arising from long term poverty in Appalachia are closely linked to the individual's health status and lead to the need for coordination between medical professionals and other social service policy makers, educators, community leaders and groups. Their combined efforts should assist the health profession in placing a program for prevention on solid ground.

Through the Kentucky Education Reform Act, the Commonwealth has called for local jurisdiction with community-based leadership to develop social programs, which include promoting good health. The rationale is that programs for the community, such as preventive medicine, should be an integral part of comprehensive care measures accessible to infant, child, youth and adults, so that families can enjoy reasonably good health. This may not be an easy task for those in the medical profession who in the past have mainly used a "curative" approach when working with the public. They will have to establish a balance between preventive and curative medicine.

Exposing the community to this program will place responsibility upon each individual for their own well-being, by choosing the right life style. They must be given the opportunity of being educated to understand the consequences of their present day health situation. People who refuse meeting the standards to a healthier life become accountable for their actions, because the medical profession will have done its job by offering preventive programs and procedures. However, even this may be a blessing in disguise, for it is known, when given the stimulus, people start caring about themselves and improve their way of life. Therefore, a comprehensive approach for improving their health status may be the starting point in attacking problems affecting the poor.

Education
Key To Appalachia's Future

The single most important educational challenge for eastern Kentucky's future is to help break the cycle of poverty that existed for many generations. In a directive from Kentucky's Supreme Court, the legislature developed one of the most outstanding reforms for education in our nation. The State worked hard to make sure that children of the poor would have a chance for a different and better way of life. No matter what political point of view policy makers of Kentucky have, they all agree that education is a vital weapon against poverty. The hope is to educate young people, which will allow them to escape economic and social problems that their parents and grandparents had to endure. Through the Kentucky Education Reform Act, schools are making sure that all children have the opportunity for a better education, by satisfying each student's need for optimum personal growth.

As of this date, reports and research indicate that school districts are showing signs of change. Though certain schools are struggling, others are following a course of accountable action. Positive results will require continued extensive and collective participation by educators, parents and community members. There is no doubt that bringing all of these participants together to achieve the goals of educational reform will not be easy, for in education, changes are often unwelcome and vigorously opposed. Revisions in education are not merely changes in an institutional structure, but also mean altering behavior of people and community. To make this effective, all participants must apply their understanding to the dynamics of school-community group formation. Emphasis on the cooperative group process, conceived as a democratic "change agent," can be enlisted in the cause toward educational advancement that will help overcome poverty in Appalachia.

Indigence has been the basis for a sense of fatalism in Appalachia's poor through the unpredictability of their economic and social conditions. Along with this, illiteracy has hindered their endeavor to succeed, and made many families insecure. People who are most of the times mentally down tend to give up on life's challenges, and when there is no hope, response is slow in accepting a helping hand because of constant humiliation. The difficult task for educators is to help undo the low self-esteem that Appalachian families and their children have lived with for so long. In focusing on child and family, Kentucky's Education Reform Act has concerned itself with the development of a full service school, or as some educators would refer to as a "community school," concentrating on a comprehensive variety of services. A major objective of this concept is to strengthen each family's role in preparing the child, and also realize that the outcome depends very much on parents. With many diversified quick changes in our society, the family comes under greater scrutiny and is pressured into making sure that their children have a better chance in life.

K.E.R.A. has provided a deliberate and systematic way for adults to become more responsible as parents by getting them involved in the educational process. By proposing comprehensive support and services, developers of the Reform Act have acknowledged that the ability for children to succeed in school depends on the quality of their early pre-school experiences. It is an undeniable fact that parents are the child's first teachers; if they are lax in that role, the youngster will enter school with disadvantages and may become a high risk for failure. With re-designing the educational program in each community, prospective and new parents are taught about parenthood, along with the necessity of proper pre-natal care. Learning experiences that children receive through cognitive, social-emotional, physical and perceptual motor development activities, are the basis for growth as they progress through their early stages of life. Parents have to understand that working with their children from birth helps them achieve skills and knowledge. However, there are some who are unable to provide for certain needs of their pre-school children. A variety of programs, supports, and services should be made available so that their offspring are prepared to function in school.

The urgency to educate children at an earlier age than kindergarten calls for development of a pre-school program that will help the disadvantaged and high risk child. Initiation of educational learning centers should enhance a child's chances of starting on equal terms with others in kindergarten. There is no doubt that getting parents involved will require great effort and commitment by educators. The direction each school takes, whether in parent services or participation, should be based on a plan that is easily understood by all parties. Education reform involves accountability, and all groups are responsible for their level of participation in preserving and improving education — including parents. Many people may raise the question: How much should a school expect of parents? The answer is unequivocal: they should be in partnership with the educational system. If parents are concerned about their children, action to build a solid foundation will increase an offspring's chances for a future productive life.

Given the present crisis of needed parent services and involvement, educators interested in school improvement must respond to these people and their children. The Reform Act, through the development of Family Resource and Youth Service Centers, projects the philosophy that everything affecting the welfare of children and their families is its concern. It further assumes that community problems can be solved through the help of educators, working cooperatively with health, social agencies and other groups. Administrators and teachers have to realize when educating children for the future that the school's role must expand to a full-service approach. To some traditionalists this is difficult to accept. They ask the question: Shouldn't schools concentrate only on educating the child with a solid academic achievement program instead of a comprehensive approach? However, this would present a problem because the two are functionally interdependent and complementary.

Furthermore, the education system of today not only has to deal with academic needs of students, but also with an increase in a number of social maladies that confront them daily. Society has changed, youth are exposed to violence, and the need to compete at an accelerated pace places stress on them as they become adults. Unfortunately, the falling apart of family life has led children to a sense of despair, and the result is that realities of life are invading classrooms since needs of today's students are different than fifteen years ago. Back then, schools were focusing on content of curriculum with emphasis on a rigorous program of study to challenge a young person.

However, for a pupil to benefit today means to change the whole system. Schools must provide youth with learning challenges that will go beyond the training of literacy and economic efficiency. They have to reflect the values and processes related to their particular social and economic settings. In order for students to achieve optimal personal growth, schools must help by developing solid learning opportunities and offer an educational environment that fosters good citizenship and responsibility. Respect for each individual's right to an equal educational opportunity should also be taught. As Kentucky goes about its way of changing the whole system, it is cognizant of the fact that unless what is being taught in schools is relevant to present conditions, the school system will stay in a time warp. The State Department of Education, school districts, and schools are also making a concerted effort to focus on teaching at every level along the educational continuum. They hope, accountability of Kentucky's new educational agenda will show that the learning experiences are applicable to today's pupil and tomorrow's adult. If results are positive, then the improved student performance through this educational approach cannot be debated.

Influence of a full-service-community school concept upon the learning situation has never been denied in modern educational theory and practice. However, only recently has it been recognized and organized by a total state system as a basic and integral factor in the educational process. Traditional education acknowledges that every student is a member of the school and community, but often has not employed the means by which each person can develop their full potential. Goals presented in K.E.R.A. are aimed at focusing on educational outcomes. So important are these intentions in the life of every student that each school is mandated to make every effort in helping and encouraging individuals to acquire a strong and positive attitude toward themselves, the learning process, school and community. As a result, particular attention should be given to ensure that Appalachian students achieve these goals, so they can find their way out of poverty and become productive citizens.

One of the greatest challenges in reform today is to provide for current educational programs that are able to change effectively in meeting projected future needs. It should be the intent of education to build a system with enough flexibility and adaptability, so that it can be altered easily to meet the changing needs of future economic, cultural, social and political conditions. In addition, Appalachians are not only confronted with local, state, and national needs, but there are now global considerations on the horizon that have to be dealt with. Today's schools will have to identify programs vital for continuous upgrading of education, which relate to a highly technological and innovative economy. Competition for educated young people with the knowledge and skills in meeting these economic needs is increasing. The role that education must play is one of involving opportunities for input from business and industry. Also, by turning over the decision-making process to local schools, this should provide for greater understanding and a stronger role in meeting community needs.

As Kentucky looks to altering its educational practices in fostering a more conducive learning environment, students must also work effectively to be part of the change. Higher achievement, responsibility, respect for oneself and others are necessary for students to achieve success in school and beyond. However, young people who assume that quitting school to get a job will secure their future, have a second guess coming. It is apparent that whatever future employment high school drop-outs aim for, opportunities and income have declined, and this trend appears more evident for the coming years. One must respond with candor and sorrow, because these individuals will face persistent joblessness, or won't earn enough for a minimum standard of living. Skepticism is mounting toward youth in our country who are non-achievers, whether in school or community life. Believing in the "American Dream" is no longer a reality for them, since trends show that there will be a decline in low-skill workers.

For schools to fail in addressing causes of student dropouts would be contrary to the reform and restructure of education. Children who come from families of poverty enter classes with severe disadvantages and have difficulty in keeping up with their peers. However, it is incumbent on educators to help the individual overcome these deficiencies, and if goals of K.E.R.A. are met, it then becomes the responsibility of every student to work toward achieving educational objectives at their own optimum level. Results are based on the student's ability of achievement, which in turn determines their future financial capabilities and social environment. Each student is the main decision maker for his or her future, and must be responsible as a citizen to work for effective self-change.

The new economic direction of our country has forced not only a re-thinking and subsequent action for reform in elementary and secondary schools, but also at the college level because higher education's role is being questioned. Poor economic conditions leading to a continuing increase of college students and graduates starting a second field of study or learning new skills, is a major concern that requires review. Having to make career changes is the result of soul-searching by young people, and reflects a growing national trend which calls for new collaborative efforts among higher education and industry regarding job opportunities. College graduates are being forced to rethink their future that may involve many employment changes. Higher education has to redefine its objectives carefully, for as it looks to a more important role in the changing of our society, its potential should be made available to increase diversity. Colleges and universities must react positively to students in response of their needs, for if higher education does not remain in the realm of reality, it will be held accountable.

Welfare — Education A Key

Appalachia's greatest concern for the future of its people is welfare, which exists throughout the region. Many poor have no financial security, some are illiterate or lack education to overcome their socioeconomic problems, with no alternative other than becoming captive to the welfare system. Since development of the Economic Opportunity Act, some federal programs fostered dependency on government handouts, which led to a fatalistic attitude among those needy who have given up hope for future employment opportunities. With welfare restricted to certain groups, there is a strong anti-sentiment in our nation that has forced the federal government toward developing reform.

There are critics who see welfare programs as giveaways of tax money to idle and lazy but able-bodied adults. This may be the case with some, however most poor who are on welfare do work. Unfortunately, their income is not sufficient to sustain themselves as well as their families, and many have very few opportunities to improve their situation. Others who are elderly or unable to work because of physical impairment struggle on a small disability or social security income. For them, realistic and sufficient funds to live on is needed. Inaccurate assumptions about welfare recipients also ignore that the largest group of poverty victims are children. If the young go without some form of welfare assistance, they wind up being robbed of their childhood, and inequality of life will take away their dignity, which leaves them with endless social and emotional scars. The unfortunate result is that many of these children grow up to be parents who will repeat the welfare cycle if it is not possible to break the bond of impoverishment. When talking about escaping welfare, we cannot ignore that economic and social opportunities must exist in order for people to find a way out of poverty.

There are many elements of political and economic resources that are important, and the role of federal government is one of them. Economic conditions of today warrant that government must continue to contribute to a wide variety of welfare needs. This is not to belittle its efforts, because the War on Poverty for example was not a total failure. Within a decade after implementation of welfare programs in 1965, the amount of people living below the poverty line was cut in half. However, with the change to a new administration in 1980, federal funds decreased. Instead of bringing together knowledge of the "thinkers, shakers and movers" of that era to improve the welfare situation, a conservative Administration created spurious images, and Americans were gullible in believing that our country was in great shape. Instead, the late 1980's and early 90's experienced an economic recession of such magnitude that it led to a greater problem of welfare not only for Appalachia, but the total country.

Today, the cry for welfare restructure is evident by a sharp increase over past years of many varied ways in which our society suffers. There are those who believe that the federal government should develop measures, such as "empowerment," bypassing the cumbersome bureaucracy and giving poor people options to improve their own conditions. The vast majority of adult welfare recipients want to work, but with present adverse conditions, there is no way of getting ahead. Whether single persons or one- and two-parent family situations, many of these people agree that welfare is not a way of life.

It should only provide temporary assistance to help people get back on their feet and become self-supporting, which was the intent and purpose by the designers of this system. Instead, as time progressed, basic causes that led the poor into their present welfare dilemma were ignored due to society's self-serving direction. Elements of economic, social, political and legal constraints presented many barriers for those who wanted to get off the welfare system. Shortsightedness and failure to recognize and realize implications of inaction impeded people from overcoming their dependency. The political system must play a fair role for the poor by making sure that opportunities of growth are available and carried out. Previously I presented elements of economic initiatives that should be considered for helping poor Appalachians, but the most important factor for future success of overcoming dependency, is ultimately contingent on providing education.

In the past, our federal government was looked upon as the only source that could lead Appalachia and the country out of poverty. Since conditions in our nation have changed so much, the President has clearly identified technology as the future for American economy. All indications are that out of necessity and the need for long sighted planning, this new direction has great implications for those people who are now on welfare. Whether government intends to develop change that will affect the present system remains to be seen. A plan to overhaul welfare is currently being processed by the Administration, which emphasizes reform, family values and education.

Through the years, "quick solutions" have been criticized, and any new directions taken by the present government will have experts leery about the aims of reform. The question is, can reform help people get off the welfare system, or will it be just another frustrating experience with not enough substance to pass Congress without a battle? All too often those who are responsible to make changes have been involved with self-serving interests rather than having "honest-to-goodness" concern for our nation's needy. As a result, government becomes the whipping boy in regard to failure of programs. Another concern is that sometimes welfare action is not carried out effectively, and wasted efforts through a cumbersome bureaucratic structure are evident. In many instances, programs would serve the people more efficiently if they were better managed.

The welfare system certainly is not responsible for conditions and disadvantages that the needy are exposed to. However, change has to occur if Appalachia is to overcome the problems that have led to generations of welfare dependents, and success in eliminating this situation starts with education. Yet, in the past, this region has never had the latitude to put much value on educating its children, youth, and adults. For today's children to be successful in an increasingly competitive society, their future financial security and social conditions will be determined by their generation's quality of education. Likewise, earning potentials and subsequent social conditions of today's parents and grandparents are based on their education and knowledge.

What happened in Kentucky, specifically Appalachia, is that Education Reform has stimulated a great amount of intellectual and practical activity in local communities. In the past, educational scenes were dominated by conservative attitudes and closed minds, and the outcome cannot be ignored. Therefore, education today is aimed toward becoming the key for change. Adult education, vocational, technical and post-secondary institutions should work in consortium with government's attempt to provide social services like counseling, job training, and education classes for low income and unemployed people.

Education provides knowledge and skills that will help people find employment instead of depending on assistance, and could serve as a force to help lower the number of welfare recipients in Appalachia. However, educating individuals who receive public aid is a critical and long term task, calling for schools, community leaders, industry, business, along with health and social services to work together by helping the poor with this first step to overcome dependency. If the federal government's reform requires mothers and fathers to participate in existing programs, it will be an undertaking that needs coordinated planning. Despite the many articles, studies, research, and reports on reform stating that welfare eventually will recede, nothing is more worrisome than the thought of today's children continuing to perpetuate their family's tradition by living on public assistance as adults. Our society must respond with compassion and understanding to people on welfare and open the door of opportunity for them. If these less fortunate succeed, there should be a dispelling of negative attitudes by critics and skeptics, for the key to eliminating the welfare drain is education.

Today's Children — Appalachia's Future

The strength of Appalachia's future lies in its children of today. Economic and social ills that afflict the poverty-stricken family have a devastating impact on their young. While past efforts and programs by the government have lost some of their effectiveness in rescuing children from a grim future, local private and public actions in eastern Kentucky are showing signs of hope for tomorrow's adults. In doing this, there is determination of certain leaders and groups to free families and children from the confinement of impoverishment.

However, a greater number of people than ever before are needed for spawning innovative humanitarian efforts if children are to attain a fulfilling life, which becomes a more confusing and difficult task in today's fast paced society. Studies have shown that there are limitations to predicting the future for poor children, if the problems are not challenged by a cooperative network of forces that work consistently and effectively. A broad concentration of services is important for helping them, since they are the most vulnerable to suffer pains of poverty. If parents are unable to escape from a life that depends on government subsidy, their children's future will be grim, for chances of becoming adults with a legacy of continued poverty appear inevitable, unless efforts are brought about to stop this growing crisis.

Leaders at local and state levels, along with federal government must come together in working toward a comprehensive strategy aimed at having a lasting impact on child poverty in Appalachia. No longer should federal decision makers ignore positive actions that started privately or publicly and were carried out successfully. Even the War on Poverty and other government programs left important impressions that should be considered. For example, Head Start, Medicare, Medicaid, Food Stamps, Low-Income Energy Assistance, the School Lunch Program or Basic Educational Opportunity Grants have been effective and serve as proof for stemming the tide toward greater poverty and deprivation.

There is no other segment of our nation's population more

attuned to the plight of child poverty than Appalachians, who are exposed to it daily . Through Kentucky's Education Reform Act, this region can meet the needs of these children so that they will be able to compete educationally, and function successfully as adults. To some people those goals may appear too lofty, but it is worth the effort by all concerned to make sure that each child will benefit. Another significant feature of the Reform Act is the development of pre-school programs for underprivileged youngsters. If schools are going to move toward their goals, educators, health and social service professionals need to identify a readiness program that is geared toward parents who have offspring ranging from birth through early grades. Identification of a systematic set of preparation goals is essential for helping a child perform better in school. Learning basic developmental skills will help the young get a head start in kindergarten. Health services for children is a significant aspect of this program, since diagnosis of any kind of impairment such as vision, speech, and hearing, is necessary to pinpoint and correct deficiencies at the earliest stage. The importance of proper diet, good health habits, rest, medical checkups as well as immunizations, is imperative for their well being.

There are other crucial elements that can improve children's health. The abundance of resources and preventive health services are useless without the knowledge of how to apply them. These services must be appropriate, and the quality of presentation will determine whether recipients gain knowledge and understanding that is so vital. Exposing parents to preventive measures will in turn affect a child's outlook on health habits that results in better learning capability. Research has shown that advances in preventive care have been astounding and one can say without exaggeration, parent knowledge is a basic requirement in teaching children good health habits for the future. Parents should be given information along with necessary training from sources of the community, such as schools, health (including dental) and social agencies. Pre-natal care is also an area of need that should be made available to every prospective mother. Health goals to overcome infant mortality, low-weight births, and insufficient care are important to improve a child's quality of life.

The major objective toward erasing poverty in Appalachia's future is a first rate educational program as a basic foundation that includes the previously mentioned health and social child care initiatives. If combined actions along with parent involvement and government sponsored resources are working together and aim toward the same direction, then families and children will function at an optimal level. Community leaders, individuals, groups, local, state and federal governments must come together and assure that children of Appalachia get a solid foundation for a productive future. In this demanding quest, the above groups have to demonstrate uniqueness in formulating a vision, which is necessary for positive results. A comprehensive plan will also inspire a camaraderie toward achieving a common approach of pragmatic and effective solutions.

In Conclusion

As one looks at records of past events, it seems that Appalachia has been endlessly marching to the beat of a different drum, while the rest of our nation grew and became wealthier. With the 20th Century entering its final years, America's common people live a life of contentment, and a growing number of elite enjoy the status of royalty. Yet the poor of Appalachia never had an opportunity to improve their living standards. For generations their stories told of frustration, defeat, and hopelessness since disparity has always separated these people from the rest of America.

Except for some concerned humanitarian government leaders, this nation has abandoned the disadvantaged and left it up to humanitarians and other concerned individuals to help the "needy." Without understanding the poor, our country labeled these people for years as being shiftless, lazy and illiterate, who would never make it out of poverty's grip. Certain outsiders erroneously think they know about Appalachians, and have portrayed a wrong image of them. This is why many people have been apathetic to the cries of the downtrodden. It is true that for generations eastern Kentucky's voice in government has not been powerful, and social programs supposed to benefit the needy were hindered by political influences from being carried out to the fullest extent. Instead of trying to understand why conditions prevailed for so long, Americans too often blame the poor for ending up this way, and tend to look at impoverishment with shallow justification, shrugging it off as a meaningless consequence.

Poverty in Appalachia is not difficult to comprehend: people are born into conditions based on elements of political, economic, social and cultural situations that have an influence on their life. Unfortunately, a future of comfort, financial security and pride is only a dream for the poor of eastern Kentucky, since opportunities for a better life were never available. These people have suffered for so many years without hope of escaping this type of existence. Consequently, this has led to the humanitarian leadership of today, who are more determined than ever to translate initiatives into action. These individuals and groups are serving as catalysts for change, and their deeds have given impetus to persons who want opportunities to escape the vicious cycle of indigence.

The myth that Appalachian culture has been non-progressive is dispelled through the selfless actions of these humanitarians, with continued efforts to show the less fortunate why "self-help" is an important factor in succeeding to alleviate their conditions. Another reason for this approach to attain acceptance is that the sense of community and values of Appalachian culture are entwined. It exposes cooperative individualism and a feeling of belonging, which is inherent in family and surroundings. The determination of these individual leaders which is based on high moral and spiritual values, has provided strength and helped restore dignity and self-esteem to those poor that they have been able to work with.

Since implementation of the War on Poverty, efforts have been made by Appalachians to overcome the many ills of impoverishment. Concerned leaders from this region know a great deal about effective programs because of their own experiences. More importantly, they have outlined varied actions that are needed for a comprehensive plan to succeed. Also, the State of Kentucky has initiated reform in its schools that may have a far-reaching impact, and no matter what point of view, policy makers agree that education is the basic foundation for a better future.

Some of eastern Kentucky's leaders and fighters, such as Governor Bert Combs, Congressman Carl Dewey Perkins, the great writers Harry Caudill and Jesse Stuart are now gone. Fortunately, their legacy lives on through Appalachians' proud craftsmanship, cohesiveness of families, and progressiveness of politicians including Benny Ray Bailey, Bill Gorman, Clayton Little, Judge Sherman Neace, John David Preston, Judge Homer Sawyer, and Greg Stumbo. The humanitarian leaders like Father Ralph W. Beiting, Sister Ida Marie Deville, Dan Greene, Eula Hall, Stella Marshall, Dr. Grady Stumbo, and other productive people such as Lois Baker, Reverend Larry Baldridge, Reverend J.S. Bell, Dr. Dennis Campbell, C. Vernon Cooper, Mike Dale, Ron Daley, Margaret Gabriel, Dr. Freddy Lawson, Gerri Martin, Dr. Lowell Martin, Mike McLaughlin, Steve Meng, Mike Mullins, Dr. Elmer Ratcliff, Dr. Anthony Stumbo, Glen Taul, Tony Turner, Teddi Vaughn, Bill Weinberg, Debbie White, who can bring Appalachia into the mainstream of American life, are still fighting the daily battle against poverty. These and other concerned citizens have seen beyond social and economic problems and know the potential of human capabilities. Education being the focal point for progress in Appalachia has always been my belief to be the foundation for overcoming poverty. There are many dedicated educators such as Jim Bergman, Pat Bingham, Wallace Campbell, Benny Moore, M. Fred Mullinax, Christine Stumbo, Peggy Taylor, Thelmarie Thornsberry, Lois Weinberg, John Wells, Alice Whitaker, and others, who have given their time and energy for the betterment of children, youth and adults in this region.

Numerous unselfish people, whom we simply call volunteers, are the unsung heroes to the needy. They have toiled for endless hours, providing a multitude of services to the less fortunate. Regretfully, their humanitarian efforts are not given enough recognition for the rest of us to acknowledge. They are common men and women who have decided to sacrifice in order to make a difference in the lives of needy people. I wish all volunteers' stories could be told, for due to their help Appalachia is getting closer to change.

We also cannot forget to pay homage to those senior citizens whose longtime contributions are immeasurable. The work of remarkable literary figures like James Still and Al Stewart have left an indelible mark on eastern Kentucky, and all who know them personally can attest to their greatness. Recognition should also be given to the brilliant song writer and voice of folk music Jean Ritchie, whose contributions will always be remembered as a leader of traditional mountain folklore. Special thanks must go to those activists of the 60's and 70's, whose passionate fight for social justice is still as strong as ever. For today's youth, who are tomorrow's future, the course of positive action leaves one with hope for better quality of life. I remember when President Kennedy was in office and "Camelot" prevailed with optimism and youthful idealism. Young people participating today in many endeavors to help the less fortunate are building not only optimism for the future, but ideally a kind of leadership that must carry on the dedicated works of today's givers.

What has been presented in this book is a view of Appalachia's people, along with initiatives and actions that are important for the needy to achieve a better quality of life. I have introduced some individuals and groups who are part of a movement of private non-profit, non-governmental organizations that are building a foundation for change. They all share similar goals in working toward betterment of Appalachia's society, and have seen the socioeconomic digression of people they care for and are concerned about.

What is needed to overcome poverty are the essentials of life: food, good education, basic health care, adequate housing, and employment opportunities. Those leaders and humanitarians I have written about represent a diverse array of groups, whose course of action may be a motivating force for the region's new direction by providing these essentials to help the needy. Vision, leadership, dedication and hard work by these individuals, groups and others must not stand alone. Every eastern Kentuckian should be concerned and committed to contribute. For change to occur throughout Appalachia, it is incumbent on the will and desire of the people to make this happen. If eastern Kentuckians come together during the years that lie ahead, there can be a positive outcome, and with strong leadership, they will achieve their goal — to finally overcome poverty.

BIBLIOGRAPHY

Aging. *Health Care In the U.S.: Meeting the Needs of the Rural Elderly.* U.S. Department of Health and Human Services. No 365, 1993

Alice Lloyd College. *A Light Unto the Mountains.* Pippa Passes, Kentucky. 1993

Alice Lloyd College. "Remembering 75 Years: Alice Lloyd's Journey to Caney Creek." *Alice Lloyd College Newsletter.* Vol 40, Number 3, Fall, 1991

Arnow, Harriette Louisa Simpson. *The Dollmaker.* New York: Macmillan, 1954

Association of America's Public Television Stations. *Star Channels Solves Educational Equity Problems: Investment in Public Television Makes Kentucky A National Model.* Learning with Public Television. Washington, D.C. 1993

Bartlett, Donald L. and James B. Steele. *America: What Went Wrong?* Kansas City: Andrews and McMeel, 1992

Beiting, Ralph W. and Constance Clark. *God Can Move Mountains: The Story of the Christian Appalachian Project.* New York: Darton, Longman, Todd and Doubleday, 1985

Bigelow V. and C.B. Trees. "A Model for Primary Care Delivery to a Widely Dispersed Medically Indigent Population." *Journal American Medical Association,* 266, 1991

Boggs, Rex and Jack G. Thomas. "Hazard: Eastern Kentucky's Queen City...Growing into the 1990's." *Hazard Herald-Voice.* June 25, 1992

Breed, Allen G. "State Stalls Company's Mining of Old Forests." *Lexington Herald-Leader.* July 22, 1993

Buffalo Evening News. "The Rich Get a Bigger Share." Buffalo, N.Y., July 29,1990

Carawan, Guy and Candie. *Voices From the Mountains.* New York: Alfred A. Knopf, 1975

Caudill, Harry M. *Night Comes to the Cumberlands: a Biography of a Depressed Area.* Boston: Little & Brown, 1962

Caudill, Harry M. *The Watches of the Night.* Boston: Little, Brown, 1976

Caudill, Rebecca. *My Appalachia: A Reminiscence.* New York: Holt, Rinehart and Winston, 1966

Clark, Thomas Dionysius. *Kentucky Land of Contrast.* New York: Harper & Row, 1968

Cleverley, William O. and Roger K. Harvey. "Critical Strategies for Successful Rural Hospitals". *Health Care Management Review.* 17(1), 27-33, 1992

Coldham, Peter Wilson. *Bonded Passengers to America.* 2 vols. Baltimore: Genealogical Pub., 1983

Commonwealth of Kentucky. *Kentucky Education Reform Act.* Regular Session Bill No. 940 enacted by General Assembly. March 29, 1990

Commonwealth of Kentucky. *An Act Relating to Education.* Regular Session House Bill No. 529 enacted by General Assembly, April 13, 1990

Daingerfield, Henderson. "Social Settlement and Educational Work in the Kentucky Mountains". *Journal of Social Science*, November, 1901.

Danziger, Sandra and Sheldon Danziger. *Child Poverty and Public Policy: Toward an Antipoverty Agenda.* Daedalus, Vol. 122, Winter. 1993

Davidson, Osha Gray. *Broken Heartland: The Rise of America's Rural Ghetto.* New York: Free Press; Collier McMillan, 1990

Dotson, Beth. "Wisdom, Sharing and Love: Visiting the Elderly in Appalachia." *The Catholic World.* November-December, 1992

Dotson, Beth. "Learning to Live." *The Mountain Spirit.* September-October, 1992

Dreiser, Theodore, et al. *Harlan Miners Speak: Report on Terrorism in the Kentucky Coal Fields.* New York: Da Capo Press, 1970

Farmer, Lizzie. *WPA Manuscript on Harlan County,* Kentucky Archives, Frankfort, 1938

Finn, Chester E. and Theodor Rebarber, eds. *Education Reform in the 90's.* New York: Macmillan, 1992

Fleishman, Jeffrey. "Appalachia's Anguish: A Way of Life Unravels." Philadelphia, (Pa.) *Inquirer.* January 10,1994

Flynt, J. Wayne. *Dixie's Forgotten People: The South's Poor Whites.* Bloomington: Indiana University Press, 1979

Ford, Arthur M. *Political Economics of Rural Poverty in the South.* Cambridge, Mass: Ballinger, 1973

Ford, Thomas A., ed. *The Southern Appalachian Region: A Survey.* Lexington: The University Press of Kentucky, 1962

Freidell, Gilbert H., et al. "Incidence of Dysplasia and Carcinoma of the Uterine Cervix in an Appalachian Population". *Journal of the National Cancer Institute*, July 1, 1992

Frook, John E. "Women Make a Difference: A Clinic for Mud Creek." *Family Circle*, January 12, 1993

Furman, Lucy. "The Quare Women: A Story of the Kentucky Mountains." *Boston: Atlantic Monthly Press,* 1923

Furman, Lucy. "Katherine Pettit", Hindman, Ky. News. May 1, 1952

Gabriel, Margaret. "People Believing in Themselves." *The Mountain Spirit.* April, 1994

Galbraith, John Kenneth. *The Affluent Society.* Boston: Houghton, Mifflin, 1984 (First published in 1958)

Gortmaker, S. et al. *Reducing Infant Mortality in Rural America: Evaluation of the Rural Infant Care Program.* Health Services Research 22, No. 1, April, 1987

Halbertstam, David. *The Next Century.* New York: William Morrow, 1991

Harrington, Michael. *The Other America: Poverty in the United States.* New York: Penquin Books, 1963

Harrington, Michael. *The New American Poverty.* New York: Holt, Rinehart, and Winston, 1984

Hofstadter, Richard. *America at 1750 (to 1865): A Social Portrait.* New York: Knopf, 1971

Hoversten, Paul. "Trimming Agriculture Department Fat." *U.S.A. Today,* June 10, 1992

Hume, A. Britt. *Death and the Mines: Rebellion and Murder in the United Mine Workers Union.* New York: Grossman, 1971

Isaacs, Barbara. "David School Ready to Make a Fresh Start." *Lexington Herald Leader.* November 7, 1993

Jones, G.C. *Growing Up Hard in Harlan County.* Lexington: University Press of Kentucky, 1985

Johnson, Fenton. "In the Fields of King Coal." *New York Times Magazine.* November 22, 1992

Johnston, Josiah Stoddard. *First Explorations of Kentucky: Doctor Thomas Walker's Journal of an Exploration of Kentucky in 1750.* Louisville, John P. Morton, 1898

Kentucky Education Reform Act of 1990. *A Citizens Handbook.* Legislative Research Commission of Kentucky. Sept. 1991

Kentucky's Health Care Reform: *A Citizens Handbook.* Legislative Research Commission of Kentucky. May 1994

Kilbourn, Peter T. "Out of Kentucky Soil, Into Their Hearts." *New York Times*. March 15, 1991

Kentucky Health Care Reform: A Citizens Handbook. Legislative Research Commission of Kentucky. May, 1994

Kosa, John, *Poverty and Health: A Sociological Analysis*. Cambridge, Mass: Harvard University Press, 1969

Kozee, William Carlos. *Early Families of Eastern and Southeastern Kentucky and Their Descendants*. Baltimore: Genealogical Pub., 1973 (c1961)

Leaf, Alexander. "Preventive Medicine for Our Ailing Health Care System". *J.A.M.A.* February 3, 1993

Levitan, Sar A. and Benjamin H. Johnston. *The Job Corps: A Social Experiment That Works*. Baltimore: Johns Hopkins University Press, 1975

Lofaro, Michael. *The Life and Adventures of Daniel Boone*. Lexington: University Press of Kentucky, 1978

Lundberg, G.D. "National Health Care Reform: An Aura of Inevitability Is Upon Us". *J.A.M.A.* Vol. 265; 1991

Lynn, Loretta and George Vecsey. *Loretta Lynn: Coal Miner's Daughter*. Chicago: Regenery, 1976

McMahon, J. Alexander. "The Health Care System in the Year 2000: Three Scenarios." *Academic Medicine*. January, 1992

Merino, Anita. "In Kentucky: Appalachian Culture Curriculum Mix." *NEA Today*. December, 1991

Neikirk, William. "Clinton's Plan Imperils Rural Health Clinics." *Lexington, Ky. Herald Leader*. July 17, 1993

Patterson, James T. *America's Struggle Against Poverty: 1900-1980*. Cambridge, Mass. Harvard University Press, 1981

Peterson, Bill. *Coaltown Revisited: An Appalachia Notebook*. Chicago: Regenery, 1972

Plunkett, H. Dudley and Mary Jean Bowman. *Elites and Change in the Kentucky Mountains*. Lexington: University Press of Kentucky, 1973

Politzer, R.M. et al. "Primary Care Physician Supply and the Medically Underserved". *J.A.M.A.*, Vol. 266, 1991

Puente, Maria. "Head Start Faces Bottom Line." *U.S.A. Today.* July 6, 1993

Ralston, Jeannie. "In the Heart of Appalachia." *National Geographic.* February, 1993

Roberts, Bruce and Nancy. *Where Time Stood Still; A Portrait of Appalachia.* New York: Crowell-Collier, 1970

Salatino, Anthony J. and Leon Lessinger, et al. *Accountability and the Educational System.* St. Bonaventure, New York: St. Bonaventure University, 1973

Samples, Karen. "Group Hopes Ruling Helps Curb Oil, Gas Drilling." *Lexington Herald-Leader.* July 23, 1993

San Francisco Chronicle. "Homeless Women's Project." San Francisco. June 10, 1991

Schaver, Mark. "Parent's Apathy Frustrates Principals; School Councils, Kentucky's New Ruling Class." *Louisville Courier-Journal.* January 30, 1994

Schlesinger, Arthur M., Jr. *The Age of Roosevelt: The Crisis of the Old Order - 1919-1933.* Boston: Houghton Mifflin, 1957

Schlesinger, Arthur M., Jr. *The Coming of the New Deal.* Boston: Houghton Mifflin, 1958

Schorr, Lisbeth B. with Daniel Schorr. *Within Our Reach: Breaking the Cycle of Disadvantage.* Anchor-Doubleday, 1988

Schwarz, John E. and Thomas J. Volgy. *The Forgotten Americans.* New York: W.W. Norton, 1992

Schwarz, Jordan A. *The New Dealers: Power Politics in the Age of Roosevelt.* New York: Alfred A. Knopf, 1993.

Selznick, A. *TVA and the Grass Roots.* Berkeley: University of California Press, 1966

Shapiro, Laura, et al. "How Hungry Is America." *Newsweek.* March 14, 1994.

Sheets, Kenneth, et al. "A Bumper Crop of Troubles." *U.S. News and World Report.* August 18, 1986

Stuart, Jesse. *The Thread That Runs So True.* New York: Charles Scribner's Sons, 1949

Surface, William. *The Hollow.* New York: Coward and McCann, 1971

Tassie, Tim. *Beaming Education Into Rural Kentucky.* Governing, October 1991, pp 42-43

U.S. Department of Agriculture. *Rural and Rural Farm Population: 1988.* Bureau of the Census and the Economic Research Service, 1989

U.S. Department of Commerce. *Public Aid Recipients as Percent of Population, by State: 1980 and 1990.* AFDC and Federal Supplemental Security Income, Bureau of the Census, 1990

U.S. Department of Commerce. *Income, Poverty, Valuation of Non Cash Benefits: 1993.* Bureau of the Census, Series P-61, No. 188, 1994

U.S. Department of Commerce. *Income, Poverty and Wealth in the U.S.* Bureau of the Census, Series P-60, No. 179, July, 1992

U.S. Department of Commerce. *Families Below Poverty Level in the U.S.* Bureau of the Census. Current Population Reports. P-60, No. 181, March, 1993

U.S. Department of Commerce. *Trends in Relative Income: 1964 to 1989.* Bureau of the Census. WDC, December, 1991

U.S. Department of Education. *A Nation At Risk: The Imperative For Educational Reform.* U.S. Govt. Printing Office, 1983

U.S. Department of Health and Human Services. *Poverty Guidelines for 1992.* Social Security Bulletin, Spring 1992

U.S. Department of Health and Human Services. *Aid To Families With Dependent Children. Benefits — Federal Share, Selected Fiscal Years 1984 Through 1993.* Family Support Administration. 1993

Voskuhl, John. "Making a Difference: W.O.R.K., Incorporated." *Louisville Courier Journal.* January 5,1994

Walls, David and John Stephenson, eds. *Appalachia in the Sixties: Decade of Reawakening.* Lexington: The University Press of Kentucky, 1972

Weller, Jack E. *Yesterday's People.* Lexington: University Press of Kentucky, 1965

Whitman, David. "The Next War on Poverty; An Agenda for Change." *U.S. News and World Report.* October 5, 1992

Whittlesey, Susan. *VISTA: Challenge to Poverty.* New York: Coward and McCann, 1970

Wilkie, Katherine E. and Elizabeth R. Moseley. *Frontier Nurse: Mary Breckinridge.* New York: Messner, 1969

Winerip, Michael. "Kentucky's Godmother To The Poor." *People Weekly,* Fall, 1991

Index

Martin, Dan, 91-92
McCoy-Hatfield feud, 15
McCreary County, 219
McDowell, 87, 184, 185
McGuffey, William Holmes, (McGuffey Reader), 38
McRoberts, 25
McLaughlin, Mike, 253
Medicare, 79, 98, 99, 250
Medicaid, 98, 250
Mental Health, 125-127, 190, 191-193, 199, 200-202
Middlesboro, 20-21, 39, 87
Migration, 69, 79, 82-83, 115-117
Mineral Rights, 21, 24, 164-166, 166-168
Moonshine, 28-29
Moore, Benny, 253
Morehead State College, 67
Mott Foundation, 216
Mountain Comprehensive Health Corporation, 209
Mountain Health Clinic, 104
Mud Creek Health Clinic, 104, 176-181
Mud Creek Water District, 178
Millinax, J. Fred, 135, 253
Mullins, Mike, 253
Murray State College, 67

N
National Association of America, 81
National Cancer Institute, 239-242
National Commission on Education, 193
National Mine Workers Union (NMWU), 59, 61
National Recovery Administration (NRA), 60
National Youth Administration (NYA), 52, 75
Neace, Sherman, 253
Neighborhood Health Center Program, 123-125
Neville, Linda, 39
Norman, Gurney, 112, 113
Nurse-midwives, 34

O
Office of Economic Opportunity (O.E.O.), 123
Office of Economic Opportunity, 123-124

Office Education Accountability, 201
Office of Price Administration, 81-82
Operation Sharing, 219
Orkney, 190
Owens, Devert, 46
Owsley County, 156, 158, 190, 215, 219

P
Patterson, James T., 52
Patton, Paul, 230
Patsy Teenagers, 211
Paxton, Mike, 112
Paxton, Tom, 113
Perkins, Carl Dewey, 99, 109, 163, 253
Perry County, 27, 190, 221-225
Pettit, Katherine, 39-40, 66, 205
Pike County, 111, 129, 163, 176-177, 190
Pikeville, 87, 93, 236
Pine Mountain Settlement School, 39-40
Pippa Passes, 42, 119, 223
Pneumoconiosis (See Black Lung)
Poverty, 9-20
    and education, 37-38, 87-90, 127-128, 129-130, 193
    and environment, 164-168
    and farmers, 61-62, 82-84, 118, 169, 171
    and health, 18-19, 31-36, 62-66, 85-87, 119-124, 172, 176-179
    and religion, 92-95
    economic conditions, 16-17, 29-30, 48, 49-52, 54-57, 69, 79-80, 97-103, 115-118, 151
    physical constraints, 31, 109-111
    recommendations for future, 227-254
    social conditions, 47-48, 110-118, 143-158
Preece, John, 223
Preston, John David, 253
Prestonsburg Community College, 131, 178
Prestonsburg, 93, 106, 177, 178, 236
Princess Elkhorn Coal Company, 210-212
Pulaski County, 219
Purcell, George, 218

265

and Center for Disease Control, 240

Center of Excellence in Health, 238

Lilly Cornett Woods Living Laboratory, 164-65

Medical School, 239

Rural Medicine program, 191-193, 239

Sanders Brown Center on Aging, 155-157

University of Louisville Medical School, 33-34, 239

U.S. Bureau of Labor Statistics, 162

U.S. Bureau of Medicine, 85

U.S. Census Bureau, 216

U.S.D.A. Agriculture Stabilization and Conversation Service, 169-171

U.S. Department of Agriculture, 169

U.S. Mine Safety and Health Administration, 163

U.S. Public Health Services, 40

U.S. Surface Mining Control and Reclamation Act of 1977, 164

V

Vaughn, Teddi, 253

VISTA, 104, 137

W

Walker, Thomas, 9

War Manpower Commission, 79

War on Poverty, 97-109

Wayland, 119, 190

Wayne County, 156

Weinberg, Bill, 137, 139-141, 253

Weinberg, Lois, 107, 253

Welfare, 247-250

     and education, 243-244

     dependency on, 154-155

     economic opportunities, 246

     restructure, 245

Wells, John, 253

Western Kentucky State College, 67

Wheelright, 25

Whitely County, 190

Whitesburg, 93, 209

Wolfe County, 190

Working Poor, 148, 155-157

lack of health insurance, 171-172

lack of job opportunities, 149

low paying jobs, 150-152

needs for the future, 242-245

Works Project Administration (WPA), 51-73

Workers of Rural Kentucky (W.O.R.K.), 214-217

Worthington, Bill, 122

Wright, Dan and Juanita and family, 166-167

Wright, Warren, 112